WORDS AND OCCASIONS

An anthology of speeches and articles

selected from his papers by

the Right Honourable L. B. Pearson

Words and Occasions

UNIVERSITY OF TORONTO PRESS

© University of Toronto Press 1970

ISBN 0-8020-1735-5

Published in the United States of America by

Harvard University Press, Cambridge, Massachusetts

Library of Congress Catalog Card Number 70–135191

ISBN 0-674-95611-7

Printed in Canada

To my Wife
for dedication beyond the call of duty

in attending so many of these

'occasions'

and listening to or reading

so many of these

'words'

Preface

IT has become normal for someone who, by accident or design, by good luck or bad, has achieved prominence in public life to publish some of the official and non-official papers that reflect his ideas and interests. I was intrigued by the idea, once I had retired from politics, that I should do this. But when I began the process of selection, I was shocked to realize the massive amount of material that I would have to examine and sift. How could anyone have written or spoken so much!

In going through all these papers, it soon became clear – another shock – that, judged as literature or thought, they were well below the level of immortality. However, there was one thing that did please me: the views expressed, the conclusions reached, and the forecasts made sometimes seem to stand up rather well in the light of later developments. My "batting average" in this regard is reasonably high, though I may, of course, be a prejudiced score-keeper. All the same, none of the selections in this book – and the contents will confirm this – were made simply to show myself, with the advantage of hindsight, as a sage and far-seeing prophet.

The material has, of course, to be read in the light of the events and emotions at the time it appeared. To this end I have tried to explain briefly before each extract the circumstances in which it was written or spoken in the first place. I hope that this will make each one more interesting and, by putting it in context, add something to its significance.

I must warn the reader that the style and, at times, the content, of some of my first contributions to posterity now seem even to me rather forced and over-dramatic. But I am anxious to include a few examples from those earlier days when no one, including myself, had any particular cause to be concerned with the effect of anything I said or wrote.

I started my "literary" career early. I recall that when I was eleven, with some encouraging pressure from my father, then minister at George Street Methodist Church in Peterborough, I submitted a moving little piece in a competition for boys and girls on the subject "Why we should abolish the bar" (not the legal, but the alcoholic bar), a subject much in the public mind in those days. I won a prize too, even though my arguments against "drinking" were not based on any experience. That manuscript, alas, has been lost.

Lost also, and I regret this even more, is an essay which won for me the Regents' Prize for English prose in my second year at Victoria College, University of Toronto. The subject we were given was from Tennyson: " 'Tis better to have loved and lost than never to have loved at all." By this time I was seventeen years of age, so once again my success was due more to imagination than experience. I received word about the prize in June 1915 when I was stationed at Shorncliffe Camp in England as Private Pearson, 1059, CAMC.

I do possess still, but have decided to omit, certain masterpieces of filial and military correspondence directed to my parents during the First World War which they chose to preserve. When I look at them now, it is like reading what a young and immature schoolboy, who had never been away from a sheltering home, wrote to his family about the Punic Wars. But war is a forcing ground for many things, including a boy's maturity, though it is often achieved in active military service in ways which are tragic and not to be recommended.

The book begins with my first appearance in print – apart from some undergraduate efforts – and it finishes with my swan-song to politics at the Liberal Convention of April 1968 which chose my successor as leader of the Liberal party and prime minister of Canada.

Between these first and last selections, I have included writings and speeches on a variety of subjects – serious and frivolous, national and international, political and non-political. Some things I have omitted because I think they are more suitable for the memoirs which I hope soon to complete. Other papers I discarded because I was assured by some good and helpful friends that they were of greater interest to me than they would be to readers of this volume. Some fell by the wayside too because they inexplicably resembled others given by myself elsewhere.

There were, however, some canons of inclusion. I have tried, for example, to show something of the range of instruments and keys that a public figure, like a public performer, employs over the years. Different occasions, different audiences, different purposes, all require different styles. As you will see, I have some favourite themes that are established quite early on and recur with variations. Speeches or articles, important in terms of their policy content, tend to be included as long as they are not duplicating too much something included elsewhere in the book. They may be of use to some future

historian as reference. There are also some selections of no great public or any other import. They are here because I enjoyed doing them
at the time and I hope that others may enjoy reading them now.

There is one selection for which I can take no responsibility (apart
from that of including it) : a short contribution from my wife made
on an official occasion. This is about the only speech she has given
during all our wonderful years together. I have been told that it is
the best thing of its kind among all the papers from which this book
derives. I would expect that. She should have done more writing.

Some selections are from a conference or a discussion, and the
words of others are included when necessary to give meaning to my
own. Where passages have been omitted for any reason, this is shown
by ellipses. Such cuts have been made for space considerations or, infrequently, to adjust the mode of the spoken to that of the printed
word. Once or twice only part of a speech dealing with two or more
related topics is provided. I have tried always to let my remarks stand
as given at the time without any major alteration. Occasionally,
however, and without changing the substance, I have improved
details of phraseology, but only when they seem to me now, a professor once again, very awkward or infelicitous, or even ungram-
matical. My editor has seen fit to make certain technical changes in
accordance with house style.

There is also in this book one rare item that has never yet impinged
upon the public ear or eye. It is an address of welcome that the Prime
Minister of Canada intended to give at the luncheon planned for
President de Gaulle when he was to convey centennial greetings from
France to Canada at the capital. He never came; but I kept the text
of my speech. I did not want it to suffer the fate of that other lost
manuscript on love and losing.

The order in which the papers appear is chronological, even though
this results in some thematic repetition; but I feel that this procedure
is better since it seems to give a feeling of development and *actualité*,
and perhaps some slight sense of history.

LBP

Contents

Preface
vii

PART I
1924–1948

1 The Game's the Thing
2

2 The New History
7

3 To a Church Group in Ottawa
11

4 Cards on the Table
15

5 Topics of the Day
21

6 Canada and the United States
24

7 At a Farewell Dinner in London
34

8 The Road to War
38

9 To the Staff of UNRRA
56

10 Canada and the San Francisco Conference
61

11 Some Principles of Canadian Foreign Policy
66

PART II
1949–1957

12 To the Ontario Municipal Association
78

13 From the Honourable Member for Algoma East
82

14 On Signing the North Atlantic Treaty
87

15 The Implications of a Free Society
89

16 In Reply to a USSR Peace Resolution
95

17 Canadian Foreign Policy in a Two-Power World
100

18 On My Installation as Chancellor of Victoria College
108

19 To the United Nations Correspondents' Association
114

20 To the Ontario Liberal Association
119

21 International Public Relations
123

22 Christian Foundations for World Order
128

23 Impressions of the Russians and Their Leaders
133

24 The Atlantic Community
140

25 On the Middle East Crisis
147

26 The Tragedy in Hungary
152

PART III
1957–1963

27 To the National Liberal Convention
159

28 St Andrew's Day Address
162

29 Politics, Opposition, and the Plight of Democracy
170

30   Education: The Creation of Finer Human Hungers
177

31   At the Toronto Freedom Festival
181

32   Tensions in the Western Hemisphere
184

33   The Canadian Partnership
191

34   On Canadian Defence Policy
198

PART IV
1963–1968

35   A l'Association des hebdomadaires de langue française du Canada
208

36   Before the Eighteenth Session of the United Nations
212

37   A Toast to the President of France
219

38   At a Parliamentary Press Gallery Dinner
223

39   To the Royal Canadian Legion
226

40   Mrs Pearson Speaks
232

41   At the Federal Provincial Conference, Charlottetown
234

42   From the Commons Flag Debate
236

43   To the Toronto and District Liberal Association
241

44   On the Inauguration of Canada's National Flag
244

45   On Television with Pierre Berton
245

46   At the Atlantic Award Dinner
253

CONTENTS

47   On Lighting the Centennial Flame
260

48   Vimy – Fifty Years After
262

49   To the Canadian Political Science Association
266

50   Expo – and a Welcome to the Queen
273

51   My Undelivered Toast to General de Gaulle
276

52   I Announce My Retirement
280

53   Adieu to the Parliamentary Press Gallery
284

54   At the Liberal Leadership Convention
287

Captions to the Illustrations
295

PART I

1924–1948

1

My first inclusion deals with sport. Both my father and grandfather managed easily and cheerfully to combine a godly life of Christian service and church responsibilities as ministers of the gospel with an almost passionate love of all outdoor games. This was a combination not usual, or even unquestioned, for Methodist preachers in those days. My father was good at all games, especially baseball. Naturally, he didn't play on Sunday, when he preached to a congregation that usually included some young men of the town who would not have been there if he had not been a "sporting parson."

I used to take my grandfather to baseball games at Hanlon's Point in Toronto in his old age. He had almost lost his eyesight, but could see the players dimly and hear what was going on. Moreover, as he wore a clerical collar, he got in free, through the courtesy of the owner of the club; and so did I, as his guide and grandson.

So my heart was in sport from the beginning.

On returning from Oxford University, in 1923, where I spent almost as much time on the playing fields as in the library, and where amateurism was so pure that you bought your own uniform when you "made" a college team or even the "Varsity," I was shocked to read about the growing professionalism and specialization in college sport in the United States. This trend, however, was certainly not noticeable at Toronto, as I could vouch from my happy, but unpaid, experience as honorary coach of the intercollegiate hockey team and the ORFU football team (we called it rugby then).

These athletic activities did not interfere with my academic duties as a lecturer in modern history and they were performed without benefit of any elaborate organization, coaching staff, pre-season training, and all that. Notwithstanding, our teams played hard and well; more important, they enjoyed the game, because the fun had not been organized out of playing. It was all so very different from the situation in American colleges both then and now, where games, for some students, are primarily a training ground for a $100,000 contract signed after graduation from a course of physical training.

I was a don at Burwash Hall, Victoria College, when I wrote this piece for *Acta Victoriana,* the college magazine. I was bending over backwards to be satirical – a posture which should not be held for too long but which on this occasion at least might be repeated to exemplify my abiding interest in games.

The Game's the Thing

Acta Victoriana, 1924

IT isn't. The "gate's" the thing. No longer is a game possible without a "gate," and that cannot be secured without publicity. The result is that before any important sporting event today there is as much ballyhooing as was used in the Middle Ages to commence a crusade. The Americans excel in this. They have become the greatest ballyhooers in history. To them the game has almost completely vanished in the frantic excitement of the spectacle, and the spectacle has become a matter of vital national importance through the feverish exertions of the press.

The amount of space devoted during the last few weeks to the baseball scandal is illustrative. Millions who have never heard of the nationalist movement in China hang on the last sentences of a Mr "Swede" Risberg. The respectable Judge Landis, who deserted the bench for baseball, and sixty-five thousand dollars a year, makes weighty pronouncements with the gravity of a Caesar Augustus. That august assembly, the United States Senate, threatens to desert the consideration of the World Court and the conquest of Nicaragua in order to be free to discuss the affairs of a Tyrus Raymond Cobb.

Look at boxing. The only occasion when it is a game today is when two urchins on the way home from school proceed to settle their recently discovered differences in the manly way, to the enjoyment and profit of them both: and they will probably be stopped by some benevolent old bystander who simply cannot bear to watch a sporting event for which he has not paid an admission fee.

Mr Gene Tunney, the heavyweight champion, only last week was guaranteed almost a million dollars to exchange a few blows in the near future with some other gentleman who in the meantime shall be found worthy of the honour. I have calculated that, if the fight should last the full number of rounds, and the average number of blows should be exchanged, the aforementioned Mr Tunney will receive for each blow the amount of money that a professor of Greek is granted for thirteen years of professional services.

Baseball and boxing are, however, professional sports. Turn to the colleges. The homes of real amateurism. There we will find, surely, that the game is played for the game's sake. Hardly! College athletics across the border are not much healthier than the two professional activities we have mentioned. Football is certainly a highly specialized, highly developed form of big business. Not long ago a paragraph appeared in one of our local dailies to the effect that the football squad – a membership of fifty entitles it to be called a squad – of the University of x had just left on its transcontinental journey to California to take part in what is known as an intersectional combat. Also, and this is what particularly attracted our attention, that to their special train with its special dining-car serving specially prepared meals for specially prepared athletes, was attached a baggage-car fitted out as a complete gymnasium, even to the extent of having shower baths to cleanse the travel-stained footballers. The battles of old England may or may not have been won on the playing fields of Eton, but certainly the future victories of the United States will have to be attributed to the gymnastic baggage-cars of the universities.

There are other indications of the trend of events. In a New York paper on 12 November last, there appeared at the top of the front page two full width, inch type headlines, one under the other, as follows:

COOLIDGE DROPS WORLD COURT PLAN
HARVARD FACES ISOLATION IN EAST

The second headline refers to a threatened rupture in athletic relations between Harvard and Princeton as a result of some ill-feeling over a football game, and I venture to suggest that most of the readers of the paper in question wondered why its importance and significance should have been obscured by associating it with such a comparatively minor matter as a world court.

Only a few weeks ago in the course of an article on Universities, a contributor to an American weekly gravely remarks that he shall not send his son to the University of x because the football shift play is used there and he does not approve of it. One may as well imagine Colet, Erasmus, and More avoiding Oxford four hundred years ago because, forsooth, the students there drew their longbows in an unorthodox fashion.

Such an amazing situation has not, as yet, reached Canadian colleges, though there are some who profess to discover the thin edge of the wedge in such phrases as "secret practices," "training tables," "professional coaches." Yet sport plays relatively as large a part in collegiate life here as it does across the border, and the task of preventing such a development as that suggested above would seem to be worthy of some attention. Why is it that those in a university with the mentality of scholars and the prestige of authority will moralize with an intensity that is awe-inspiring over their own particular divisions of history and philosophy, science and sociology, and yet scorn to consider or attempt to influence by their thought a phase of activity that touches so many so intimately?

Unless we draw our ideals from the universities of the old land our games will soon enough be Americanized. Unless we succeed in avoiding the two great evils that threaten to destroy the athletic life of American universities, the evils of too much organization and too much money, the football tail will soon start wagging the academic dog.

As regards too much money: A successful college will now receive some half-million dollars from its football games during one season. I realize perfectly well that football carries practically every other college sport, but no university has the slightest right to spend half of that amount in the conduct of the whole of its athletic activities. Amateur sport and a half-million dollars are mutually exclusive. If the money comes in it will be spent. The more there is to spend the less praiseworthy will be some of the ways of spending it. Ten thousand a year will probably be given the successful coach. That is a lot of money, and it is going to be rather difficult, I should imagine, to persuade the man who has a chance to earn it by winning games that the playing of the game is greater than the winning of it.

So far as too much organization is concerned: Look at the pampering of football players as if they were Russian ballet dancers; the strenuous training rules which make drudgery out of what should be fun; alumni organizations for enticing budding experts from high school to dear old alma mater, by fair means or foul, for the sole purpose of playing football; the scouting system to steal an opponent's plays; the football managers, the assistant managers, the assistants to the assistants; the student mass-meetings before the big games for the purpose of lashing the undergraduate body into a fury of "Old X Spirit"; "pep talks," organized howling, girl cheer leaders, and all that fantastic rot. The Americans have it all. We do not want it here.

Now that there are national marble championships and national horseshoe pitching contests, the only games I can discover in the Great Republic that have not been organized and commercialized are ping-pong and blind man's buff. But they are doomed. I expect to read in a year or two something like this:

In the Yale bowl before a howling hundred thousand, Yale and Harvard met in their annual Blind Man's Buff combat. Yale lost the toss and went "blind" first. Six trainers adjusted the bandages over his eyes, while nine referees inspected them. Three timekeepers blew their whistles and the great contest was on. Yale lunged forward, but Harvard, alert, avoided him, with a neat crawl under his legs. The crowd went wild. Pandemonium broke loose. The Blue Rooters roared a "Find Him, Yale." The Crimson countered by singing "Dodge Him, Fair Harvard." Yale fought doggedly on after this first rebuff, with that invincible Eli spirit, and groping feverishly he almost caught the over-confident Harvard with a neat feint into the corner and a quick reverse to the centre. Rapid fire instructions shouted from the eleven coaches on the side-lines just managed to save the Cambridge warrior. Then the whistle blew and the first period was over. During the intermission it was broadcast that there had been 113,000 paid admissions, at four dollars per head. If 137 would volunteer to leave and enter again, Yale would have made an all time record for men in and money paid. A hush swept over the vast multitude. Were there 137 there who would pay another four dollars for the honour of Old Eli? Volunteers were seen to spring up. Over 659 were counted, including one member of the Yale faculty. The crowd broke into a frenzy of cheering. Women fainted, strong graduates of former years were seen to weep quietly. The honour of Yale was saved. A record had been made. Then the gong clanged for round two. The game was on again.

And so on; and so on.

Oh, if these words could only be read in every college of North America, before it is too late! What a wave of reform would sweep over our fair continent. Students would sink to sleep whispering "The Game's the Thing." They would creep to nine o'clock lectures murmuring "Sport for Sport's Sake." Next fall we would read how the Varsity Stadium was deserted for the Queen's game as all the students were engaged in interclass ping-pong contests, and the newspapers had not announced the Rugby match to the general public.

The college would have been saved for the classroom.

2

THIS was another contribution to *Acta*, four years later.

It was a time when the literary style of Michael Arlen and his "Green Hat" was popular, and "smart" young historians – I was trying to be one – aped Philip Guedalla and Harry Elmer Barnes when they wrote. This selection is meant to be witty advice to students on how to use this kind of writing to impress professors. I doubt if my older academic colleagues in the history department were much impressed by either my advice or my attempt at humour. However, it didn't prevent that greatly respected and highly respectable dean of Canadian historians, Professor G. M. Wrong, from recommending me for promotion to assistant professor in that year, 1928. Perhaps he had heard that I might soon be joining the Department of External Affairs in Ottawa! At least, he knew that I had entered the civil service competition for the position of first secretary in that department. So I never did become an assistant professor. More than forty years later, however, I became a full professor at Carleton University. In between, I had taken a long non-academic detour (where tenure was at times very dubious) before achieving this promotion.

The New History

Acta Victoriana, 1928

To those unfortunate individuals who find the writing of history essays an unwelcome intrusion on the enjoyment of a university career, the following remarks may prove to be of some interest and value. They will explain the method of acquiring a "first class" with a minimum of effort and a maximum of certainty. It is, of course, notorious that one's efforts in the direction of historical composition are not sufficiently rewarded at this university, and that serious disaffection, culminating in mass meetings of protest, has been caused thereby. Indeed, it is most humiliating and exasperating to receive a D— for your contribution on "Henry VIII's Attitude to Companionate Marriage" when you have slaved for all of two hours on the subject and have thoroughly digested all the pertinent material in the *Public School History for Beginners*. This lamentable lack of recognition for historical effort is due, not to the cold-blooded brutality of those amiable gentlemen who inhabit Baldwin House, but to their negligence in explaining to undergraduates the mysteries of the new history, without a knowledge of which an A++ is quite impossible. It is to rectify what has been a serious dereliction of duty on their part that these few sentences have been hastily written.

The writing of the new history may take any one of four forms, or a combination of all four. First, there is the "picturesque" method. To its devotees, all history is romance, and should be written in a highly coloured style of epigrammatic brilliancy. There must be imagination, life, vividness in every paragraph. Effect must be heaped on effect, metaphor on metaphor, until the reader is ready to fall into an ecstatic swoon. Fifty years ago, for instance, if one of the classic historians of the old, old school wished to open a chapter with the information that 1848 was a year of revolutions, he would merely repeat that alarming fact in a quiet, emphatic, dignified and well-documented sentence. Thus, "1848[1] was a year[2] of revolutions."[3] There is an impressiveness and grandeur about this method much to be admired, but the "picturesque" historian of the year 1928 scoffs at such dull, Victorian solidity.

Philip Guedalla is, perhaps, the leader of this modern school. Along with Michael Arlen and Noel Coward he makes up a frothy trinity, *les enfants terribles* of modern letters. Now, if the effervescent Philip wished to introduce his reader to the afore-mentioned fact that 1848 was a year of revolutions, he would inflict the following on him: "The great clock in Westminster's ancient tower tolled twelve, each toll groaning as in

[1]Trans. Roy. Soc. 1878, VIII, 32, sec. 6–7
[2]See ss. 24–7; G. of I. Act, 556–67B
[3]23 Wm. Cong. c. 22, 1066

anguish. A hush spread o'er the world. 'Twas 1848. Far off in China sweat-bedewed coolies toiled in dampened fields of rice. Beneath the setting Arctic sun a polar bear slipped wearily into an icy sea. In crude but coming Illinois, Lincoln, that gaunt man of destiny, had just finished splitting another rail. But in Europe, faint rumblings were heard, growing louder, louder. The drum of revolution began to beat ere the last faint gleams of the old year had faded into distance. 'Twas 1848." Try that style in your next essay. Results will be immediate. A++, or even A+++.

If you find it difficult, however, to be picturesque you can join the "revisionist" branch of the new history school, and become a soldier in that gallant army fighting the battle of "de-Bunker Hill." To be a success at this method, one need only prove that all the villains of the past have been heroes, and all the heroes, villains. For instance, if you are asked to write an essay on Alfred the Great, you would commence as follows: "It has been the fashion of credulous historians in the past to portray Alfred as a paragon of all the kingly virtues. Of late, however, an immense amount of new material has been uncovered concerning this man. To wit, five sentences from a hitherto lost letter written by Alfred to his father while he was a freshman at Oxford; and three candles, which, from the peculiar notches made on them, were undoubtedly once owned by the Saxon King. This new evidence has been carefully investigated by Professor Fenley Pearbrooke, and the results prove conclusively that this pseudo-saint, Alfred, was in reality a wife-beater, a coward, and a Bolshevik. This impostor should be torn from his pedestal. In the following essay I propose to tear him down." Or the subject might be one of history's traditional bad men – Nero, for instance. The conclusion our conscientious de-bunker arrives at with respect to Nero would be something like the following: "A much misjudged and misinterpreted man, Nero. It is my privilege to show in this essay that Nero was really a hero. Recent documents brought to light from the ruins of Casa Loma show that Nero did not fiddle in fiendish glee as Rome burned. Rather, that Nero had collected thousands of poor, homeless refugees in the palace gardens, and there, his eyes brimming over with tears of compassion, he tried to take their minds off their awful plight by playing, softly and tenderly, 'Just a Song at Twilight.' And so, I repeat, Nero, a hero."

Such de-bunking efforts will always receive the coveted A++ from the liberal-minded, truth-seeking members of the history staff.

Then there is the "hidden cause" school. Its method is to shun the obvious, to probe behind every superficial reason for human action until the ultimate cause is made clear. As a matter of fact, it is closely allied with the previous "de-bunking" method. Take, for instance, the statement that Austerlitz killed Pitt. A trite remark, the truth of which is taken for granted because it has appeared so often. But really quite false.

Was Pitt at the Battle of Austerlitz? No. Was he of a highly-emotional nature, liable to collapse on the receipt of unpleasant news? No. Then Austerlitz could not have killed Pitt. What did? Back to the sources. The medical report on the death of the great Commoner reads, "Wm. Pitt died of gout." Ah, gout! A discovery! What caused Pitt's gout? Port wine, indubitably. How did Pitt come to consume enough port wine to bring on the gout? It was the custom of the age. Why? Back in 1660 Charles ii married a Portuguese princess, Catherine of Braganza. The gallants about the court, to honour the new Queen, began to drink her country's native wine, port, hitherto not much in favour. The custom spread until nobody that was anybody drank anything else. Hence this popular habit brought to England her eighteenth century national infirmity, gout, of which Pitt died. So not Austerlitz, but Catherine of Braganza killed Pitt.

Finally we have the "psychological school" of historians, those who believe that all human action is due to emotional reactions, reflexes, submerged desires, and what-nots. Emil Ludwig is the most distinguished of this group. In his brilliant portrait of the Kaiser he has proved beyond a shadow of doubt that the great war was due to the psychological effect of a withered arm on a sensitive, neurotic, imperial nature. If you are doing honours history in the second year, it will be easy and profitable for you to prove that the English civil war was caused by the wart on Cromwell's nose. If you are in the third year, you can show that the destiny of the modern world was changed when Napoleon decided to be a soldier, not a Corsican farmer, and that this decision was made when the Bonaparte baby was eleven months old. Purely psychological reasons again. The young Napoleon was looking out of the front window one morning in the old homestead at Ajaccio when a regiment marched by with band playing. The spirit of military glory, the lust for martial conquest at that very moment entered into the subconscious nervous organism of the hitherto agriculturally-inclined infant who from that day began to develop a behaviouristic emotional super-complex for war. If the student wished to follow up this last idea, he could establish a direct connection between this Corsican parade and the Arabian revolt of Ibn Saud.

This, then, is the new history. When confronted with the next essay or the next examination be sure to adopt its methods. If you follow its technique carefully, your reward will be swift and sure, for it is well known that the history department is partial to new ideas. May approaches, but, in its historical aspect, it brings no fear to the initiated, to those who have read and understood these lines. For them there is no skeleton in the closet, and the sword of Damocles is secured by a cable. Fortified by their secret knowledge, they laugh at Baldwin House and all its tutors. Calm and unafraid, they examine the future, confident that where once there had been naught but failure, there can now be nothing but success.

3

PERHAPS it was because I had just left university where I gave lectures not only to undergraduates but also, extramurally, to adults, that I departed on occasions after I had moved to Ottawa from the public silence and anonymity that befits a civil servant. From 1928 to 1935, when I was transferred to London, I accepted some invitations to speak to church groups and service clubs in Ottawa and to one or two audiences outside. I even went to New York once to explain to the Council on Foreign Relations there the reaction in Canada to President Roosevelt's New Deal.

I must have been careful not to say anything politically controversial on these occasions because I don't recall ever having been reprimanded, or even cautioned, by my immediate chief, Dr O. D. Skelton, a very wise and dedicated but cautious public servant.

This "Survey of the International Situation" was a talk I gave to a church group in Ottawa in 1934. In my gloom over apparent failure to deal with the depression or do anything effective about peace and disarmament, I lamented, as I have done so often since, that scientific advance was outstripping social and political progress. During this lament I made a reference, which must have seemed quite fantastic to my listeners, to the release of atomic energy and its catastrophic use for destruction. I also expressed alarm and discouragement because in 1931 world expenditure on armaments had reached four-and-a-half billion dollars. In 1969 it was more than two hundred billions. This is a measure of our progress.

To a Church Group in Ottawa

11 April 1934

IT is the duty of officers of the Department of External Affairs, when not attending international conferences for the protection of homeless cats or preparing answers to questions by inquisitive members of the House of Commons as to the amount of money being spent on blotting paper, to survey the international scene and try to keep track of what is going on in the outside world. It is a cheerless duty because the scene itself is a depressing one.

I have no doubt that the historian of the future will consider the period through which we are now passing as one of the most complex and chaotic since the barbarians from the north climbed the walls of Rome and destroyed European civilization and order. In fact any survey, however cursory, of the world today gives one an uneasy feeling that George Bernard Shaw was right when he said: "If the other planets are inhabited, this world is their lunatic asylum." With all our boasted technical and scientific progress which has enabled us to count the stars and remove mountains, to fly through space at the rate of 430 miles an hour and listen to King George say "Merry Christmas" to all the world over the radio, we are unable to keep the economic machinery functioning without periodic crashes; or to prevent ourselves from flying at each others' throats, in a manner usually associated with savages, whenever our national honour or patriotic interest is involved. Never have there been such amazing examples of man's ingenuity to harness the forces of nature to his own productive ends. Yet in the midst of all this, millions look for work and suffer want and destitution. Though there are bread-lines in this brave new world and starving peasants in China, Brazilians dump their coffee by the boatload in the Atlantic Ocean, in order to force up the price, while we contemplate hopefully the possibility of grasshoppers decreasing wheat production. The greatest benefactor of humanity today is the man who can make one blade of grass grow where two grew previously. The peasant of old starved because there was no food. The producer of today suffers because there is too much. It is an "Alice in Wonderland" system of economics.

In order to carry out their plans for control of production the Administration in Washington has, during the last six months, handed out 300 million dollars to farmers who promised to produce less wheat, cotton, tobacco, corn, and hogs. Unfortunately the authorities were unable to persuade nature to subscribe to a production code. So in spite of the decreased wheat and cotton acreage, and the bonus for acreage reduction, there was more cotton produced in the States last year than the year before, while estimates for winter wheat visualize an increase over last year's harvest of more than 150 million bushels.

We find an equally complex and Gilbertian situation in respect to international trade and exchanges. It is almost as difficult for one country to send a shipment of goods to another country in this enlightened age as it would be for Adolph Hitler to be elected mayor of Jerusalem.

Society is lopsided and our physical and scientific progress has been infinitely faster and further than our social, political, or spiritual advance. Take, for instance, the postwar movement toward disarmament and world peace. During the last war the unfortunate soldiers of His Majesty were told to "grin and bear it." If an arm was suddenly removed from its accustomed place, or a rodent wandered across one's face during an uneasy sleep in a muddy hole, we were encouraged by three comforting thoughts:

1 we were making the world safe for democracy;
2 back home there was being prepared a land fit for heroes to live in;
3 this was the war to end war.

As to the first, making the world safe for democracy, I suggest that you gaze at Russia, Japan, Germany, Italy, Poland, Yugoslavia and some other countries. Even in Anglo-Saxon states which, as we know, are inhabited by a people of superior political virtue where men "never, never will be slaves," there is a growing tendency to question the divine right of 51 per cent to rule 49; to murmur that Mussolini saved Italy and made the trains run on time; and to cast sidelong glances at coloured shirts. Though personally I prefer the boiled shirt of Mr Bennett or Mr King to the black shirt of Mussolini, or the brown shirt of Hitler, there seem to be increasing numbers of people in various parts of the world who do not agree with me. In short, we do not seem to have made the world safe for democracy.

As to making the world fit for heroes to live in, I have a strong suspicion (made even stronger since the failure to restore my 10 per cent civil service cut) that the world has been made a place in which only heroes can live.

Then, finally, it was the war to end war. We were to convert our swords into ploughshares and our spears into pruning hooks, and the lion and the lamb were to lie down peacefully together for all time. Unfortunately, statistics now show that there are more men under arms in Europe than there were in 1914, while world expenditure on armaments, which was roughly two-and-one-half billion in 1913, was four-and-one-half billion in 1931, and has increased since then. Germany, which was disarmed in 1918, and technically remains disarmed, is now spending 538 million dollars on armaments in the year 1934, of which 100 million was set aside for the Nazi militia.

At the moment there is more talk of war than at any time since 1918 and more, I venture to say, than in July 1914. Much of it is stupid and ill-informed, but some is profoundly significant and depressing. Much is due to the failure of the Disarmament Conference which commenced in Geneva more than two years ago with such high hopes. Reduction of armaments itself cannot, of course, prevent war any more than the powdering of a rash can cure a fever. Men can fight with fists as well as machine guns. And in any case even if machine guns had been limited, or even abolished, in Geneva there was always the danger that new types of armaments might have replaced them. Any attempt to reduce existing armaments without taking into consideration new methods of chemical and scientific warfare would prove as futile as a conference would have been in 1914 to cut down the number of swords without considering high explosives. It is altogether likely that in twenty-five years from now the weapons of today will be as out-of-date as pikes and tomahawks. In the next war it will not be the charge of the Light Brigade but the flight of the gas brigade, or the advance of the bacteriologists. Scientists make our blood run even colder when they describe warfare by the transference of specific forms of energy from machines to the body with specific effects destroying that body. We get almost into the realm of the fantastic when we consider the release of atomic energy as a destructive agency. We are told that a drop of water contains sufficient of such energy to run a motor car continuously for twenty years. If that energy is ever released (and scientists are hopeful that it will be in the near future) and applied to destructive purposes, we would doubtless have world peace, because the world would be blown to bits.

Therefore, a mere agreement at Geneva to reduce weapons which in a few years would be archaic might not of itself have any lasting effect unless at the same time steps were taken to limit the basic causes of conflict. Though I feel one might have easily exaggerated the success of the Disarmament Conference, it is quite impossible to exaggerate its failure; and that failure is imminent unless developments soon take place to alter the current of events. The conference itself practically ceased functioning when the Germans withdrew, and has since remained in a state of suspended animation. The great powers are now indulging in what they politely call "diplomatic conversations" (another name for which is the old diplomacy). Notes are exchanged and re-exchanged in what the press communiqués call "a spirit of perfect frankness and friendship," but so far all that has been done is to have kept the ball in play. It reminds me of one of those long drawn out defensive hockey games where a forward makes a lone rush and take a feeble shot; a member of the other team takes the puck, makes in his turn a lone rush with another feeble shot; but there is never any danger of a goal.

The failure of the Disarmament Conference merely means two things:
1 It will result in an armaments race; and an armaments race has never yet had anything but evil consequence for anybody taking part in it.
2 It may involve the failure of the collective security system based on the League of Nations – that system by which we were, so we hoped, building up an organization to outlaw war and peacefully settle disputes. We are in danger of sliding back into the morass of prewar politics; into that condition lauded by George Canning when he said: "We are returning to a hopeful state of affairs – each nation for itself and God for us all." It is more likely to be "each nation for itself and ruin for us all."

The whole postwar peace movement is in grave danger. The time to consolidate that movement and to build up a new world society was in the ten years after the World War when men still remembered the horror and unutterable degradation of that conflict; in which ten million men were killed and thirteen million were missing; where the daily loss of life amounted to 16,585 men; where the parade of dead marching ten abreast from sunrise to sunset would take forty-six days to pass a given spot. With the sheer physical revulsion against war caused by these horrible facts, a revulsion which ruled in every country, there was a chance to build up a better order of things. That chance is now rapidly passing, for a new generation is appearing on the stage for whom the sound of the trumpet is a call to adventure rather than a summons to death.

4

WHILE serving as first secretary of the Office of the High Commissioner in London, I was asked by the BBC in 1936 to do a broadcast about Canada. They must have approved of what I said because later I was invited to take part in a series of talks over their overseas transmission with a well-known broadcaster who was also a Harley Street physician, Dr Geikie-Cobb. He disguised himself on the air as "Anthony Weymouth" and was a charming and intelligent person. The BBC offered me all of eight guineas per broadcast, and, as the Canadian government didn't pay me very much more than that per week, I, with a wife and two children, could hardly afford not to be enticed. The broadcasts did not interfere in any way with my work at Canada House, as they were done late in the evening. However, I thought I had better play safe, and disguised myself as "Michael Macdonald." This became my identity in this series and other BBC talks over short-wave which I gave from time to time until I left London in the summer of 1941.

My disguise, in name and voice, must have been very good – or else no one in Canada listened to my BBC broadcasts – because, apart from my family and one or two others who had been told about my "moonlighting," no one apparently knew who Michael Macdonald was.

Extracts from this talk in the Empire Programme series have Weymouth and Macdonald reminiscing about the First World War. It seems now far away in time and even further away in spirit.

Cards on the Table

11 November 1937

w Where were you this morning at eleven o'clock, Macdonald?
m I had intended to go down towards the Cenotaph and listen to the service of remembrance there, but I couldn't get away. So I went up

to the top of my office building and saw the motionless crowds from there. It was, in a sense, I think, even more impressive than being actually at the Cenotaph itself; to look far below you at the very heart of London and see everything stop dead at a given moment; not a move, not a sound, except the pigeons of Trafalgar Square who started to flutter about in some alarm at the unaccustomed silence – a silence which fairly shrieked. I even heard the waters of the Thames lapping against the embankment. Then the "maroons" went – seven million people came back to life – and the city went on with its work. Where were you Weymouth?

w I was in my study which faces on to a busy road where there is always a rumble of traffic. I had been very busy writing and it had escaped me that we were approaching eleven o'clock. I didn't actually hear a maroon; possibly I should have if there had been less noise from the traffic. I had my back to the window and the first intimation I had was something that made me stop writing, and that was complete silence. I stood quite still during the two minutes' silence with the pen in my hand. I realised that I should know when it was over because I should hear the traffic start again. It is a marvellous idea, I think, this two minutes' silence; extraordinarily effective.

m Yes, it never seems to lose its impressiveness. But one wonders how long it can go on and maintain that impressiveness. You would have thought that twenty years after, the solemnity, the emotion, would somehow have become a little less intense. But that doesn't seem to be the case – certainly not in London.

w I doubt whether it is the case anywhere really ... What did you think about during that long two minutes?

m Trudging in the mud; the sound of a bugle in camp at nightfall; the rusty old squadron gramophone playing – what's that old song – "Goodbye my dearie." You remember it? Friends who never saw Canada again – but who'll never see old age, distress, or disillusionment either ...

w I always think the most poignant moment that any soldier really had was when he said goodbye at Victoria Station after his leaves, because, however much he might try to hide it, or his relatives might, in both their minds was the same thought: it was as likely as not to be goodbye for always.

m Most Canadians were spared that. At least I was, not having any relatives of my own here. In fact, when I first arrived during the war I did not know a single solitary person in the British Isles. When I got leave – after I had been overseas nearly two years and hadn't had a day's leave – and I arrived at Victoria I saw crowds of people there to meet the men coming back who were English, or Irish, or Scotch; I remember wondering if there wasn't somebody among them who knew me. I waited till they had all disappeared, and then I went off to the hotel alone.

w That was all very well when you were coming back on leave, but it was compensated for by the fact that there was nobody to see you off when you left.

m And also compensated for by the fact that it was a Canadian's own fault if he remained friendless in London for long. Once when I had only been twenty-four hours or so on leave, that first one, and hadn't had time to get in touch with the organizations which looked after stray "colonials," I was standing in the Piccadilly tube station – incidentally, I knew so little about your tubes then that the first time I bought an underground ticket, from Piccadilly, I walked down the stairs – I hadn't heard of the lifts.

w That must have used up most of your leave.

m Well, it used up most of my energy. I couldn't figure out why there was nobody else on the stairs – this is the middle of London, I thought, and so few people travelling. However, to get back to my efforts to get out of this state of loneliness. When I was standing there I saw a very pretty girl lining up to get a ticket. I was an extremely shy youth then, but I thought, now I've got to do something about this, otherwise this leave is going to be wasted. I summoned up a lot of courage. As a matter of fact it was one of the most courageous things I ever did; nothing previously or subsequently required half so much courage. I walked up to this lovely girl who was about to buy a ticket and said: "I am a Canadian; I don't know anybody in London, why don't you come out to dinner and a theatre with me – do your bit for your country, and all that." She looked at me with a mixture of pity and pleasure. At any rate she didn't seem unfriendly, and said, "Well, I'd like to very much, but that's mother over there. I'll have to ask her." Whereupon she pointed to a most formidable-looking middle-aged woman. I was about to slink away, thinking I had taken on more than I bargained for, when the young lady said: "Leave it to me. What's your name?" Whereupon she took me by the arm and led me over to the mother, saying, "Mother, you remember I was speaking about my Canadian soldier friend, Macdonald, whom I met in the canteen the other day." The mother, who looked a bit dazed, rose to the occasion and said, "Yes, my dear, I remember, of course I remember." My newly-won friend said, "Well, he wants me to go and have dinner and to a theatre," and the lady, who had by this time softened perceptibly, said, "Oh yes, my dear, you run along, you two young people, and have a good time." We did. We had a very good time. That was English informal hospitality. What war will do to you people!

w I remember when I was on leave from France ... I arrived some time in the evening and went to dine at a restaurant with some friends. We had hardly got inside when they pulled down the shutters in front of the restaurant. A first-class zeppelin raid had begun. This one seemed to me a good deal noisier than the front.

m It was a zeppelin raid in London that finished me with the war.

w How was that?

m I was in the Flying Corps towards the end of the war, and I was stationed at Hendon, where, among other things, they were supposed to
keep zeppelins from bothering people. I, unfortunately, was at the
Trocadero in Piccadilly when the maroons went up this time. But, like
a good soldier, I fled for my post of duty, which was some miles away.
You will remember how all the lights went out during a raid, how
even the buses travelled without them.

w Do I not!

m I had gone as far as I could towards Hendon on one bus when it
stopped because of the raid, and I was rushing away at full speed to
the aerodrome on foot when I saw another bus; it wouldn't stop, so,
after it had gone by, I crossed the street behind it and, as I crossed, a
bus, without lights, came full speed down the other side. I walked in
front of it. A bus, you know, can hit you an awful wallop.

w And did this one hit you an awful wallop?

m It must have. You know how tough I am, yet it knocked me out! It
was a very unheroic but a very effective method of ending my military
career. Some hours later I found myself in hospital, where I rested for
some time. I was in a small ward with two or three other officers. We
were, of course, visited by the usual coterie of kindly old ladies who
asked us questions about our wounds and how we got them. Unfortunately, the three of us in this ward were not – well, our wounds, and
the cause of them bore little relation to the charge of the Light
Brigade. It was most embarrassing, because I had been hit by a bus,
the gentleman on my left had been kicked by a mule, and the gentleman on my right had a touch of asthma ...

w Another thing I remember on leave was a VAD having tea with my wife
at a rather swish hotel in the West End. She had just come back from
France and after tea, without thinking, she lit a cigarette just as
she'd have done in France. The head waiter came up to her at once
and asked her to leave the hotel, because in those days nice women
were not supposed to smoke in public.

m And I remember being asked to leave a swish restaurant in 1915
because I was not an officer, ergo, not a gentleman. That was one of
the things that really disturbed me about your country during the war,
that private soldiers (I was one for a couple of years) were treated
like that. In our army we didn't take very easily to social distinctions
between soldiers and officers.

w I agree that that sort of distinction, in an army recruited from civilians, was disgraceful. The only excuse one could make is that in the
old prewar days there was a great gulf between the social class of the
officers – who all came out of the top-drawer – and the private. But I
never realised to the full how true this was until one night I was going
up the line and stopped to sleep on the floor of a more or less ruined

building. In the morning my batman came in and called me in the usual respectful manner. Next door to me, also on the floor, was an Australian major. Looking back now I see how funny it was, but I was literally horrified when, in the morning, his batman came in, gave him a kick in the ribs, and said, "Will yer get up, Bill, it's half-past seven!"

M That's the spirit! I once had as company commander the man who ran a little cleaning and pressing establishment in our town at home.

W Was he your officer, then, and were you in the ranks?

M I was his subaltern. He was one of the best officers we had. Most of the men in his company were from his town and were, of course, in civil life rather his superiors, financially at least. My own brother was washing dishes in the officers' mess in his battery once when he was summoned to meet the CO. As he was famous for getting into rows, he thought, "I'm in for it again. More CB." He paraded from the kitchen to the orderly room and was told that he would have to stop washing dishes – he had been recommended for a commission.

W By the end of war we, too, had learned to regard the non-commissioned officer and the private as human beings.

M To give the other side of the picture. I recall being violently defended by a very senior British officer once when I was a private soldier because a headwaiter was rude to me in a restaurant. That headwaiter got a grand tongue-lashing from my friendly staff officer.

W I call that very refreshing. Served that waiter jolly well right. That shows we weren't all so bad as you might think.

M But what we couldn't always understand was the necessity of emphasizing these social distinctions in order to preserve discipline.

W Well, I want to make this point. I don't see how any commanding officer can sit cheek by jowl in a railway-carriage with a man of his own unit and still retain that rather distant manner which is necessary to discipline.

M It seems to me a distant manner makes for distrust rather than discipline. Of course, we had no military tradition to break down.

W You see, Lord Kitchener's army was not a new army in that sense – it was moulded as near as possible on our old regular army ... But it's interesting the different ways discipline was maintained in our two forces. Ours was a different type of discipline from yours. I am sure you had discipline. You must have had it to do that what you did in the war. For I suppose you'd agree with me that discipline is absolutely essential in any warfare.

M Oh, absolutely.

W It's amusing looking back. I was what was known as a "temporary gent" – and I was always tickled by the respect paid by the regulars to administration ...

M Yes, that passion for administration – red tape is a better word. It would follow you into the front line. In the middle of a bombardment you would be asked by headquarters to send in at once in triplicate the middle names of the aunts of all the unmarried corporals in your battalion.

w Or how many tins of plum and apple you had. Fill in form R.I.49 ...

m I suppose that sort of thing has helped to account for the fact that for every man in the front line there were fifteen men behind!

w I should think you underestimate the number. Looking back over those nineteen years, Macdonald, a thing that sticks in my mind most was the universal good temper shown by all the soldiers, whether they were tramping through the mud or filth, in discomfort, fear, pain – whatever they were doing they were good-tempered and could see the funny side to it and make the best of a damned bad job. Remember the chap who saw two signposts a mile apart which both said the next town was still twenty kilometres away – and he thanked goodness that he was keeping up with the [bleep] place?

m Yes, it was wonderful – the comradeship and the good fellowship. The fine qualities that were brought out under terrible conditions. Why should it require war to bring out those qualities to that extent? ... It's only when there's a wolf near the flock that the flock huddles together.

w I am one of those who do not believe we have sunk back – that is, those of us who are still alive. I wonder whether we should have acted as regards the unemployed had the war not forced us to realize what suffering really meant.

m I think that is true. One's sense of social obligation in peacetime has, I think, been strengthened by the sacrifices of the war. But in my view the only possible justification for the last war would be not such incidental benefits as that which you have mentioned, but if it made war in the future impossible or at the very least more difficult. Yet the two minutes' silence this year is accompanied by the falling of bombs in China and the crash of shells in Spain. There's the tragedy of it all ...

w And just as one never appreciates what one's always had – so I never thought how lovely peace was until it had been blown sky-high. Now I know that peace is our right – we've got every reason to have peace – just as a human being's got every reason to be sane – insanity is not normal. And national insanity – that is, war – is not normal. It's a wild beast which destroys everything which is worth while – and makes life impossible. Look how today the mere fear of war has given the stock markets the jitters. Peace means stability and freedom to spend one's life in a way which leads somewhere – somewhere useful – both to us and to those who'll come after. So you'll see that I think our job – those of us who went through the last war – is to make peace as certain as possible, is to make sure that there isn't another war.

m You're right – and there are millions of veterans who were on both sides who think so, too. The old soldier, after all, is the bulwark of peace.

5

THIS talk was one of another series I did, but solo this time and over the empire transmission of the BBC. It was called "Topics of the Day" and I didn't have Weymouth to support and needle me. I am trying to describe the reactions of the British people at the critical and desperate time of the Munich crisis. Its "solution" resulted in a year's reprieve from catastrophe. That was all. We seized on that reprieve with a joyous sense of escape that should have made us more charitable to Mr Chamberlain later, when the reprieve ended and the execution took place. But the feeling of escape was mixed in many hearts with one of guilt, humiliation, and outrage. We had thrown Czechoslovakia to the wolves but had not appeased their appetite.

Personally, like so many, I soon recovered from the delirium – because it was that – of temporary release. Though I had for some years felt we should be patient and understanding about the Nazis because Germany would throw off this infection in due course, my views changed after the take-over of Austria. I became convinced that a show-down with Hitler was now inevitable and that if he did not back down (which he was not likely to do), war could not be avoided. In Ottawa I was considered rather an alarmist.

Topics of the Day

12 September 1938

PEOPLE have been going through anxious times the last few weeks, over here in Great Britain. True, the recurring alarms and crises of the last year or two have, in a sense, conditioned the population so that its shock-absorbing capacity has increased even beyond its normal admirable point. But whereas the crises of recent years have, it seems to me, never really impressed the man in the street as anything over which, in the last analysis, he would himself ever conceivably have to fight, the situation of recent days has brought him up against the ghastly possibility.

Well, this has, of course, been a shock to him; but to an outsider – if a Canadian can be considered an outsider – who is accustomed to the more violent reactions of transatlantic people to events which disturb and disconcert them, the Englishman has taken it all pretty calmly and, of course, without getting panicky or all worked up ... The English, you know, aren't a demonstrative lot. They're not as cold or unemotional or unsentimental as so many foreigners suggest – quite the contrary – but they're not given to the easy demonstration of emotions which they feel deeply; just as some of the more volatile races across the channel are not given to the concealment of emotions which they don't feel deeply.

Today, as always, the topics of real interest are football and the weather and the Missus and the "pictures." It is about these concerns that arguments most often develop over a pint in the pub, rather than Czechoslovakia.

Foreigners often have a difficult time understanding English psychology. How could they help but be a bit baffled when they are told that a huge news sign reading "Arsenal in Danger" has no reference to international politics, but is a warning to a famous football team to get a new half-back and a couple of forwards!

But don't make the mistake of thinking that Czechoslovakia and foreign affairs are not in their minds. They are. Somebody writing in a weekly review last month said that his idea of a perfect place to spend a holiday was one where nobody had ever heard of Czechoslovakia. He wouldn't find many such places in Britain tonight.

Behind the calm there is no indifference, but sober realization of an increasingly serious situation. Yesterday, especially, when we were all awaiting Herr Hitler's speech, with almost feverish anxiety, one felt a tension in the atmosphere. The crowds that gather in Downing Street, that small one-block street where so much of the world's history has been made, are a pretty good barometer of public interest in political events in this country. Well, I went by there twice yesterday. In the morning, when the Cabinet was in session, and in the evening about 10 o'clock.

The street was empty both times because crowds were so great that it had
been cleared. But the Whitehall and Horse Guards ends were massed
with people – not idle or curious people, not tourists, but earnest, intensely serious, yet quiet and calm Londoners, driven by some irresistible
inclination to be near the spot where, who knows, the destiny of themselves and their children may have been under discussion ...

As I walked away to my tube station to catch a train for home, news-
boys were shouting the latest special editions with the reports of Hitler's
speech. I've never seen papers go so quickly, or read so earnestly; people
in evening dress scanning them under street lamps; maids and butlers
coming to doorsteps and shouting for a copy. Around a coffee stall everyone was reading while they drank. But no talk. And in my tube coach,
every person but three was poring over those fateful words from that city
of Nuremberg which was once the centre of the toy industry.

I watched those reading faces: anxiety, yes, but no fear. The Englishman is roused to the possibility of danger. As always, he is sober and
restrained, yet ready to face any eventuality. I find this attitude infinitely
more impressive as a demonstration of national strength than all the
parades, fireworks, bands, and goose-stepping which have been so often
used in the past to whip up martial excitement; and are still used in some
countries.

That is one thing I haven't discovered a trace of, these last few weeks –
martial excitement. Not a bit of it. Nobody that I have met hates his
opposite number in any other country. Very few people have even mentioned war. No single person has ever suggested in word or print that
war at this time, or any time, is anything but, as one chap put it, "a
mug's game." Could there have ever before been an international crisis
of such seriousness with such catastrophic possibilities, where there is
such a complete absence of jingoism, or even of the martial spirit?

But, we needn't talk of war – yet. There are people in other countries
too who know what war means and are just as anxious to avoid it as
Englishmen.

There is another impression I have received during recent days – the
essential solidarity and unity of the people. To me that has been most
impressive, and, because I believe in democracy, most encouraging.
There is freedom in this country, and so there is division of opinion. That
is what freedom means. There have been viewpoints, controversies; there
have been sections of opinion which have said the whole of Central
Europe was not worth a war or widows' tears; there have been those who
have taken exactly the opposite view ... And yet no clarion appeal for
unity was shouted. It wasn't necessary. The nation closed its ranks almost
automatically in the face of a great national emergency. There is order
and discipline, self-imposed and without loss of liberty.

Yet, not long ago, I heard public speakers violently denouncing
courses now being pursued. I find no denunciation now, either in the

press or on the platform, or even in conversation. England's disunity has not for a long time been Europe's opportunity. But England's unity has often recently been Europe's salvation.

But I come back to where I started – the calm, the sober but determined facing of facts without being unstrung by their implications.

Don't think there is any panic or fear over here. There isn't. Life goes on. People flock to see a picture called "The Rage of Paris" which has nothing to do with the French reception of Herr Hitler's speech. They go to the dogs and lose sixpence on each race. They try to get that double six on the dart board over the last pint before closing time.

I hope no one will think I am an Anglomaniac, but they have some great qualities, these British. It often takes a crisis to make us aware of them.

6

I HAD been asked to do an extension course lecture at University College, Nottingham, on "Canada and the United States." London was being heavily and regularly bombed, and I thought it would be nice to get out of town for a couple of nights, even to give a lecture at a place and time which had otherwise little to commend itself to me and on a subject which was of less interest to me at that moment in my life than it had been earlier and was to be later. So I turned up in Nottingham, and my views on Canada and its neighbour were submitted to a reasonably large audience that night.

The only vivid recollection that I have of the lecture was an incident at its end, as I reached my peroration. I had just said the most welcome words of so many lectures, "In conclusion," when a note was sent up to the chairman. He read it and, with apologies, interrupted me to inform the audience that the air-raid alert – which I confess I hadn't heard, so caught up was I by my own eloquence – had been sounded. With the distinguished speaker's permission, and further apologies to him, he would give those who wished to leave and hurry home or to a shelter a few minutes for that purpose. To my great satisfaction, as evidence of the gripping nature of my performance, practically no one departed.

So I resumed my closing remarks, when a minute or so later the procedure was repeated; a second note was handed to the chairman. He rose, I sat down, and there was another announcement: this time that enemy aircraft were overhead and bombs had begun to fall in another part of the city. There would be a further pause for voluntary departure. This time I lost about half my audience. Not bad under the circumstances, I thought, but the whole thing made it difficult for me to start again with any enthusiasm. By this time the peroration was a warmed-up soufflé!

Doggedly, however, I began a third time and had almost finished when there was a sudden and final announcement without any formalities that fire bombs were burning the neighbouring building. Hurriedly I lost the brave survivors of the earlier warnings.

Canada and the United States

31 January 1941

MY own experience suggests that the average Briton, if there is such a person, gets most of his knowledge of the United States from Hollywood; and that he knows even less about Canada. Indeed, he is very often, or was before the war, inclined to think of a Canadian as a species of American. In one sense he is. After all, he comes from North America. That is why I accept now with equanimity the question so constantly addressed to me, "Are you an American?" and merely return the accurate answer, "Yes, I am a Canadian" ...

It is inevitable that, as a North American country, Canada should develop North American points of view on political, social, and economic questions, and possess certain North American social and racial characteristics ... We read American newspapers and American magazines. We cannot help it. We play American games. We won't drink anything that hasn't ice in it. We refuse to move except in motor cars, and occasionally even indulge in chewing gum. American singers, actors, and lecturers are continually among us, while Hollywood has, of course, enveloped us. Then there is the radio, which knows no international boundary. The Canadian listener is, I suspect, more often found searching for swing music from privately-owned stations in New York than listening to educational broadcasts from the government radio corporation in Ottawa.

The most important thing, I suppose, about any country – and about the relationship between any two countries – is geography. Certainly geography is a unifying influence between Canada and the United States, and makes for that identity of customs and outlook I have mentioned.

A glance at the map shows how large Canada bulks on the North American continent. The first geographical impression one gets is of a huge blob of imperial red, from the Atlantic to the Pacific, from the American border to the North Pole. This impression of enormous size is

confirmed by statistics of square miles and by such factual embroidery
that you could put the whole of England in Great Bear Lake; or the
whole of Europe, except Russia, in the three Prairie provinces. These are
rather misleading boasts, however, because, in fact, the area of Canada
which is settled, or even likely to be settled, is much smaller ...

Even more important than actual or economic size is Canada's geographical position in relation to the rest of the world. In this respect
Canada is fortunate in its boundaries and in its lack of boundaries. On
the east and west there are oceans which separate the dominion by
thousands of miles from the political storm centres of Europe and Asia.
Our northern boundary, the Arctic ice, invokes no fear of invasion, and
until recently has aroused no particular interest. There remains the south,
our only land frontier, where we march for some thousands of miles
alongside the United States. Not so long ago this boundary aroused the
same uncertainties and fears that European boundaries do. But not now.
We have few fundamental political differences with our "good neighbour," no fear of her, and, at the same time, the conviction that we would
be helpless to protect ourselves, in any case, against the most powerful
state in the world. So we make the most of a situation beyond our control, and boast in after-dinner speeches of the three thousand miles of
unguarded boundary, which is as much an admission of Canada's relative strategic weakness as a proof of the superior political virtue and
pacific restraint of North Americans ...

There is another respect in which the two countries are, at least super-
ficially, similar. I refer to the racial composition of the population ...
There is none of the homogeneity which now – though this was not
always the case – characterizes England ... In Canada, we are a country
of racial and linguistic groups, with all that this means in our social,
political and economic life. The second largest French-speaking city in
the world is not in France. It is in Canada. There are also large groups
of Germans, Italians, Scandinavians, Ukrainians, and others. It is in the
West that Canada's polyglot character is most striking. In Winnipeg
there are twenty-two newspapers published in languages other than
English or French.

The racial characteristics of the two North American countries are,
then, similar in their variety. Also the constant flow of people between
them brings them closer together. The Canadian-American border was
crossed thirty million times in 1938 by citizens of the two countries. May
I quote Stephen Leacock on this point:

If anyone wants to understand our relations with one another better than history can tell or statistics teach, let him go and stand anywhere along the
Niagara-Buffalo frontier at holiday time – fourth of July or first of July,
either one, they're all one to us. Here are the Stars and Stripes and the Union
Jacks all mixed up together and the tourists pouring back and forward over

the International Bridge; immigration men trying in vain to sort them out; Niagara mingling its American and Canadian waters and its honeymoon couples ... or go to the Detroit-Windsor frontier and move back and forward with the flood of commuters, of Americans sampling ale in Windsor and Canadians sampling lager in Detroit ... or come here to Montreal and meet the Dartmouth boys playing hockey against McGill ... or if that sounds too cold, come to Lake Memphremagog in July and go out bass fishing and hook up the International Boundary itself.

There has also been a permanent as well as a temporary flow of people between the two countries. The population statistics of both nations provide some interesting evidence on this point. During the thirty years, 1901-31, approximately five million immigrants entered Canada (350,000 from the USA). But during those same years, Canada lost by emigration three and one-half million – practically all to the United States. It is almost startling, and to a Canadian a shade depressing, to realize that such has been the attraction of the fleshpots of New York and Chicago that one-third of *all* the people of Canadian origin are now living in the US.

Important also are the economic and financial relationships – closer and more extensive than those between any other two foreign countries. We are the largest customer of the United States and she imports more of our products than does any other country, except the United Kingdom. In 1938 the trade between our two countries was almost two billions of dollars, gradually working up again to the high point of 2,780,000,000 reached in 1929. In 1938, 40 per cent of all our exports went to the United States, and 61 per cent of our imports came from that country ...

Our financial relationships are equally close. In 1938 our foreign indebtedness amounted to approximately seven billions of dollars of which two and three-quarters billions were held in Great Britain and nearly four billions in the USA. Our currency, our dollar, hangs uneasily on New York, when it is not being pushed about by London. Mr Roosevelt signs a decree in Washington, or the Director of the Bank of England writes a letter to the Treasury, and the Canadian dollar wobbles in Montreal. A prominent broker sneezes in Wall Street, stocks go down, and doctors, housemaids, and college professors lose millions in Canada.

Mutterings of alarm are often heard that the United States is getting such a grip on the raw materials, the resources, and the manufacturers of our country that in a few decades, by means of peaceful, even friendly, penetration, the Canadian economy will be completely Americanized. This penetration is so much easier in Canada because Canadian business, Canadian industry, and Canadian labour are organized in fundamentally the same way as that of the United States.

The result? At the end of 1934 there were more than 1350 companies in Canada controlled by or definitely affiliated with American firms. Almost a fourth of the manufacturing in Canada was done by United States controlled companies.

You will now ask, with all these influences pulling the two countries together, will Canada be able to maintain her own separate national existence? I think the answer is undoubtedly "yes," and I shall try to tell you why.

I admit, of course, that there is a tremendous force exercised in Canada by the proximity of more than 130 million neighbours – who are like us in so many respects; and that we ourselves exercise very little pull in the opposite direction. I admit also that Canada must react in some way to this pull. But I think that she more often reacts against it than with it; that it often forces Canadians to develop their own individuality, rather than to imitate that of the United States. With one hundred and thirty millions of Americans right on top of us, if we are to survive as a separate people we are forced, in self-defence, to emphasize the fact of our own existence and of our separateness. The United States, in short, makes Canadians think more about Canada.

Therefore, in one sense, the pull of the United States, far from destroying the three thousand miles of unguarded boundary, has emphasized it. That boundary, though it never will divide in the sense that European boundaries divide, will continue to exist as two different peoples, expressing themselves in different ways, grow and develop on either side of it; for it is a boundary marking deep-rooted identities which are not removed by the assimilating influences that I have outlined, important though they be. As close as they are, our relations with the United States have not, and will not, mean absorption by her. We possess now and are going to maintain our separate national identity. Although we are alike in so many respects, we are unlike in others. The boundary between us may be unguarded but it is not invisible. Let me explain.

There is the boundary raised by history. The story of Canadian-American relations is not such as to make a Canadian forget that he is different from an American. We often hear eloquent passages about the 125 years of peace between our two countries. But it is more than that. It has been 125 years of peace with friction. Anyone can keep the peace if there has been no friction. It is the glory of the British and American and Canadian peoples that they have kept the peace in spite of friction. But this very friction has for Canada emphasized her separateness.

Furthermore, the national development of the two countries has been based on different foundations. The United States was born out of a struggle against Great Britain and hence a struggle against Canada. Its origins are based on fear and suspicion of the Old World and a passionate desire for isolation from its affairs. An American once said: "We Americans left Europe for our own good and we have been marching away from her ever since." That is true, though it might be pointed out that, the world being a round one, if you continued to march away from Europe you eventually get back to Europe again.

In contrast, Canada's political tradition is, in its Anglo-Saxon part at least, intensely British, inherited largely from those American settlers who refused to acknowledge the Stars and Stripes, left their homes after the revolution, and brought their colonial loyalties into a northern wilderness. Whatever military tradition we had up to 1914 was based almost entirely on war with the United States. True, in course of time, we also grew up and became a nation, but while the US could only win its nationhood by fighting against the mother country, we won ours by peaceful means and we are fighting today by Britain's side. So complete, however, is our control now over our own affairs, foreign and domestic, that in September 1939 we had the power to decide, without any pressure or even advice from Britain, whether we would or would not take part in the present war. It's not my purpose now to try to explain why we made the choice we did. The fact that we made it, unanimously and without hesitation, showed that, in spite of all the similarities I have mentioned above, we remain in at least one vital matter different from our neighbours.

There are also other differences in development between the two countries. Canada, with its membership in the British commonwealth, has its roots deeply in the history and traditions of an older political society. For us there has been no declaration of independence to break the line of development from Magna Carta to the Statute of Westminster. A bomb dropped on the Guildhall is a bomb on our past as well as yours, in a sense that it can never be to an American. This makes for unity and indigenous stability. It means that there is less turbulence in Canada than in the United States and more of the social order that accompanies the inheritance of an ancient tradition. That is why life in the dominion moves, if faster than in this country, slower than in the US, even though the manner of our life may be similar to that of our neighbours. There are still in Canada, though their number is decreasing, a good many who subscribe to the Greek conception that the supreme end of existence is the intelligent employment of leisure. The only gentlemen of leisure in the United States are in jail.

Furthermore, in Canada – and this is important – our race problem lies fundamentally in the relationship between the two parent stocks, British and French. The problem of the US is to develop, out of a score of unrelated, newly-arrived, and sometimes antagonistic peoples, an entirely new race.

This leads me to a very important phase of this whole subject, the influence of the French-speaking Canadians on our relations with the United States. Someone has said that the last shot in favour of a British connection in North America will be fired by a French Canadian. That may be true, but only if the alternative to British connection is American absorption. Certainly the strongest bulwark against such absorption is provided by Quebec. It must be remembered that most of the observations I have made about the similarity in habits, customs, and modes of life between Canadians and Americans do not apply – or apply to a much smaller extent – to French Canadians. There is little in common between Quebec and the USA – so little, that we have exploited in the US the tourist value of French Canada as a quaint, mediaeval survival which Americans, if they want to see something different, should certainly visit.

At present Quebec is a powerful, almost a dominating, element in the dominion, with all its own rights of language, law, and religion guaranteed and respected. But that position would be very different if Canada and the United States were one nation. The French Canadians would then be a tiny minority in an overwhelming Anglo-Saxon majority. That is sufficient reason for French Canada strongly to oppose any tendency which might lead to the political absorption of the dominion by her great neighbour. Even those French Canadians – and there are many – who accept with some reluctance a position in the British commonwealth which involves them in Europe's wars, would not willingly replace that situation by one in which Canada's provinces would become states in a greater American union.

It is, of course, this position of ours in the British commonwealth, with all that it implies economically, politically, and sentimentally, which differentiates us most from the United States.

We like to think that, because we have never cut the political tie with the Old Country, we have a somewhat broader international outlook than our neighbours and a greater sense of international responsibility. For instance, we had no hesitation in joining the League of Nations after the last war, nor did we hesitate to take our place in the ranks of those states now fighting the world menace of Hitlerism. Indeed, so long as we are in the British commonwealth, so long as a shot across the Vistula echoes in Vancouver, there can be no isolation for us.

There were Canadians before this war began who thought otherwise. As one of them put it: "We must make it clear ... that the poppies blooming in Flanders field have no further interest for us. We should close our ears to these European blandishments and, like Ulysses and his men, sail past the European siren, our ears stuffed with tax-bills from the last war."

But we didn't sail by.

For better or for worse, 1939 showed again that we couldn't keep out of European wars – or at least this kind of European war. What is the significance of this in Canadian-American relations? It means that in any major war in which Great Britain is engaged, the United States must be at least benevolently neutral. The alternative would be fatal for Canada.

As in war, so in the field of international relations in peace, Canada's dual destiny as a North American state and a British dominion is apparent. Again, her primary problem in this field is to ensure that British and American policies do not diverge to a degree which would make it necessary for Canada to choose between them. For such a choice would, for Canada, be an impossible one, fatal to her national unity and indeed to her national existence.

This was not always a problem. While Canada was a colony ruled from Downing Street she had little influence on policy in London and none on policy in Washington. She was a mere pawn in the game of Anglo-American relations. Once or twice Canadians felt, in the Alaska boundary dispute, for instance, that her interests had been sacrificed to imperial considerations. On the other hand, London, until towards the end of the nineteenth century, considered Canada as rather a nuisance, a "millstone around the neck of the mother country," and a standing source of trouble with the United States.

Now all that has changed. We run our own affairs, and we even have the privilege of sacrificing our own interests. Furthermore, we feel that in our new grown-up state we are well qualified to assist rather than disturb Anglo-American relations. We like to think that the Washington-London Axis – to use the phrase that has a rather disreputable political parentage – runs through Ottawa. While Canadian delegations in the USA are often in a position to give the British point of view, at imperial conferences in London and at League assemblies at Geneva they are prone to adopt a North American attitude. At these European meetings, almost instinctively our reaction to proposals for international action is, first, what effect will it have on British relations with the United States. It was, for instance, Canada that was primarily responsible for the abrogation of the Anglo-Japanese Alliance in 1921, because she felt that that alliance would make relations between the empire and the United States more difficult. It was Canada, as much as any other country, that prevented the League of Nations developing into a security system based on mutual guarantees and sanctions, because she shared the American suspicion of European entanglements which would follow the adoption of any such system.

It is, in short, Canada's fundamental policy to keep on the best possible terms with the US and do what she can to promote the friendliest possible relations between London and Washington as well.

What about American policy towards Canada? Originally there was none, apart from that towards Great Britain. Canada was merely a poor, struggling colony which soon, of its own accord, would ask for the priceless boon of freedom as a new state in the Union. But when Canada got her freedom without ceasing to be British; when she became a flourishing, fast-growing state, one of the first half-dozen trading countries of the world; and when she took her place, in 1914, not 1917, as a partner in the first war against Germany, the Americans began to acquire a more respectful attitude towards us. Not only had we suffered more battle casualties than had they, but we had also become their most important customer. Yet we didn't enter very largely into the Washington scheme of politics, defence, and diplomacy. Pan-Americanism was then – after 1920 – the vogue, and that meant looking south. But with President Roosevelt's accession there came a change, and with that change Canada began to loom larger on the American horizon. This change is concerned with the worsening of the American security position, the transformation of the Monroe doctrine to meet this new situation, and the strategic importance of Canada in the conditions thus created ...

Canada had nothing to do with the Monroe doctrine nor with Pan-Americanism. Her position, first as a British colony and then as a dominion, has excluded her. In the last four or five years, however, there has been a change. First, growing tension in the Far East and the possibility of a clash between the United States and an aggressive Japan emphasized the importance of Canada's strategic position in the Pacific. It would be, I think, quite impossible for us to remain neutral in any major Pacific conflict in which the United States was engaged, and it is equally impossible for the United States to allow Japan to attack Canada. Second, the rise of Nazi aggression in Europe also meant a threat to Canada on the Atlantic, and, as such, became a matter of interest to the US. The climax of this growth of American interest in Canada's defence was Mr Roosevelt's speech at Kingston, Ontario, in 1938, when he brought Canada formally and definitely under the protective umbrella of the Monroe doctrine. That was notice to Hitler – even more than to Japan – that whatever the Nazis might do to Europe, or even to Great Britain, they would have to leave North America, even British North America, alone.

At the time the pledge was given, there seemed to Washington to be no immediate risk of having to implement it. We were still at peace. Even after September 1939, though Canada was at war, the British navy and the French army would together ensure that no German could touch Canadian – let alone American – soil.

Then came the collapse of France. The incredible had happened, and the United States began to realize that for the last century it had been the British fleet that stood behind the Monroe doctrine – that American isolation was based on British naval supremacy. But now it seemed that Great Britain was doomed to follow France to defeat and disaster. The Nazis were in Paris. It was only a step to London and British capitulation; then Iceland, Greenland, the Gulf of St Lawrence. From the Gulf, it was merely a short flight to Boston, New York, Washington. This must be prevented at all costs. And so Canada became a vital part of North American defence. The Americans became more aware of Canada than ever before ... An American writer has said: "Don't forget that this country cannot afford to see Canada go into a tail spin. You are part of our defensive system as we are part of yours. You must be kept strong. Even if we didn't like you, we would have to help you in a pinch."

The result of this interest was the American-Canadian Defence Agreement of last June, which has been acclaimed in the United Kingdom as well as in the two countries most concerned. By this agreement, for defence purposes, the United States and Canada may be considered as one.

This is, of course, a development of tremendous importance, both for the present and for the future. It is, in fact, almost unprecedented, and certainly of great significance, that a neutral and a belligerent should enter into an agreement of this kind. It was one thing for the President of the United States to say on a formal ceremonial occasion in time of peace: "We will protect Canada." It is quite another to say the same thing when the British empire, with Canada, but without any effective foreign allies at the time, is fighting Germany and Italy, with a none too friendly Russia and a distinctly unfriendly Japan.

Are American naval forces to assist us in repelling the attack of a raiding German cruiser against Halifax; or in driving off a German force from Iceland, in the event of the Germans attempting to land there?

An agreement of this kind, therefore, which can be put forward to the American public as a purely North American idea – and therefore above suspicion – is nevertheless a step from isolation to involvement ...

But what are the implications of this agreement, and the tendency it represents, for the future? Remember, in this union for defence, one country has 130 millions of people, and the other less than 12 millions.

While all Canadians appreciate their good fortune in having as their northern neighbours the Arctic ice and polar bears and as their southern, a friendly United States, some are a little bit apprehensive of the future, remembering, I suppose, that when the stalwart young hero jumps into the angry waters to rescue the beautiful young heiress, afterwards he usually wants to marry her – or worse. A well-known Canadian editor has recently voiced these doubts when he said: "The willingness of one nation to defend another is seldom the result of pure affection or even of a pure passion for international justice" ...

I do not think these fears will be realized. Canada is certainly not going to become a subservient protectorate of her neighbour – a North American Manchukuo. My own view is that we will be able to maintain our position as a separate national entity in the British Commonwealth of Nations, while making concessions to our "manifest destiny" as a North American state in close association with our neighbour. In this association we may find it desirable to make adjustments in respect of some aspects of legal sovereignty in return for larger advantages. Such concessions do not, however, worry me. If we are to remove the recurring anarchy of war, *all* states will have to abandon some of the attributes of sovereignty in the interest of larger associations of nations. One such larger association will, we hope, be that of the freedom-loving nations of the British empire and of the United States. If Canada can do anything to foster and encourage this development, I, for one, would not be unduly disturbed if in the process we lose some of our legal title to full sovereignty in the Austinian sense. So I think that we can, without fear, leave the development of Canadian-American relations in the confident hope that they will, to use Mr Churchill's phrase, keep "rolling along" to the benefit of both nations and, I hope, of the whole British empire and commonwealth as well.

7

DR Skelton, under-secretary of state for External Affairs, died very suddenly in 1941. To succeed him, Mr King appointed Norman Robertson, who had become a close and trusted adviser to the Prime Minister. If anyone could take the place of "ODS," it was "NAR." He was one of the most brilliant and at the same time, like his predecessor, one of the most modest and self-effacing civil servants Canada has ever produced. We were close friends as well as colleagues, and he asked me to return to Ottawa and join him as assistant under-secretary. I was very happy to rejoin my family, whom I had sent home from London, and not reluctant to see the end of bombs and blackouts and wartime difficulties. At the same time I was sad to be leaving the gallant citizens of that beleaguered city and, in particular, Canada House. I tried to describe my feelings in a little speech at a dinner given for me by my Canada House colleagues.

I would miss the six-foot, ramrod-straight, ex-Guardsman porter at our block of flats who prevented me one very noisy night from going up to the roof where a fire bomb had landed. I would put it out, be a hero, and win the George Cross. But the porter courteously but firmly reminded me that tenants were not permited on the roof and that *he* would deal with the emergency; which he did.

I would miss my ancient caddy at Roehampton who, one Sunday morning when I was teeing off for my weekly game, blitz or no blitz, advised me to slice a little more than usual because there was an unexploded bomb in the middle of the fairway; a red flag had been placed over its resting place.

At a Farewell Dinner in London

15 May, 1941

Iᴛ is not easy for me to speak on this occasion. You wouldn't wish me to be serious but I do not feel like being too light-hearted. I wish, in fact, that I could combine the inconsequential and the impressive as skilfully as a member of the House of Commons in Ottawa once did when he said: "Mr Speaker, returning as I do from the duty of paying a last tribute to my beloved and revered father, I feel it my duty to rise in my place and protest with great earnestness against any increase in the duty upon corn meal."

Another difficulty in the way of my eloquence is that I have eaten too well for words. There is a story of two diplomats at an international conference who found themselves sitting beside each other for the sixth successive official dinner. One opened the conversation: "How is your constitution standing up under all this?" The other, whose knowledge of English was rudimentary, got only the word "constitution." "Oh," he replied, "in my country we have an upper and a lower chamber."

Well, even if my lower or upper chamber or both were not acting normally, I would still be grateful for your hospitality tonight; and for this opportunity to foregather with so many of those who have made my work here so easy, and made my off-duty hours even easier. Canada House has been for me a good and a busy place in which to work. I hope that when I go back I may be able to convince any Canadians, if such there be, who wonder whether we have enough to do over here.

Once upon a time, I am sorry to state, there was a real suspicion in Canada on this score. I read not long ago a story of a candidate for election in Canada, in the 1890s, who was belabouring the government of the day for extravagance, more particularly in connection with a list of articles for the furnishing of the High Commissioner's house in London. In reading this list at an election meeting he came to the item, "dinner-wagon." Someone in the audience asked what a dinner-wagon was. The orator had not the slightest idea of its purpose, but this did not deter him from the following vivid explanation:

I am glad that question was asked. This man, Tupper [Sir Charles Tupper was then High Commissioner in London] gives great dinner parties, paid for by your money and mine, to which he invites the swells of London. At these dinners every kind of wine is served, paid for by your money and mine. In great flowing goblets, it is passed around and the toffs whom Tupper invites to his dinners drink it until they can drink no more. Finally one of them slips off his chair and falls under the table. Then two of Tupper's flunkeys, paid for by your money and mine, haul the guest from under the table, place him on the dinner-wagon, take him to the front door, call a cab, and send him home. Then another goes under the table and the flunkeys bring the dinner-wagon again and so on until all the guests are disposed of. That, ladies and gentlemen, is the purpose and use of this dinner-wagon, paid for by your money and mine.

The audience, marvellously enlightened, went home full of indignation at this scandalous and iniquitous misuse of public funds. I think, however, in later years Canada has acquired a truer appreciation of the position and work of the high commissioner's office.

So far as I am concerned I can only say that I owe the present head of this office a very special debt of gratitude. I have worked with Mr Massey now in London for more than five years, but my association with him goes back far beyond then, back to 1913, in fact, when as dean of Burwash Hall, Victoria College, he tried to make me and other undergraduates wear an academic gown at dinner in hall and listen to a Latin grace. We freshmen knew everything then, and so we knew that this was just a bit of Balliol swank to be resisted. Resist we did, but without success, and so I was for the first time forcibly introduced to that formality in dress and demeanour which has been so characteristic of me ever since.

Then in the autumn of 1914 Mr Massey used to bark military orders at me, a private in the COTC; orders which, because I was so essentially civilian, I always had difficulty in understanding, let alone in carrying out.

After the war I went to Oxford on a Massey Fellowship, and on returning I joined the history department at the University of Toronto, which the High Commissioner himself once adorned. He it was, also, who first gave me the idea of joining External Affairs.

I give you these biographical details merely to show you that the Massey and Pearson fortunes have for long now been intimately connected, to the great advantage of the latter. I admit that there have been moments during the last few months when the less courageous aspects of my nature asserted themselves and I longed for this connection with the High Commissioner to be broken before the next bomb fell. Indeed, there have been moments when, gazing at the under-side of the bed, I have thought that the happiest fate that could befall a human being would be to return to a country where men crawl under beds to escape husbands, not bombs; where the light shining in the window is a welcome, and not a crime; and where bacon and eggs for breakfast is neither a miracle nor treason.

But now that I am actually going, I realize acutely that it is a great wrench to leave London at this time. The enemy has made the rooftops and shelters of this old city a field of battle. That, of course, has its liabilities, but it also has its assets. One of these is that we work together in a comradeship and co-operation which the front line seems to inspire, and which often is more difficult to find at general headquarters.

It has been no hard duty, but a great privilege to have worked in London during these months of war; to have seen something and felt something of the spirit which now animates the people of this island.

God knows those people are not perfect. They have defects enough. At times their methods seem to me to be based on Plantagenet ideas, applied with Victorian ease. They often make me tear my hair. But, by and large, I feel that this country represents the furthest and finest stage mankind has yet reached in political and social development. As a Canadian I am glad we still have our roots deep in its past, that the line of our national development runs without interruption from the Magna Carta to the Sirois Commission. With our roots so deep, our branches should be able to swing wide and high.

Like many another Canadian I was, before 1939, isolationist, in the sense that I hoped that the British empire might evade those European entanglements that made for war. I even thought that the war, if it came, might be of such a nature that Canada at least could keep clear of it ... That was not to be, and no Canadian can quarrel with the choice which we freely made. Now only one thing matters – to win through. We shall do that by the combination, which is rapidly taking place, of the moral resources of this country and the material resources of the Western world.

Then when it is over, I hope that this country, having helped clean up the European mess, may turn westward and realize that its boundaries in the future are to be not so much the Rhine as the St Lawrence and the Mississippi.

As for me, I regret that I am returning to those frontiers prematurely. To you who remain behind and have to submit not merely to bombs and blast, but even to the rationing restrictions so impressively exemplified by a Coq d'Or dinner, I wish all the best of luck.

Thank you very much.

8

I HAD not been back for long in the Department of External Affairs on my return from London when I was asked to go to Washington as minister-counsellor in our embassy. While there, I was invited to return to Toronto to give the Armstrong Lectures at Victoria College. In them, I outlined the sad story of the road to war – which I attributed largely to failure to build up an effective international organization for peace and security after the First World War. The thesis I advanced in these lectures, that only by restrictions on national sovereignty in the interest of collective action for security could peace be preserved, is one that I have always advocated, in and out of season. But it is not one that is yet acceptable to public opinion. Are we to be destroyed before we are convinced?

These lectures, from which I have here had to omit much, were, of course, given in the midst of war – a time when our feelings and emotions ran high. It is necessary now to recall those emotions in order to appreciate some of the words most of us used in expressing them.

The Road to War

January 1942

As an official of that department of the Canadian government charged with the conduct of our external relations; as one who has served that department both at home and abroad, in various countries, and at a number of conferences, I have had a better opportunity than most to study history in the making. The fact that I participated in these events in humble capacities – at conferences I was usually one of that busy, but unhonoured, species referred to in the directory as "advisers" or "secretaries" – was, in one sense, an advantage. I was on the stage, but at the back of it – a good place for an observer of the drama. Without lines to declaim or a principal's role to play, or any worries about my professional reputation to distract me, but knowing something of the actors and the play itself, I was in a good position to make up my own mind about the whole business; why the play had to be tragedy with a bloody end, rather than a drama with everybody living together happily ever afterwards ...

The subject I have chosen for these lectures – The Road to War – touches the eternal and baffling paradox why nations, and the individuals who compose them, most of whom wish for peace, are continually being plunged into war. I know, of course, that the only way we can get out of this war is by victory, and I realize that everything must be subordinated to that end. But I am not one of those who believe that while we are fighting our way to victory in war, we should not, at the same time, be working to achieve victory at the peace conference. We can do this by studying the causes of this war now, and, by doing so, help to ensure a firmer foundation for peace when it is over. We don't want any half-baked, hastily contrived improvisations at the next peace conference. If we make that mistake, we will have deserved this war and ensured yet another.

This problem of peace and war – of why men fight who aren't necessarily fighting men – was posed for me in a new and dramatic way one evening in Christmas week a year ago in London. The air-raid sirens had sounded their now accustomed message. Almost before the last dismal moan had ended, the guns began to crash. In between their bursts, I could hear the deeper, more menacing sound of bombs. It wasn't much of a raid, really, but one or two of the bombs seemed to fall somewhat too close to my flat. I was reading in bed, and to drown out, or at least to take my mind off, the bombs, I reached out and turned on the radio. I was fumbling aimlessly with the dial when the room was flooded with the loveliest carol music I had ever heard. Glorious waves of it wiped out the sounds of war and conjured up visions of happier peacetime Christmases. Then the announcer spoke – in German. For it was a German station and they were Germans who were singing those carols. German bombs screaming through the air; German music drifting through the air. Whosoever can resolve the paradox of those two sounds from a single source will understand the problem of peace and war.

It is, of course, true to say, though it is not the whole truth, that this war began at the end of the last. Some of you may remember – I certainly remember – the high hopes, the joyous release, the burning enthusiasms of 1919. We had fought for four long hard years. Now it was over, and it would never happen again. "Never again" was the cry on the lips of almost every soldier who was able to thank God he was alive. I say "almost" because even then there was a small group of neurotic, savage, frustrated Germans with a tragi-comic corporal in their midst whose failure in peace had been matched by his lack of distinction of any kind in war. Even then this group was vowing that the day would soon come when they would fight again.

But with this exception, and a few others like it, the whole world resolved that the tragic futility of war should not recur. It *must* not recur
because, we were warned, if it did, it would be the end of all.

What happened then at Versailles? Why did that treaty become a
reason for war instead of a foundation for peace? Why is it that Hitler
shouts with venom every time he mentions it – which is in almost every
paragraph of every speech he ever makes? There were, of course, many
and grave defects in this treaty – "the most abused and least perused
treaty in history," as Lloyd George once termed it. But these defects are
to be found in every treaty made after a hard, bitter, and decisive war.
Versailles was not, in fact, nearly so bad a peace settlement as we ourselves have often charged it with being. It does not remotely resemble
the caricatures made of it by the Nazis for their own nefarious purposes.
Indeed, a more important cause of failure than its terms was the refusal
of certain states to accept the responsibility for carrying it into effect;
and the determination of other states to use it for narrow, selfish, national ends.

Furthermore, the treaty's defects were largely due to the uncontrol-
lable emotions that four years of hate and slaughter had let loose. These
created the atmosphere in which it was made. The final and grimmest
act of the tragedy of the last war was that the hatred it aroused made
any plans to prevent its recurrence difficult to the point of impossibility.
There were almost insuperable obstacles to a cool, objective, and wise
approach to the problem of the organization of Europe in the millions of
the victors' dead; in the thousands of square miles of devastation in the
lands of the conquerors; in sharpened national hatreds, new class anta-
gonisms, strange fanaticisms.

It might be wondered why this atmosphere of hatred and this understandable insistence on punishment of the guilty and defeated did not
bring about a clear and deep-cut surgical solution; did not bring about a
reduction of Germany to an impotence so complete as to ensure that
never again would she be able to commit an act of armed aggression
against any state, however small.

For that, the United States and the United Kingdom are largely responsible. The former country had suffered, relatively, neither very
much nor very long in the war. Physically remote from the scene of the
conflict, the US began to move spiritually and politically back to its traditional aloofness almost as soon as the last gun had been fired. Disil-
lusioned by the bickerings and the backbiting, the jealousies and the
hatreds of Versailles, the United States withdrew from the European
scene in the pardonable but mistaken hope that isolation meant immunity; that to leave Europe to stew in its own dark juice might permit
America to bask forever in its own peaceful light. We know now – and I

hope we will never forget – how vain such a hope must be in an interdependent world, where bombers can fly non-stop for 3000 miles and
submarines can circle the globe. But in 1919 that lesson had not yet been
learned, and the American government, for a time, withdrew unto itself,
even so completely as to return letters "unopened" addressed to it by
that new instrument of Europe entanglement, the League of Nations.

The loss of the United States was one of the greatest blows to the
possibility of the Versailles settlement proving satisfactory and enduring.
There was another such blow when Great Britain, exhausted after a ti-
tanic struggle which had barely snatched victory from the grave of the
ocean, decided that if the United States could retire across the Atlantic,
she would, so far as possible, retire across the channel. Therefore, Great
Britain refused to guarantee the peace, and was reluctant to help police
the Continent. She attempted instead to maintain a series of uneasy
balances, displaying once again that Anglo-Saxon genius for compromise; that tendency to shake hands with the vanquished foe, to let bygones be bygones, and to turn a suspicious eye on the too powerful continental conquerer. Another name for it is "balance of power." In the
pursuit of this policy the British continued to mystify and irritate the
logical Latin by their fondness for organizing peace, as well as waging
war, on the playing fields of Eton; by trying to adapt the rules of cricket
to international affairs. It was a case of, if not three cheers for the losers,
at least a refusal to make certain that in the return match the result
should not be reversed. This was all bewildering and infuriating to the
French, to whom international relations is not a game, as M. Briand
once found to his cost when an outraged opinion forced him from office
after he had spent a weekend playing golf instead of politics with Lloyd
George at Cannes ...

At Versailles, alongside the two wavering Anglo-Saxon powers, stood
France, the tottering victor, bleeding from a million wounds, and gashed
by devastation; grim and determined to end once and for all the menace
of a Germany found guilty by her on all counts, without any extenuating
circumstances and with no recommendation to mercy. Either Germany
must be destroyed completely or France's security guaranteed by an
alliance of the victors, designed to hold down a beaten foe and hold up
a European settlement based on that foe's defeat. France – a victor, but
conscious of a dreadful insecurity; Germany – defeated, but not in her
own mind, and still conscious of military superiority. That combination
gives you the clue to the history of the twenty years after 1918 ...

The Treaty of Versailles, then, was a combination of kicks and kindness; of a severity which the Germans resented and an idealism which
they didn't understand; of a severity, however, which the French felt to
be insufficient, and of an idealism which they determined, therefore, to
use to get that security which had been refused them by the rejection of
an alliance of the victors.

Could this somewhat shaky foundation of 1919 have been strengthened to support an enduring edifice of peace? Up to 1936 the answer was, I think, "yes." After 1936, the answer was "no." For as I see it, the die had by then been cast, in Geneva, when the League of Nations defaulted on sanctions against Italy. If I am right, how might this strengthening of the peace settlement have been carried out in those earlier years before Europe's doom had been decreed? By using the mechanism which had been created for working out that settlement in such a way that just and necessary changes could have been made peacefully; but that aggression by any one would have been met with swift, automatic, decisive, and collective police action.

Such a development was certainly in the minds of the peace makers – or most of them – at Versailles. That was the reason for the League of Nations.

GERMAN REACTIONS

It has been said that the League was damned from birth by making it the child of the peace treaties. But that need not have been the case if the League had itself given birth to those heavenly twins, peaceful change and collective security. Versailles should have been revised at Geneva as revision became necessary; altered, improved, extended. Do not think that much was not accomplished in this direction. Hitler may forget, but we should not, that Germany was admitted to the League, reparations scaled down to a figure below that which Germany received in loans; the Rhineland was evacuated; Locarno was signed; and bit by bit the worst features of the treaty – the worst for Germany that is – were removed by the decision of the victors; but without gratitude from the vanquished. Nothing could, of course, have satisfied that increasing band of Nazi fanatics who, even in those early twenties, were determined to exploit Germany's economic misery and the burning humiliations of defeat in order to climb to power – if necessary over the corpse of Europe. We could never have done anything to satisfy them. But we might have done more to prevent them achieving, first, power in Germany, and finally, domination over Europe. Too often we gave them specious excuses for whipping up German hatred and German frenzy which they exploited with devilish cunning. We considered the Nazis almost as figures of fun; until in 1933, never having received a majority of the votes of their own people, they bullied and beat their way into power. And what then? The concessions we refused Streseman and Bruening – I heard him beg for them in Geneva – we gave to Hitler. But by the time we started to appease Hitler, Germany was strong again; and instead of our concessions gaining Hitler's gratitude, they inspired his scorn; instead of being received as an evidence of our willingness to bring about peaceful change, they were interpreted by the Nazis as proof of fear and decay.

There is another theory – that war was inevitable, not because of the

Nazi triumph in Germany, but because of the German people's lust for conquest. According to this argument not a party but a people are to blame. Hitler is but Frederick the Great and the Kaiser writ large; or to put it another way, "Hitler is merely the old Junker gone mad." German nature, German aggression, German brutishness remain constant whether it is expressed through a Bismarck or a Himmler. This is the national guilt theory, with Lord Vansittart as probably its most persuasive contemporary exponent.

Those who hold this view, that the German character is the cause of it all, do not deny the existence of German idealism, culture, kindliness. Anyone who has lived in Germany – as I have – has experienced these qualities in a Tyrol peasant village, in a Bavarian cafe, or with a group of wandering German students in the Black Forest. There is a Germany of the war of liberation against Napoleon, of the '48, and of the Weimar socialists. But alongside and always undermining this Germany, and always crushing it when the chance presented itself, were the Prussian bullies, the Junker tyrants, the Nazi brutes. The development of Germany is, in short, the application of Gresham's law to politics, "Bad money drives out good." Who said that "the hope of expunging war from the world is not merely absurd but deeply immoral"? It was Treitschke – but it might have been Hitler. Indeed it might have been almost any Prussian leader of the last 150 years.

This poison might have been driven out of the German body politic by a peaceful national growth and the healthy development of representative institutions. Britain, remember, once had this disease but, greatly favoured by history and geography, managed to cure it by combining political progress and administrative order. Britain once had her Prussians, her feudal robber barons, but she turned them into country squires, justices of the peace, local MPs. No such transformation took place in Prussia – and Prussia, in all this, means Germany. There was no "broadening down," no Magna Carta, no Long Parliament, no Bill of Rights, no Fox and no Pitt, no Great Reform Bill, no Tory Democrats, no Labour aristocrats. Consequently there were Hitler, Himmler, and Goebbels in 1939.

Personally, I can't go the whole way with this "blame it all on the German character" school of thought, but I go so far as this. The German people must share the guilt of war with their Nazi overlords. No peace settlement can be permanent which overlooks this fact; just as no peace settlement can, I think, be permanent which is based entirely on the personal guilt of eighty-five million German individuals.

Whatever may be the truth here, I feel profoundly that in the years after Versailles, Europe's rulers should have kept two objectives completely and constantly in view: firstly, to keep the Nazis and those who thought like them out of power in Germany; and secondly, if this was impossible, to make certain that a powerful and collective front was built up so that, if they broke out, they would be punished by international action. This collective European front should, I think, have acted through the League of Nations, not through mere alliances. It should have had as its watchword that which we have adopted today: "Whoever is attacked by the Nazi or the Fascist, we will help."

If we study the years between the two wars, we can follow the disappearance of the hope of a Europe organized in this way. Such a study may prove instructive for the future.

Immediately after the peace conference and the satellite meetings which followed, Germany began the policy of whittling away at Versailles; and other states soon began the policy of whittling away at Geneva. Germany's policy in respect of the peace treaties, though it has occasionally done lip service to "fulfilment," was bent on "destruction." Therefore after a decent interval of mourning and official self-condemnation, Germany concentrated every atom of her diplomatic skill on altering the treaty and securing a position of, first, equality and, later, superiority in the European family.

The test of equality became armaments. In all the diplomatic history of these years, there is no more revealing, no more depressing story than that of the effort to disarm, or to put it more accurately, that of the effort by some states to avoid disarming. After the dramatic initial success of the Washington Conference of 1921 – and even that left its heritage of bitterness – attempts towards the further conversion of swords into ploughshares were nullified by counter-efforts carried on silently but effectively behind smoke screens of eloquence and idealism ...

Why did the disarmament movement fail? The reason is simple enough. The French and their continental allies, the smaller states who owed their existence to the defeat of Germany, would not disarm or let Germany rearm until their own security had been made sure. There is the problem in all its naked simplicity. "No disarmament without security." And so, even for us in far away, so-safe Canada, the struggle for peace became the search of French, Czechs, Poles, and others for security in Europe; but a security based on the preservation of the status quo; therefore security against Germany.

The problem, indeed, from the beginning had been a political and not a technical one. It always has been so in history.

FRENCH POLICIES

Armaments were a symptom, not the cause of the European disease. You cannot cure that disease, war, merely by abolishing tanks or airplanes. Take away all arms – and man can fight with clubs, and stones, and even fists.

Security, then, before disarmament. At Geneva we called this the French thesis. I have heard it argued there so brilliantly and so often, with all that persuasive French eloquence and that fatal French logic, that I know it by heart. Said France: "Let Germany frankly accept Versailles and let our friends help us police that settlement, and there will be security, and, therefore, disarmament and peace." "Let peace be organized," was the cry of every French statesman from Clemenceau to Blum.

What steps did France take to gain this security? First, there was the Anglo-American guarantee of 1919, to be given in return for France's abandonment of the Rhine frontier. But the United States would have none of this, and her refusal released Great Britain from any pledge. Second, there was the Anglo-French guarantee pact of 1922 by which, in the event of unprovoked German aggression, Great Britain would place her forces at France's side. M. Briand tried to widen this military guarantee into a political alliance, failed, and the pact died.

Then there was a series of general security conventions drawn up within the framework of the League. First, the Draft Treaty of Mutual Assistance. This laid down a series of guarantees and provided the machinery for applying them. It combined a general pact with regional agreements for co-operative and immediate action against an aggressor. But this was rejected by various states including all those of the British empire and commonwealth. The British objection emphasized the fact that the treaty was immensely complicated (so is war) and of uncertain practical effect; that it was unwise to superimpose a series of regional agreements on a general treaty. Next there was the famous Geneva Protocol of 1924, the nearest the French ever came to reaching their objective of organized security.

One great weakness of the Draft Treaty had been that no criterion for establishing aggression had been laid down. This was corrected by the Protocol which made provision for the pacific settlement of all disputes, prohibited aggressive war, established tests for aggression, and defined the application of sanctions against an aggressor so established. This was the most elaborate and far-reaching security pact yet attempted, but Great Britain rejected it. Her reason was that she could not accept these new and general obligations as long as the United States and other countries remained outside the League. For such acceptance might conceivably bring her into conflict with those countries. Consequently, the British government stated it preferred special arrangements to meet special needs. Canada rejected the Protocol on similar grounds.

There followed the Locarno Treaties of 1927. These did come into effect and had a most beneficial political result at the time. France received by them a measure of that security by guarantee which she had previously sought in vain.

Other agreements were also signed or negotiated through the League to provide for arbitration and conciliation. But they had no sanctions behind them and, from the French point of view, were, therefore, of no real value for security. Defeated in their efforts to achieve security in this way, the French had recourse to other methods: by military alliances with the Little Entente, with Poland, and later, Russia; and by interpreting and amending the Covenant of the League so as to provide for obligatory and automatic sanctions against an aggressor state. This was known as "putting teeth in the Covenant."

Almost before the ink on the Covenant of the League was dry, the French and their European allies were busy strengthening its sanctions clauses while the Anglo-Saxon states and the Scandinavians were busy scaling down their obligations. The two articles of the League Covenant which dealt specifically with sanctions and security were x and xvi. Great things were once expected from these articles. But the legal fortress which the French saw in them, an impregnable structure with guns in every turret, became a feeble shelter indeed. The walls stood, but the guns were spiked by interpretations.

Canada had a good deal to do with this spiking. We never felt, indeed, that the League should be a fortress at all, but rather a centre for consultation and co-operation. Take Article x:

The Members of the League undertake to respect and preserve as against external aggression the territorial integrity and existing political independence of all Members of the League. In the case of any such aggression or in case of any threat or danger of such aggression, the Council shall advise upon the means by which this obligation shall be fulfilled.

This article was opposed by the Canadian representatives at the peace conference when the Covenant was being drafted. It was opposed in the House of Commons in Ottawa when the Treaty of Versailles was being debated. Its deletion was moved by the Canadian delegation at the first League assembly at Geneva. Failing to secure this, Canada moved an amendment to it at the third and the fourth assemblies, which would have removed from it any obligatory force. Our amendment was defeated, but instead we got an interpretative resolution which left to each member state the right to determine to what extent it would employ its military forces in preserving the independence and integrity of its fellow members. In other words, we weren't guaranteeing any European boundaries in those days. Public opinion felt differently in 1939 – because we knew that our own boundaries had moved over to Poland.

The other security article was xvi. It reads:

Should any Member of the League resort to war in disregard of the covenants under Articles xii, xiii, or xv, it shall *ipso facto* be deemed to have committed an act of war against all other Members of the League, which hereby undertake immediately to subject it to the severance of all trade or financial relations, the prohibition of all intercourse between their nationals and the nationals of the covenant-breaking State, and the prevention of all financial, commercial, or personal intercourse between the nationals of the covenant-breaking State and the nationals of any other State, whether a Member of the League or not.

It shall be the duty of the Council in such case to recommend to the several Governments concerned what effective military, naval, or air force the Members of the League shall severally contribute to the armed forces to be used to protect the Covenants of the League.

The French, and those who thought like them, argued that the meaning of this article was clear and decisive. It meant automatic and obligatory sanctions, military and economic, against any aggressor so determined by the League. All that remained was to work out a method of application. The British empire and the Scandinavian states said, "Not at all. All that the League can do under Article xvi is to recommend. It cannot order us to do anything. There is nothing automatic and obligatory about it at all." These two viewpoints of the League, as an international police force or as an organization for consultation and co-operation, as an executive or as a merely consultative body, came continuously into conflict.

Germany, after her admission to the League, became one of the strongest supporters of the "debating assembly only" view of the League. She, of all its members, had the most to fear from a League whose policing power would be used, if certain members had their way, to ensure the preservation of the status quo.

The League, of course, was not meant to freeze the European territorial and economic settlement. On the contrary, in its Covenant was included an article (xix) designed to facilitate peaceful change as such change became necessary ... The members of the League, however, who were most insistent on the strictest possible interpretation of Articles x and xvi showed a marked inclination to ignore Article xix. For them it was full of explosive dangers just as it was full of hopeful possibilities for the defeated states, Germany, Hungary, Austria, and Bulgaria ...

In the result, the French and their European allies failed in their efforts to make the League into an effective executive instrument for the preservation of peace. For that failure, they were as much to blame as those who opposed them. But whatever the reason, it became increasingly clear that Articles x and xvi were not going to mean what the French wanted them to mean; that the decision of the League to apply force was merely an authorization, and not an order, to the member states. In other words, the Covenant of the League imposed no legal obligation on any of its members to use force – even for international police action against an aggressor. Force remained under national control. We know what national control has done with it. That "sacred idol," unrestricted national sovereignty, was preserved, but the League became "half a League." It was a case of "half a League downward."

CANADIAN POLICY

It is, I think, of the utmost importance to understand why Canada and other states refused to put teeth into the Covenant of the League at this time; why we rejected that collective system in peace which is now our only hope in war.

In the first place, we didn't know then how right the Russian commissar for Foreign Affairs, M. Litvinov, was when he kept repeating at Geneva, gutturally but emphatically, that peace was indivisible. Twenty-six states paid tribute to that truth in Washington a few weeks ago; but only after the world had been at war for more than two years. Until 1940 the non-Axis world – or a great part of it – thought that the plague could be isolated; that peace *was* divisible. Therefore, it was also felt that automatic sanctions would make every little war a world war. This was, of course, true, but we ignored the vital corollary, that if every war was a world war, the odds were against any war, because it would be one aggressor against the world; that the deeper and wider the commitment, the less likelihood that it would ever involve action. We forgot that the more extended the obligations of all, the less danger there would be of any of them having to be carried out.

Those who did not accept this view argued that the League should base its strength on morality and not on force; on consultation rather than coercion; on prevention rather than punishment. It should become a forum from which world opinion would speak, not a platform from which orders would be given to shoot. Further, a League with automatic sanctions might be used to freeze a European status quo which should be changed. Better even half a League than a League used for wrong and selfish purposes. We also suspected – and events in 1936 justified many of our suspicions – that the territorial integrity we were to preserve was that of European states only; that boundaries in America, in Asia, in Africa, were less sacred, though possibly much older, than boundaries in Europe. We didn't expect much help from Europe in the unlikely event of someone attacking us. We felt, in short, that some countries, Canada for instance, were to be asked to produce security which others were to consume.

Security, you know, is the ideal of the insecure, and we felt pretty safe in Canada not so many years ago. In spite of 1914, we still thought that a shot fired across the Rhine might raise no echoes on the St Lawrence. We had just won control of our own affairs. We had just achieved dominion status from Downing Street. Were we to abdicate our new rights to an assembly of foreigners in a Swiss city? Above all, for Canada and the British empire, we could not become part of an armed collective system with automatic sanctions behind it when the United States remained outside that system, even hostile to it. The use of such sanctions might conceivably, it was feared, bring us into conflict with our neighbour. That was something not to be contemplated, even as a remote contingency.

All these reasons, and many others, caused Canada, and numerous other states that felt like her, to resist the wiles of that French siren, collective security, who was attempting to seduce us for her own dubious purposes.

THE ITALO-ABYSSINIAN WAR

Then came the great test – the Italian attack on Abyssinia. I know there had been other occasions in which the League might have prevented wars, might have come to the rescue of the victim, might have punished aggression: the Italian attack on Corfu; the Bolivia-Paraguay war – a bloody struggle which aroused no interest in those Europeans who were clamouring for guarantees in their own continent; above all, the Japan-China "incident." The League failed in all these. But the final, tragic failure, was Abyssinia, for it was here that the new idealism came into the most direct conflict with the power politics of old. To me the present war began in Geneva in September 1935, when the Italo-Abyssinian dispute had to be faced.

This was our greatest and, as it happened, our last chance to make the League work. I, for one, am convinced that it could have worked, and would have worked, if we had then given it a chance; especially if those states who had been for years clamouring for teeth in the Covenant had now decided to use those teeth, which had at last been put at their disposal. But they didn't, and the League failed. No, the League didn't fail, its members failed.

The pitiable tragedy of that failure is that it brushed success. In September 1935, the Assembly of the League met to listen to the statesmen declare the policies of their governments on the unprovoked attack of Italy, the self-styled great and powerful fascist state, on weak and primitive Abyssinia. Would the aggressor get away with it? We looked for an answer on the afternoon of 11 September, for we knew that the Foreign Secretary of Great Britain was going to speak that day. We listened to Sir Samuel Hoare's speech with growing excitement in an atmosphere of tense strain. Then, in solemn and measured tones he ended: "In conformity with its precise and explicit obligations, the League stands and my Country stands with it, for the collective maintenance of the Covenant in its entirety, and particularly for steady and collective resistance to all acts of unprovoked aggression." That was a grand moment in which to have lived, the climax of the postwar struggle for peace. The opening of the Disarmament Conference had been a high point. The emotion of that day, however, sprang from idealism and aspiration. This was something else; it was based on reality and achievement. It was the highest point reached by the League, the summit before the descent. This flood-tide of hope, which was mixed with wonderment, increased as one after another member state voted for the application of sanctions against the guilty aggressor, Italy.

Then the League set up a committee to decide what sanctions should be applied, and how. If there was ever an opportunity to make sanctions work it was now. Italy's aggression was obvious and admitted. Her position was particularly vulnerable to punitive pressure. She had no friends – not yet even Germany – to come to her assistance. In spite of the puffing and boasting of the "sawdust Caesar" who dictated to her, she was in a military sense a weak power, though not until 1940 did we know how weak she was. In an economic sense she was even weaker. Finally, the United States, though not a member of the League, had showed every willingness to co-operate with the League on this issue.

Surely France, the apostle of organized peace with international force behind it, would have seized this occasion, when her own sanctions doctrine had been accepted by a practically unanimous League, to drive home once and for all the lesson that aggression does not pay. If she had, it would have gone a long way to ending all aggression. France, however, took no such course. The sorry retreat from the ideals of collective resistance began almost with the first meeting of the committee appointed to apply those ideals. Nations began to get frightened of the daring decision they had made. Especially was this true of the more powerful nations who were in honour bound to take the lead. And of those powerful ones, France, which had for so many years been advocating, so we thought, the policy which was now being tried, proved weakest. Or was this merely the final and complete confirmation of the suspicion that sanctions were meant to be applied for one particular purpose only – the maintenance of the European structure of 1919?

During the meeting of the Sanctions Committee, my place as a Canadian representative was by alphabetical accident beside that of the representative of France. His name was Pierre Laval. An unlucky fate, unlucky for the world, had decreed that that evil, shifty, treacherous man should be in a key position at this crucial time. There were more honest statesmen, however, who also began to worry about sanctions. If we tighten the sanctions noose, they thought, the Italians will fight to get loose. Sanctions to accomplish their purpose must be effective. But effective sanctions mean war.

The answer to that argument was an easy one. What of it? Is war on these terms and on this issue something to dread? Italy, alone, against the world; Italy, remember, the fascist Italy whose power we now know. That Italy against the world – and it frightened us? Britons who would have fought till death if any Italian foot had been laid on Malta, Mauritius, the Pitcairn Islands, British Honduras, or Bechuanaland, began to discover how weak they were, and how risky and dangerous it was to fight for an abstraction – collective action for peace. Five centuries of history, of traditions, of education in national as opposed to international patriotism could not be overcome in a day or a year.

What a great opportunity was lost in that small room in Geneva when the nations of the world surrendered to Mussolini's sneering challenge! Sanctions were imposed, but only mild ones. They had the effect of a dart in a jackal. They pained enough to infuriate, but not enough to deter. Soon a British statesman could say in the House of Commons that to continue them was "midsummer madness." In the circumstances, and for those circumstances nearly all the governments concerned must accept some share of responsibility, he was right ... That was the end of the League of Nations as we knew it. It was also the beginning, I think, of the present war.

This last is, I know, a controversial and arguable statement. I should try to explain it. We had tried a new deal in international relations at Geneva. But this new deal had failed. It proved to be for some a double deal, and for others, too difficult to be understood. It was thrown aside; the old pack was brought out and reshuffled. The cards were dirty and bloodstained and the four suits were national hatreds, national fears, national armaments, and national wars.

THE BEGINNINGS OF GERMAN AGGRESSION

Across the Rhine were a group of men who knew how to play this old game with a crooked skill and a disregard for morality that made us appear childish amateurs. By 1936, these Nazis had firmly fixed their yoke on the neck of a not too difficult Germany. It is not possible here to discuss their rise to power. They exploited our mistakes and Germany's weaknesses with a fine disregard for every form of decency, honesty, and truth. They beat their way to power. They promised all things to all men, and tortured where promise did not prevail. They played on the desire of the little man in Germany for national respect and economic security. There would be work for all, honour for all, glory for all. At the same time, they played on our desire for peace; peace at almost any cost.

But of one thing Hitler and his crowd were mortally afraid – Geneva. Not the Geneva of 1927 or 1937, but the Geneva of that afternoon of September 1935. Their grandiose and barbaric schemes for domination would have become cloudy phantasies devoid of reality in the face of a collective system at Geneva which worked. That was why the Nazis watched with keen, hungry, but venomous eyes the outcome of the "sanctions against Italy" drama. If the League had succeeded on this occasion; if it had defeated the Fascist aggressor by the united power of its member states, acting as the agents of international authority; if, in short, it had seen sanctions through, come what may, the Nazis were doomed to failure in their plans for European domination.

As we know, nothing like this happened. The League failed. Fascism triumphed. The effect of this was twofold. Firstly, Mussolini, the victorious aggressor, tied himself body and soul to Germany, the potential aggressor, and the Axis was built on the ruins of the League. Secondly, the Nazis knew that they no longer had anything to fear, morally or physically, from the collective action of the nations of the League. Therefore, having divided their enemies, the Nazis felt that it would be easy to destroy them, one by one. As each victim was crushed, the others would be lulled into false security by German promises of "this is our last demand on Europe" and would take refuge in a neutrality which was, in fact, as much protection as a spear against a twenty-ton tank.

This "one by one" gobbling policy ended when Great Britain and France, now alive to the German menace, and arming – though all too slowly – to meet it, gave that blank cheque to Poland which they had refused to Czechoslovakia. The British honoured that cheque, and themselves, in September 1939. This was, however, no League war. It was too late for that now. The British and French with their Polish ally fought alone. No one even thought of invoking Articles x and xvi of the League Covenant, or so much as whispered about sanctions against an aggressor. The League was dead, so complete and rapid had been the deterioration in less than four years.

The smaller European states still thought it possible to be neutral in the old sense. They clung to this hope of immunity right up to the moment and, indeed, even after the moment when Nazi parachutists began to swarm down on their lands and Nazi aeroplanes began to bomb their cities. The Norwegian Foreign Minister, for instance, was hard at work in his study late one night writing a note to the British to protest against some alleged technical violation of international law at the very moment when the Nazis, against whom the British actions had been designed to protect him, were murderously attacking his defenceless and unprepared country. He naturally just couldn't believe it when the news reached him. Only a week before Holland was assaulted, the Netherlands government received authentic information from its intelligence service of the approaching invasion. Not only were no steps taken to concert – even at the last moment – plans of defence with the allies, but the allies were not even warned of the attack. The Netherlands Foreign Minister explained why: "We wanted," he said, "to be absolutely certain that an unfounded accusation could never be made against us for having secretly abandoned the neutrality we had so consistently observed." The reward from Germany for this consistent observance was the slaughter of 20,000 citizens of Rotterdam a week or so later.

And so the German policy "divide and destroy" triumphed over the policy of "unite and survive." Or rather, it would have triumphed if one country, Great Britain, had not stood firm and unshaken against the Nazi might, and, by so doing, provided a core of resistance around which could gather once again the forces of collective defence. As a result, there now exists another league of nations; a league, if you like, of nations at war, working together, pooling their resources, removing barriers between them, subordinating their individual interests to the common good, because only by doing so can any of them survive. This "collective system" will ensure victory. If it could have been achieved ten years ago, it might have ensured peace.

LESSONS FROM THE PAST

What of the future? What have we learned from the past, what are we learning from the present? And how can we apply these lessons to the next peace settlement? ... I have time only to skirt the outside edge of this subject, but I make so bold as to lay down certain principles, the soundness of which has, I think, been clearly shown by the events of the last twenty years. I, personally, am convinced that our refusal to accept these principles, our obstinate clinging to false and destroying gods, brought us from one war into another. I feel, however, even more strongly, that the mere acceptance of principles is nothing; their application is everything. What are they?

In the first place, I quote from a speech of the Prime Minister of Canada in the House of Commons in Ottawa on 3 November 1941:

What all have still to learn is that today no nation is sufficient unto itself, no continent and no hemisphere great enough, in its own strength, to maintain its own freedom. A recognition of interdependence and combined action based thereon is necessary to the democracies of the world, if they are to maintain their freedom, more than it is to the Axis powers in the furtherance of their acts of agression.

We can no longer afford to think of our own freedom and the freedom of others as two things which may be considered apart from one another. We are all members one of another. The freedom of all is bound up in the lives of all.

If this is true, and I think it is profoundly true, then those political concepts "self-determination" and "sovereign rights," which were the guiding principles of the last peace, must be modified at the next peace conference in the light of this interdependence. Furthermore, no country can any longer expect peace and security by basing its policy on isolation or the absence of formal international obligations. Recognition of this interdependence may well, in turn, result in the grouping of small nations – of their own free will – around larger nations.

I am not now suggesting some easy and immediate transition from a world of independent states to a federation of mankind. All-embracing and grandiose concepts of that kind invite their own defeat. I doubt, for instance, whether after this war we will have the will or the desire to cover the whole globe with the same League and Covenant. We tried that in 1919 when we seemed to have both the will and the power. But as E. H. Carr has said, "it is important to remember that the durability of a settlement will depend, insofar as it depends on power, not on the amount of power available to support it at the moment it is made but on the amount of power which will be available to support it ten or twenty years later." The wisdom of those words is proven by comparing the power at the disposal of the League of Nations in 1919 with the power at its disposal in 1939.

We should move gradually, in organizing on a world scale this idea of interdependence. There might first, therefore, be regional associations, all members of which will act together and each one of which will have to yield something of its own rights and its own authority in the interest of the group. This will be the easier because the group will be composed of states whose interests make close associations natural and desirable. There should be room in the world for more than one British Commonwealth of Nations.

The principle on which these associations are founded should, I think, be twofold. In the first place, there must be no veto by any one member state on change, economic or political, desired by all the others. We don't want a frozen organization which can only be altered by an explosion. Next, all change must be peaceful and any effort to use force by one state will be met by the total force of the others exercised under group control. Having formed these regional associations, they, in turn, may form a larger world organization where the bond of union will be looser, the obligations less stringent. A league of nations, in fact, on the model supported by the Anglo-Saxon states at Geneva.

This is no "new order" after the Nazi model, with the base of the pyramid a hundred million slaves and at the top a few swaggering bullies. These regional associations would be voluntary groups of free states which have accepted and applied the principle of interdependence as opposed to independence; who have realized that economic health and prosperity cannot be achieved at the expense of your neighbour; who know that the price of freedom is peace and that peace can only be secured by co-operation. It should be less difficult for the smaller states to accept this development after the war because it has now been proven that there is as little political security for them in formal neutrality as there is economic security in legal control over their own trade and tariffs. This being the case, the whole traditional concept of neutrality may have to be radically revised.

This revision is not dictated primarily by political or moral considerations. It is dictated by military and industrial facts. In 1914 neutrality was possible for most of the smaller European states because their subjugation presented some difficulty. Their nuisance value was high. Those were the days when a soldier was a fighting individual with a gun and a bayonet. Now he is a mechanic who directs swift but huge and complicated mechanized monsters, on land and in the air. Whereas a hundred thousand brave men, skilfully led, could once defeat three hundred thousand, and check twice that many, now a hundred thousand men against a thousand bombing planes and a thousand tanks are impotent. Unless a state has enough machines to ensure its protection, it might as well have none. A small country fighting a big country may as well have no air force as a small air force; no tanks, as a few tanks. Norway, and Holland, and Belgium know this now. Ireland, and Portugal, and Switzerland still talk bravely and sincerely about fighting to the bitter end against any violation of their neutrality. But without help – swiftly and substantially given – that end would be as short as it would be bitter. For only large industrial states can produce the machines without which defence against modern attack is futile.

This means that small states cannot rely on their own efforts for protection. As a result, to be safe, they will have to subordinate their policies and their military plans to those of larger powers. But this is itself an admission that neutrality, on the old model, cannot exist for them. The Russia paper, *Izvestia*, wrote in April 1940: "Absolute neutrality is a fantasy unless real power is present capable of sustaining it. Small states lack such power." That being the case, collective action for individual security has become an inescapable military as well as an inescapable political necessity ...

We may, therefore, have to do some hard thinking about the nature and functions of the state. I cannot, obviously, go into this now. But I suggest that the first essential in this regard will be a recognition of the difference between a "state" and a "nation." In 1919 "self-determination" was taken to mean that all members of a national group had the right, almost the duty, to become one state, irrespective of economic and other considerations. We must remember next time that nations and states do not, and should not, coincide in all cases and in all circumstances. We must, in short, have more nations like Wales and Scotland, and more states like Great Britain, which includes these nations. We must place less emphasis on the rights of national self-determination and more on its limitations; less emphasis indeed on national right of any kind and more on international obligations.

To me, however, almost the most important thing of all – and the most difficult to achieve – it to make sure that there will be no complete reversion to the so-called "good old" prewar days. There is great danger in the fact that during and immediately after years of bitter warfare with all its sacrifices and privations, peacetime, any peacetime, even a "slump," seems something infinitely desirable. That is why in 1919 we were only interested in the road back. We know where that led. We must now keep our eyes on the road ahead ... This time we must maintain, for the organization and application of the peace, the spirit and the forms of international co-operation which we are forging in the heat and flames of war. Let us not deceive ourselves that a new world can be made by going back to the old; or that we can sign a treaty and, presto, there is peace. Peace is far more than the absence of war, and we may have to work for it long years after the guns stop firing. If we don't, we are lost. Let us not think otherwise. Let us not take refuge in the confidence of the drowning man who thinks because he has gone down twice he can keep going down indefinitely without fatal results.

I am of the opinion, therefore, that the co-operation and controls of war must be maintained after war for as long as it is necessary to ensure that peace and security are solidly established. Otherwise, we will once again enter the wasteland of another postwar world, where millions can be spent on munitions but dollars only on nutrition; where a budget of fifty million for social security means ruin, but five hundred million for military security is a privilege; where a hoard of gold cannot reduce hordes of unemployed; where wheat is burned, while humans starve.

9

WHILE in Washington at the Canadian Embassy, I became involved in many activities concerned with the war and its aftermath. This led to various international assignments as Canadian representative at conferences and on committees. It was an interesting experience which later led to many others at the United Nations.

My first of these appointments was to the Preparatory Committee – of which I was chosen chairman – that set up what later became the Food and Agriculture Organization of the United Nations. President Roosevelt once told me that he was particularly interested in this work because he was convinced that the "welfare approach" to peace and happiness was the strongest incentive to bring peoples together after the war.

As part of this approach, the allied nations, before the end of the war, began to consider measures for relief and rehabilitation which would be desperately needed in stricken countries. It was bound to be an enormous task, and UNRRA (United Nations Relief and Rehabilitation Administration) was brought into being to deal with it. I was chairman of the Committee of Supplies for UNRRA, with headquarters in Washington. It was felt that a Canadian should have this responsibility because Canada was expected to and did contribute much to relief in the way of food and other supplies.

This talk was given to the international staff of UNRRA at its first birthday party. The staff, inevitably, had been hurriedly recruited and, partly because of this, the organization was later to show some weaknesses in the field. But the work that was done was of essential importance in the recovery of devastated areas. It was, on the whole, an encouraging beginning to postwar international organization.

To the Staff of UNRRA

5 November 1944

TONIGHT, we are not only inaugurating an UNRRA staff association, we are celebrating also the first birthday of UNRRA itself. I am told that the hazards of life for an infant in the first year of its existence are greater than that of any other period until three-score-and-ten is reached. UNRRA therefore can, at least, congratulate itself in having gotten over this difficult and dangerous period. The infant is alive, flourishing, and learning to walk. It could write and talk from birth ...

What has been done? I don't want to try to answer that question by a lot of superlatives and adjectival generalities. After all, this is a family celebration – not a public meeting. In any event, I don't think I could fool you, even if I wanted to, by any exaggeration of enthusiasm.

Nor do I wish to bore you with a lot of soporific statistics, to befuddle you with data, like the veteran who paraded up and down the street with a sign on his back reading:

Years	52
Campaigns	3
Battles	7
Wounds	2
Wives	1
Children	6
Total	71

With strict accuracy, however, it can be said that the past year for UNRRA has been one of solid and steady achievement. Yet that achievement has, I think, been underestimated in the public mind because it has not been spectacular. The work has been planning, preparing, blueprinting, organizing. All this has been essential, but undramatic. The drama of relief work, like the drama of war, lies in action, in rescue, in sacrifice, in the overcoming of physical obstacles, the storming of concrete objectives. This is the stuff of which song and story are made. But no one, I fear, will ever write a poem about the "charge of the Deputy

Director General for Finance," or paint a picture of "the last stand of the sub-committee appointed under Resolution 23."

There is another reason why the work already done by UNRRA is not fully appreciated. The administration was launched at the White House and at Atlantic City, and, quite properly, in a blaze of publicity and with a fanfare of trumpets. Something new had been added to the international scene, and the press, radio, and movies took notice. There were high hopes and great expectations. But the spotlight was possibly a little too dazzling to last. Even if UNRRA the very next week had begun the practical work of relief and rehabilitation, there would have been inevitably some reduction of attention. So when the hosannas and the hurrahs of Atlantic City were followed, not by action in the field, but by the dull if essential jobs of enlisting staff and organizing duties, of writing memos and drawing up agreements, there was a natural and inevitable let-down which, I think, lessened public interest and may, no doubt, have even affected, temporarily of course, the enthusiasm and morale of UNRRA's staff itself.

However that long period of preparation is about over. There is now a sense of urgency and imminent practical activity. I know you feel that. We felt it at the council meeting in Montreal. The public in our various countries is feeling it. UNRRA is about to go over the top.

There must also, I think, have existed during these months in some of your minds a sense of frustration; a feeling of "Why can't we get on with the things that must be done? Why all this official red tape and delay?"

As one who has been concerned over the years with the ham-stringing effect of red tape, I can certainly sympathize with that feeling. But I have also learned that there is one thing even more delaying and destructive than red tape; that is misguided and premature efforts to cut across wise and well-established procedures. You can, I suppose, get more toothpaste more quickly by squeezing the top of the tube; but it is not a procedure that I would recommend. The result is quick, but messy and wasteful. Conversely, you can go too far to the other extreme, in observing all the fussy niceties and formalities of official procedures. I hope, for instance, that UNRRA will never become strangled with its own forms. I hope you don't feel too often like a staff-officer friend of mine once did. It was during the grim days of September 1940 in London and I expressed some natural anxiety about the future. He cheered me up by replying, "Don't worry, we'll win this war alright, if the supply of carbon paper holds out."

There is another aspect of UNRRA which is to me heartening, but which to many of you, in some respects at least, must seem to make for delays and difficulties. UNRRA is genuinely international. It is international in many ways, but I need mention only two. First, it has an international staff in fact and in spirit. I am informed that there are more than twenty-six nations represented on that staff. There are even some Canadians, who supply, no doubt, the spice and seasoning for this international salad. I have to admit that, in numbers at least, citizens of the United States overshadow the rest. But when I visit UNRRA headquarters, I am always encouraged to feel the cosmopolitan atmosphere of the corridors. There are times when it even reminds me of the old days at Geneva, though the illusion is usually shattered when I leave the elevator, for which I have been waiting some seventeen minutes, and am confronted at once by a Coca-Cola stand. Yet even Coca-Cola, I gather, has gone international these days ...

Don't let anyone tell you that an international staff can't be efficient or harmonious. I know from experience that it can. There never was a national civil service, even in London where my British friends tell me the best civil service in the world resides, which was more efficient, more eager, more energetic, and less hidebound by tradition or timidity, than the old League of Nations secretariat. And I assure you *that* was international. There is no reason why UNRRA should not be as internationally efficient in the organization of the new United Nations as ever the Geneva secretariat was in the old League. The international work that is being done here; the techniques and principles of collaboration that are being developed in doing that work; the organizing of international effort which is going on; the traditions of international service which are being established; all these are going to prove of tremendous value in the days ahead. You are, in fact, an administrative link between the prewar world organization that failed, only because governments wouldn't let it succeed, and the new United Nations organization which will, we hope and pray, be given the chance to succeed.

There is a second important respect in which UNRRA is international. The administration is responsible, not to one, but to forty-four governments. That is, no doubt, inspiring, but it also means, and this may seem a shade disturbing, that every UNRRA employee, in his capacity as such, owes allegiance and loyalty to Ethiopia, Luxembourg, and Iran as well as to the United States, the United Kingdom, and the Soviet Union ... John Galsworthy might write a drama of conflicting loyalties about a situation like this, but there is no necessity for such a conflict. Reconciliation of national and international patriotism is only difficult when we make it so.

Loyalty today should include far more than devotion to a city, a state, or even a country. It must include loyalty to the international ideal for which UNRRA stands. Without this wider allegiance – if you wish to call it that – the deeper, more intimate, more appealing loyalties to the land and the people closest to us will be dissolved and lost in a welter of recurring bloodshed.

The loyalties of the citizen of today need not be exclusive; they are inclusive and overlapping. The municipal loyalty of a Washingtonian does not result in an irresistible desire to lead an expeditionary force against Baltimore. In the fourteenth century, however, such a desire, and such an armed excursion against a neighbouring city would have appeared to be a perfectly normal proceeding; and anyone who protested against it in the market place would have been labelled as unpatriotic or a dreamy idealist. We have progressed beyond that insularity, but we have still one lesson to learn, and this the most difficult of all – that just as mediaeval England or France became too small for warring and competing feudal magnates, so a world of flying bombs and flying fortresses has now become too small for suspicious, warring, sovereign nations. UNRRA is going to be a good place to learn and to teach that lesson ...

Whatever the future may bring to UNRRA, one thing is clear. The task ahead of healing and rebuilding is as hard as it is vital. There is no question as to its urgency, in spite of misleadingly optimistic stories of fashion shows in Paris and seven-course meals in Brussels.

The liberated peoples face shortages, in some cases distressing shortages, of food and clothing and shelter. They are menaced by disease. Many of their factories are in ruins and their fields scorched or flooded. Millions of them are far from their own homes and communities, and need help to return.

Every liberated nation will do its utmost with its own resources to help in this work of relief. They are proud and sensitive people. Let us never forget this – they dislike charity, as you or I would. But not all of them will be able themselves to import all the supplies and services required to relieve their own suffering and reopen the doors of opportunity. This is where UNRRA comes in, to help them help themselves. But UNRRA does more. It gives us a chance to help ourselves by helping others, because chaos, destruction, and despair anywhere are a menace to welfare, happiness, and order everywhere.

UNRRA is therefore a challenge both to our hearts and our heads. It is more than a challenge – it is an opportunity. If this work, organized on a co-operative and international basis, succeeds, it will help and hearten the work of international organization generally. The results of our success will overflow into other fields and will irrigate and enrich the whole international scene.

If UNRRA, however, should fail or falter in its task, much more will be lost than relief for liberated lands. The cause of international collaboration itself would suffer. If UNRRA, which makes its appeal both to our highest feelings of human compassion and to our instinct of enlightened self-interest, cannot prove by its actions and its results that nations can work together, effectively and harmoniously, then, believe me, the outlook for international peace and progress is bleak indeed.

10

THE San Francisco Conference is never likely to be forgotten by those who took part in it. Once again the victors were organizing peace in a way, so the world hoped, that would prevent another world war. Surely, two such wars in half a century were enough.

So the hopes and aspirations of all peoples were centred on San Francisco. For a few weeks it seemed as if those hopes were to be realized. But it was not to be. The record of the conference was one of solid achievement, but there was also increasing doubt. The achievement was in the writing and signing of the Charter. The doubt was in the signs of division between the Great Powers which would prevent the United Nations from operating as effectively as it should for peace, progress, and security.

In this talk given to the Town Hall Club in Los Angeles during the conference, I was more concerned with our hopes than our doubts. I also tried to explain, because I had been asked to speak about this, how Canada as a middle power, and one whose men had twice in this century to cross the sea to fight in war, was anxious that this time a world organization would have the power and will to prevent a third world tragedy. I also tried to explain why Canada and countries like it wished to be able to play an appropriate role, through the United Nations, in the maintenance of security and the promotion of world progress and good relations between states. To this end, we, and others, tried to make changes to the Dumbarton Oaks proposals which had been agreed on by the Big Three – the USA, USSR, and UK – before the conference opened. We had our successes and our failures, but the Charter emanating from San Francisco, though not as good as we hoped, was far better than the draft submitted by the Dumbarton Powers to the conference.

The Charter and the United Nations that resulted from it was capable of serving as a good foundation for peace; but only if the big powers worked closely together. The icy winds of the cold war soon succeeded the warm breezes of San Francisco and blew away hopes of such co-operation.

As ambassador from Washington, I was one of the advisers to the Canadian delegation to this conference. The delegates were from all Canadian political parties: Mr King and Mr St Laurent from the government side; Mr Graydon and Mr Coldwell for the Conservative and CCF oppositions. They soon had to return to Canada, however, where an election was in the offing. This left the permanent officials to carry on during most of the conference. We had a strong team and I think we acquitted ourselves respectably.

Canada and the San Francisco Conference

4 June 1945

CANADA's position at the San Francisco Conference is influenced primarily by three factors:

First, our geographic situation as a North American nation. This often results in Canada taking an attitude towards questions that come before the conference similar to that taken by the United States delegation. The facts of geography are, however, in our case often influenced by facts of history and tradition.

This brings me to the second factor – our position in the British Commonwealth of Nations. That position is based on two things: friendly co-operation with other parts of the commonwealth and the complete independence of all those parts. There is a persistent ignorance in this country and in others of the nature of this British commonwealth and of Canada's place in it. There was, for instance, much talk before the conference began of a British empire bloc – of six British votes, and all that. It is as foolish to talk about six British empire votes at the conference as of twenty-one Latin American votes. In fact, voting at San Francisco often illustrates that the dominions are "chips off the old bloc." We do, however, want to co-operate fully with the other states in the commonwealth within the world organization, and we have no desire to give up our special relationship with those states, especially as it does not prejudice co-operation in a wider field.

The third factor influencing our position at San Francisco is our strength and our resources as a middle power. This results in close co-operation with such states as Brazil, the Netherlands, Norway, Belgium, and others in that "middle" category.

We approach the problems of this world conference from the point of view of a state which has made a contribution to international security in the past and which knows that if war breaks out again, it will be asked to make a similar contribution. In that respect, our position is as different from that of the smallest power as it is from the largest. We do not see why the sovereign equality of states, a principle which must be accepted in theory, should be modified in practice only by giving special rights and privileges to great powers. We agree that power and responsibility should be related, that absolute equality in any world organization would mean absolute futility. No country will be able to play its proper part in international affairs if its influence bears no adequate relation to its obligations and its power. This, however, means not only abandoning the fiction that Salvador and Russia are equal on the World Security Council, but also abandoning the fiction that outside the group of four or five great powers, all other states must have an exactly equal position.

This feeling, based on our experience, has coloured our views. No special position of any state, or any group, or any regional association must destroy universality. We also know that there is no permanent basis for a world organization on any alliance of a few powers, however great. There must be an international framework within which great powers can work with each other, but also with all other powers. The world organization must be a symphony, not a string quartet. We also realize, however, that the symphony must have a leader. The Big Three are the leaders here, and if they don't lead in harmony together, if they appeal separately to different instruments, strange and discordant music will result.

In the last analysis, unless the big powers work together and have faith in the organization and in the whole idea of international co-operation, the charter of San Francisco, however perfect in all its details, will be merely a shiny, beautiful motor car without an engine. Conversely, if the great powers have the will and the desire to co-operate, even if the machine isn't perfect, it won't matter very much. It will work.

Therefore, Canada's preoccupation with San Francisco is based on the hard realities of the existing international situation.

There are dangers in seeking perfection. Whatever comes out of San Francisco will be a compromise. It will not, it cannot, be ideal. There is no use in hoping to reform the world by any single plan. If we insist on perfection, we might not get anything. We would merely make the *best* the enemy of the *good*. The compromise which will result from San Francisco may be well fitted to postwar conditions, to transition from war to peace. Some of its provisions, however, may prove later to be not so well suited to normal peacetime conditions. It is therefore essential that the charter be flexible and relatively easy to amend.

Nevertheless, our main purpose is to get an organization going which everyone will accept and which will help to ease international difficulties by adding to the machinery for international co-operation. To make that machinery as efficient as possible, our delegation has – as others have also – proposed certain changes to the Draft Charter which, we hope, will improve it.

The changes in which we have been specially interested are based fundamentally on one idea – to make the charter one which will appeal to public opinion in *every* country, by giving the people of that country, through their governments, a real sense of participation in the work and responsibility of the new world organization. We don't want to make easier the work of isolationists in any country.

Many of our changes are not going to be adopted, because the sponsoring powers will not accept them. We accept that fact, that the charter must represent the highest common denominator of agreement among the four great powers. The veto, for instance, is unavoidable now simply because unanimity among the great powers is essential.

This veto power given to the great powers, however, simply means that, though our new league of nations will have more teeth than the old one ever had (and that is a great improvement), those teeth can be used only to bite the smaller countries when they misbehave. For this reason, it may be argued that the teeth need dental attention. Well, they will probably get it in Committee Three of Commission Two. Remember, however, dentistry consists of filling teeth as well as in pulling them out.

Remember, also, that a great power, though it has a veto on decisions to use force against it, is pledged equally with a small power not to commit aggression which would necessitate the use of such force. If it breaks that pledge, its right of veto, or the absence of that right, is of little practical consequence ...

The veto is not a protection for unanimity. It may even be an evidence of disunity. I hope that in the future the powers will have sufficient faith in each other, and in the organization, to base their unanimity on deeper and higher considerations than the possession of a veto on decisions of the Security Council. But this is not the case now.

Other changes to the Draft Charter, however, have been possible. The prestige and power of the Assembly have been increased without interfering with the work of the Security Council which is, of course, the primary agency for settling disputes and preventing aggression. The Assembly will be the forum through which international public opinion, through which the world conscience, can express itself. It is the town meeting of the world.

We of the Canadian delegation are especially interested in the committee of the conference dealing with economic and social matters. We feel that the primary task of the new world organization must be to remove the social and economic as well as the political causes of international friction and international dispute. What we are trying to create here is a league for peace, not a league for war. There must always be in reserve overwhelming force on the side of peace, but the use of that force, or even the threat of its use, must become the deplorable exception, not the general rule. The new international organization must therefore come to think and act less and less in terms of force and more and more in terms of forces – the forces that create or destroy international amity and goodwill, the forces that create poverty or promote well-being. To that end, we welcome the fact that the powers and position of the Social and Economic Council have been greatly increased.

As for the Security Council, we wish special consideration to be given to middle powers in election to it because they will be expected to contribute substantially to the enforcement of any decision taken. We also feel strongly that states which are directly concerned with a question on the agenda of the Council should participate in its discussion. This is especially essential if a state is being asked to contribute armed forces for any collective police action that may be decided. Indeed, in this case, the non-member state concerned should take part not only in the discussion but in the decision of the Security Council.

The Draft Charter for a United Nations which was agreed on at Dumbarton Oaks by the big powers will, I am confident, be substantially improved by the decisions made at the San Francisco Conference under pressure from smaller countries.

It has been good that the big powers have had to discuss and argue with the others and that on occasions they have been outvoted and accepted the resulting changes. The smaller powers in their turn have shown a proper sense of responsibility and have yielded in respect of many of their proposals which they considered to be good ones, when they were convinced that the sponsoring powers were not able to accept them, without creating disunity and division that would have made any charter impossible.

There has – at least to some extent – been a healthy give and take of international debate on a wide front and most of it has been constructive.

But remember, whatever we accomplish at San Francisco is a beginning, not a conclusion. It will be something which will have within it the seed of hope and progress and achievement. That is all we have any right to expect. Whether that seed grows and flourishes depends entirely on what the nations do about it. Remember this also – the proposals we are discussing now, and which I think will be accepted, embody the pledge of all the United Nations, not some of them, but *all* of them, great and small, to co-operate in the work of ensuring peace and promoting welfare. They also establish – even if they do not reach – the objective which we must seek to attain: that national force must ultimately be brought under international control if peace is to be safeguarded. Starting from, not ending with, Dumbarton Oaks and San Francisco, we must seek to make certain that never again shall an aggressor be permitted to strike down one nation after another before the peace-loving nations of the world organize and take concerted action against it. If we have not learned, from the history of the last thirty years, that that must be the supreme objective towards which we must all strive, we are incapable of learning any lesson.

There is no use fooling ourselves that it is going to be easy to attain this objective or, having attained it, to consolidate our position and defend it against counterattacks. The struggle for victory over war is even harder than the struggle for victory in war. It will be a slow, tough process. There must be superb organization. There must be brilliant improvisation. At times caution; at other times, a willingness to run great risks for great objectives. At all times a refusal to permit temporary reverses to shake our belief in ultimate victory. Above all, there must be no false optimism about the possibility of an early victory. There is no easy and upholstered way from the foxhole to the millenium. We shall not secure victory over war at San Francisco. But we must, as Commander Stassen has said, win at San Francisco a "beachhead in the battle for a just and lasting peace," the beachhead not being "the final goal, but only the jumping-off place for the long, hard drive toward victory." We must be very sure that we get at San Francisco as large and effective a beachhead as possible.

To that high endeavour, for which our men have died in every far corner of this shrinking world, the least we can do, every one of us, is to pledge our hearts, and our minds, and our souls. If we fail, then we might as well agree with the cynic who referred to this war as "the little one before the last."

11

THIS was the last time I discussed the principles influencing Canadian foreign policies before I abandoned the security and satisfaction of the Foreign Service for the excitement and uncertainty of politics. It will be noticed, however, that I talked about policies, not politics;

and I believe I did so in terms that were non-controversial in any partisan sense. Certainly at that time I had no partisan feelings and not the slightest idea that, in a few months, I would be a Liberal member of Parliament and secretary of state for External Affairs. How that happened, suddenly and in a way to change my subsequent life, is another story.

This speech to the Vancouver Branch of the Canadian Institute of International Affairs may have some interest in the fact that the views I gave them on Canadian foreign policy, which would later lead us to membership in NATO, were substantially unchanged after twenty years in office and opposition. I would not, however, have been quite so dogmatic in 1968 in my warning about communist conspiracy as I was in 1948 when we were feeling the worst effects of the cold war and the first aggression against Czechoslovakia by the Kremlin was taking place. I would be more concerned now with Soviet imperial policy than with communist ideology.

To a great extent, Canada's foreign policy has been determined for her by circumstances and conditions which she did not create and some of which she cannot alter. I doubt, however, whether we can expect these factors to remain unchanged during the years ahead. Even our geography is being altered, to say nothing of new economic and constitutional problems.

Some Principles of Canadian Foreign Policy

January 1948

THE principles that should direct and control a national foreign policy in this interdependent, atomic age are almost as difficult to define as they are to implement. Our age is one of swift-moving change. In our political and economic thinking and in our foreign policy, we are trying to catch up with the implications, the shattering implications, of the scientific revolution that has taken place. We have made some progress in our thinking. But the translation of thought and understanding into national and international political action is agonizingly slow. And time is neither on our side nor at our disposal.

Foreign policy still tends to be expressed in terms of the sovereign national state, though these terms are as out of date as a battle axe at Chalk River. We cling, if I may switch metaphors, to the ancient and respectable reluctance to change horses in mid-stream. Though we know that this particular horse – the sovereign nation state – will never get us across to security on the other bank, it seems at times as if we are nevertheless willing to be carried downstream and over the falls, rather than abandon it ...

The foreign policy of a country, especially of a country like Canada, cannot in the circumstances of today be determined by national considerations alone. There are, however, national and local factors which influence, to a great extent, the nature and value of the contribution that a country can make to a collective international policy; that measure the extent and character of its co-operation with other and friendly states.

Foreign policy, after all, is merely "domestic policy with its hat on." The donning of some head-gear, and going outside, doesn't itself alter our nature, our strength, and our quality very much. If we are weak and timid and disunited and jumpy at home, we will be the same away from home. Canada's foreign policy, in so far as it is Canadian policy at all, is, in fact, largely the consequence of domestic factors, some of which remain constant and others which are not easily altered. Geography (especially air geography), climate, natural resources, the racial composition of our population, historical and political development, our dependence on foreign trade, our physical and economic relationship to the United States, our historic association with Britain in a commonwealth of nations – these are the factors that influence, and often determine, the decisions which the Canadian government has to make on individual problems which require action. It is the collectivity of these decisions, made in a variety of ways, with great thought or little thought, for good reasons or for no reason, which make up what we call "foreign policy."

A Canadian government is not only restricted by domestic factors in its external plans; it is limited also by the policies and attitudes of other governments. Of course we are independent now, constitutionally. But that independence is only relative. The pride at being able to cast a vote at Lake Success, which counts as much as the vote of the US or of Liberia, should not obscure the fact that decisions can be taken in Washington, or in London, which often have as important, and sometimes almost as immediate, an effect on the well-being and security of our people as a Canadian act of Parliament or an order-in-council.

When we talk of Canadian foreign policy, therefore, we are not talking of clear-cut, long-range plans and policies under national direction and control. We are certainly not without power to influence our own external policies – and in many matters the influence is of course decisive. But we needn't exaggerate our power, or deceive ourselves about it, by talk of sovereign rights and unrestricted independence.

This becomes all the more apparent when we look realistically and without self-delusion at the objectives which Canadian foreign policy seeks to achieve. Few of these objectives are concrete or positive, except in the realm of international economic policy, where again the major decisions are outside our sole control. We have no territorial desires, having already quite as much geography as we need. We certainly have no expansionist political ambitions. When from time to time it is suggested, for instance, that we enlarge our sphere of influence and accept certain responsibilities in connection with the British West Indies, we become very modest and timid. We are satisfied with our present boundaries – even though we have lost more territory than most countries by unjust international arbitrations. We can leave *terra irredenta* foolishness to other countries. No British Columbian schoolboy need spring to attention, turn north, and salute the flag whenever the Pan-Handle is mentioned. We have inherited no legacies of hatred or distrust with which to excite and inflame our people. We are, of course, worried about the ability of our neighbour to use its great new power in a way which will ensure peace and security for the world and will not infringe our own legitimate national rights. But this is not a worry which we express in any positive way. At best, we adopt an "on guard" posture.

Our modesty, our timidity, if you like to call it that, does not, I think, mean that we are isolationist. It may once have been based on that not unreasonable reaction to the follies of Europe. Our timidity, now, is a sensible recognition of the fact that middle powers who once might have expanded in a rewarding, an imperialist, way can now merely expand their responsibilities and their worries. It is also a recognition of the internationalist view that countries must come closer together inside a United Nations rather than take over areas and responsibilities outside it. We can most effectively influence international affairs not by aggressive nationalism but by earning the respect of the nations with whom we cooperate, and who will therefore be glad to discuss their international policies with us. This principle is based on both political and economic considerations. We instinctively know that Canada cannot easily secure and maintain prosperity except on the broadest basis of multilateralism – which is another name for internationalism. Even the British Commonwealth of Nations, which we quite properly consider to be a cornerstone of our external relations, is not wide enough for our needs in the postwar world. We also know, or should know, that there can be no political security except on the widest possible basis of co-operation. If that basis can be a universal one – so much the better. If it cannot, then on the broadest possible basis and inside the United Nations.

Canadian political leaders, even Canadian civil servants, have been preaching that doctrine vigorously and constantly during the last year. Our government has, I think, given a lead in this vital matter, and has made more specific and unreserved commitments concerning it than has any other government. All this is far removed from the spirit of timidity over the British West Indies, which I have mentioned. It is far removed from the cautious, somewhat inglorious attitude we adopted at Lake

Geneva in the twenties whenever sanctions or collective security was mentioned.

What has come over us? Or are we just talking big? If another Ethiopian issue arose would we act as we did in 1935? Weren't we rather timid about accepting obligations on the UN Korean Commission and haven't we, after a somewhat adventurous beginning, backed well away from the implications of our earlier words in the sorry and tragic Palestine business? ...

I feel very definitely, in spite of evidence here and there to the contrary, that Canadian policy at Lake Success in New York, in regard to collective security, is different from, and much more positive than, that which we followed at Lake Geneva in Switzerland in prewar days. The difference in policy is, I think, explained by changes in circumstances. What are these changes?

1 The UN is in the United States;
2 we have had a second world war;
3 the crusading and subversive power of communism has been harnessed by a cold-blooded, calculating, victoriously powerful Slav empire for its own political purposes.

Let us look at these in turn.

First, the fact that the United States is not only a member of but the leader in the UN, and has been from the beginning, radically alters the position compared with that of the old League of Nations. It will be remembered that the one great nightmare of prewar Canadian governments was a clash, or even a divergence, of policy between the two governments – American and British – with both of which Canada wished to keep in step. It seemed in those days that the League of Nations, in some of its manifestations, notably French insistence on using the League to keep Germany down, might bring about differences between London and Washington. That helps to explain, though it may not justify, Canadian negative, timid policy in regard to such matters as Article x of the Covenant of the League and sanctions under it. The United States, you remember, was not a member of the League.

There is no danger of that kind in the United Nations, in which British and American policies now usually march side by side. We can stride along beside them, and even on occasions indulge ourselves by slipping ahead. It is, of course, to our interest to strengthen any organization which brings London and Washington into closer alignment. The UN, in the face of the menace of communism, does that. When in specific cases this result is not achieved, and a divergence of view between London and Washington develops inside the UN, then all the old Canadian fears come to the surface.

The Palestine issue is a good case in point. The more bitter the dispute between the US and the British points of view on this issue – and it once became bitter – the more cautious Canada became in supporting one side or the other; or in actively participating in UN committees or agencies set up to deal with the question. At the same time we worked hard, but well behind the scenes, to reconcile the US and British points of view. The whole episode is revealing. It shows that the earlier postulates of policy still, if almost unconsciously, apply, though possibly with less force as Canada grows in confidence and strength. It shows that, almost automatically, we stop playing the triangle in the international symphony when the British and American instruments are out of harmony.

Personally, I would have liked in this Palestine issue to have taken a strong independent stand for what we thought was the proper and right solution and to have dismissed the British and Americans with "a plague on both your houses; on votes in New York; and oil in Arabia." But then "irresponsible" civil servants can always afford the luxury of these courageous fancies.

The second difference of 1948 over 1928 is that we have had a second world war. This has shown us:

1 that war is indeed indivisible from now on in;
2 that war is annihilative;
3 that we cannot escape it by national action alone, either by isolation or by preparedness;
4 that in the future, not our European but our North American connections may bring us into a world conflict. It seems a long time since a Lindbergh could demand that Canada break her association with the UK lest it drag the US into war.

The Second World War has left us, and everybody else, not with the rosy feeling of 1919 that the world has been made safe for democracy and a place fit for heroes to live in, but with a feeling of insecurity amounting almost to panic. This springs in part from the horrible implications of atomic, supersonic, and bacteriological warfare; in part from the depressing and bitter division of the victors over fascism into two hostile camps, a division which is both ideological and political.

This brings up the third difference between the current situation in the United Nations and that formerly in the League of Nations. The chief menace now is subversive, aggressive communism, the servant of power politics. The change is sufficiently indicated by comparing the plausible, pleading speeches of Litvinoff at Geneva with the snarling, vituperative outbursts of Vishinsky last October. In the face of the menace of aggressive communism, the democracies are brought closer together, *all* of them, and are willing to make concessions of national rights which they would never have thought of doing ten years ago.

Security has always been the ideal of the insecure and the search for it, now in 1948, is much more widespread and more intense than in the days when the French tried to use the League of Nations for this purpose. We now know that there is no security in distance; that incapacity to harm does not mean immunity from attack; that indifference does not mean isolation. There are no fire-proof houses in the atomic age, or little countries far away, like Czechoslovakia in 1938, whose fate means nothing to us. Our frontier is now not even on the Rhine or rivers further east. It is wherever free men are struggling against totalitarian tyranny, of right or left. It may run through the middle of our own cities, or it may be on the crest of the remotest mountain. Above all, no longer do we insist that we are the producers of security to be consumed by others, a feeling which is a basic source of isolationism.

If all this is true, and I think it is, it explains why it is possible, indeed inevitable, that certain principles of conduct and policy can be followed more openly by Canada today than would have been possible a few short years ago. These principles are now the easier for any Canadian government to adopt, not merely because our close connections with London and Washington would involve us, in any event, in any major war in which they were both involved, but also because of the spiritual – if I can use that word without misunderstanding – nature of the struggle against revolutionary communism which makes its appeal, on ideological grounds, to a large section of our people who previously had been suspicious of overseas entanglements.

It seems to me that this search for security requires decisions on two matters: firstly, the policy to be adopted towards aggressive communism; and secondly, the policy to be adopted towards the UN, as it becomes increasingly impotent in the face of the East-West division between free democracy and totalitarian communism, with a superpower at the head of each side. As to the first, Canada cannot, of course, play the leading role. But we should not blindly follow British or, more important, US policy in this matter. We have opportunities of influencing, both by example and by precept, the policy of others who count for more than us, and we should use them. We should not support the policy of others, at the United Nations or elsewhere, merely because it is put forward as a defence against communism. Nor should we support communist appeasement measures which are dictated purely by tactical considerations of power or politics.

All this is easier said than done. I suggest the principle which should guide us is support for any policy of steady and consistent, firm but unprovocative resistance to communist aggression or indeed to any aggression. We should oppose panicky and provocative moves when things deteriorate. We should not, however, allow ourselves to be fooled into a sense of false security when there *seems* to be an improvement in the international climate, an improvement which may have been manufactured merely to create complacency. To keep our Canadian balance between the extremes of hope and fear, altruism and interest, which so often seem to characterize the policy of our neighbour, is going to require steadiness and good sense. It is going to require, on occasions, firm but friendly resistance to pressure for support which is all the more difficult to resist because it will be made in good faith and with good will.

The most immediate danger is, I think, the illusion of improvement in the communist picture, which improvement may have been created by those who wish to prevent the type of international security arrangement which alone in present circumstances can bring about a real and lasting improvement. We are becoming familiar with the practice of communist dictators giving reasonable and pacific answers to the carefully selected questions of favoured correspondents, designed to create certain impressions and encourage certain delusions. We should not be deceived by such tactics, especially at this time when the outlines of a democratic security system are beginning to appear.

It would, of course, be folly to accept as inevitable or irrevocable the breach between communist and democratic states. There is nothing inevitable in the shifting currents of history or politics. Régimes come and go, peoples rise and fall, they submit and they revolt. The eternal spirit of man can never be permanently bound by slave institutions, even in the least advanced states. But I *do* suggest that our present attitude towards communist despotism should be based on the pure, or impure, doctrine of that creed as enunciated by its leaders and its prophets, and not on "answers to questions" which make the headlines on the afternoon editions five thousand miles away from the Kremlin where they are not taken seriously and from the people who are not allowed to savour their sweetness and light.

Mr Stalin, for instance, may pick out six or seven questions from twelve or fourteen, and answer them in a way which should earn him a lot of merchandise on any quiz programme. But we would be better advised in finding out what the totalitarian communist state means to study other statements of Mr Stalin which were meant to be taken seriously by communists as a permanent doctrine for action. You will recall that we did not take very seriously the preposterous statements of the slightly ridiculous author of *Mein Kampf*. We preferred the friendly remarks of "jolly old Goering" at his hunting lodge. But *Mein Kampf* laid out – for all who cared to see it – the authentic plan of Nazi aggression. Let us look, therefore, not at Premier Stalin's answers to half of Mr Wallace's questions, the ones he chose to answer, but at some of Mr Stalin's statements which form the basic dogma on which the policy of the USSR is inflexibly based.

Regarding the external opposition and irreconcilability of capitalism and communism, Premier Stalin reaffirmed, at the Fourteenth Congress of the Communist party on 9 May 1925, Lenin's candid dictum that "we are living not merely in one State but in a system of States, and it is inconceivable that the Soviet Republic should continue to exist interminably side-by-side with imperialist states. Ultimately one or the other must conquer." Stalin also asked: "Who will defeat whom? This is the essence of the question." Regarding flexibility of tactics, he quoted Lenin: "... tactics change dozens of times, whereas the strategical plans remain unchanged. Tactics deal with the forms of struggle and the forms of organization of the proletariat, with their changes and combinations. During a given stage of the revolution tactics may change several times, depending on the flow or ebb, the rise or decline, of the revolution"; and again: "To carry on a war for the overthrow of the international bourgeoisie, a war which is a hundred times more difficult, prolonged, and complicated than the most stubborn of ordinary wars between States, and to refuse beforehand to manœuvre, to utilise the conflict of interests (even though temporarily) among one's enemies, to refuse to temporise and to compromise with possible (even though transient, unstable, vacillating, and conditional) allies – is not this ridiculous in the extreme? Is it not as though, in the difficult ascent of an unexplored and heretofore inaccessible mountain, we were to renounce beforehand the idea that at times we might have to go in zig-zags, sometimes retracing our steps, sometimes giving up the course once selected and trying various others?" ... "The object of this strategy is to gain time, to demoralise the enemy, and to accumulate forces in order later to assume the offensive." (*Problems of Leninism*, quoted by Stalin.)

These utterances, which were not for foreign consumption, reveal that the fundamental aim of Soviet policy is to make the Soviet Union strong enough to prevail in the decisive struggle which should result from the next inevitable crisis of monopoly capitalism. Tactics may change, but the fundamental strategy remains the same. The clash with monopoly capitalism, however, is not necessarily imminent, and in the meantime the Soviet Union may at times be prepared to go along with the rest of the world, provided always that this entails no weakening of its fundamental position for the ultimate and inevitable struggle.

It is a first essential, then, to understand communist doctrine which lies behind and guides Russian policy. In his book *Russia and the Russians*, Edward Crankshaw gives a balanced and enlightening analysis of this subject. May I quote just two thoughts from that book?

The truth ... lies all around you ... Violence, arbitrary law, sustained privation and undernourishment, blind, trampling stupidity, the uttermost harshness of rule over body and soul impartially, bodily slavery with no compensating freedom for the spirit, forced atrophy of the independent mind without bread and circuses to fill the gap, physical drabness and squalor over all, reflecting perfectly a mood of hopeless apathy ...

Unless we ... realize that they stand for a faith, a faith which is transforming the face of Russia and has the power to transform the face of the world, unless we do this we shall soon find ourselves transformed or liquidated. The great mistake of many pagan societies blotted out by the Christians was that they never found out what it was that was hitting them until it was too late. At the moment most of us in the West have not the faintest idea of what is hitting us.

In the face of this situation and having done our best to understand what we are up against, what should a country like Canada do, in association with other free countries?

I suggest that, in the first place, we should recognize that we cannot remove the menace of aggressive communism, at home or from abroad, merely by damning it and by including in that damnation, as a communist, anyone who votes the other way. If democracy is to flourish, or even survive, it must be far more than anti-communism. It must become, and remain, a positive and dynamic doctrine which proves, by results, that it can contribute more to the welfare and happiness of the individual than communism can. We need not fear communism from within or from without as long as nations, in their foreign policies, are willing to co-operate in the prevention of war and give up some of their old and outworn sovereign rights in the interest of greater security; and as long as, at home, they keep their democratic societies strong, healthy, and progressive. But, as it has been said: "Being strong and healthy is not the same as beating our chests and staging war-dances in front of the iron curtain. Being strong and healthy means keeping our own house in order and arranging the life within it so that all the members of the household are proud to belong to it and do not look elsewhere for their salvation from oppression."

Furthermore, in this struggle of free, expanding, progressive democracy against tyrannical and reactionary communism, we should be careful not to use our weapons in such a way that we win battles but lose the war. We must not allow freedom to be used to impose slavery. But neither must we lose our freedom in the name of security.

While democracy, then, is proving by its contribution to human welfare its superiority as a form of government and a way of life, what steps must the free states take to protect themselves from the threat of a sudden attack by an aggressor communist state?

The United Nations, as at present constituted, cannot give that protection. But within the UN there is no reason why free states, on a regional basis, should not form a security system, the members of which are willing to accept greater responsibilities for co-operative defence in the interest of greater security.

Canadian official policy on this matter is well known and I need not elaborate it. May I mention very briefly, however, what such an association of free states must not become.

1 It must not be a provocative, aggressive alliance against any *one* state. It must be purely defensive, non-exclusive, and acting solely within the letter and spirit of the United Nations Charter.

2 It must not become the instrument of the power or imperialist policies of any of its members.

3 It must not be merely a military alliance, purely negative in character, with provisions for defence only against the old form of armed aggression, provisions which may be as futile as defence against a muzzle loader in the atomic age.

4 It must include provisions, as does the Brussels Pact, for dealing at least by consultation with indirect aggression against states, carried on through the spreading of subversive, soul-destroying ideological germs as the prelude to revolution inside and conquest from without. This is, of course, a far more difficult problem than throwing back battalions of soldiers who have crossed frontiers. There is no effective Maginot Line against ideas.

5 Our security league, therefore, must include provisions, as does the Brussels Pact, not merely for defence against armed aggression, but for peacetime co-operation in economic, social, and cultural fields.

In the development of this kind of association lies our best hope for peace. Through it, we can ensure a decisive superiority of physical, economic, and moral power on the side of those who do not believe in power alone, but will use it, together, if there is no alternative. It is in this kind of association that Canada can best exert its influence for peace and progress.

PART II

1949-1957

12

THIS speech was given only a few days after I joined the government. It was not an easy occasion for a very new and inexperienced politician, and the relations between the civil and political services seemed a good subject in the circumstances. Some newspapers had begun to wonder whether my change of status might lead to a weakening of that political impartiality for which our civil service had deservedly acquired such a high reputation. But any such fears proved to be groundless. In my own department, External Affairs, those with whom I had worked so closely as a colleague and who now advised me as their minister gave equal loyalty and service to my successor when the Liberal government was defeated ten years later. That is the way a civil service should work and does work in Ottawa.

To the Ontario Municipal Association

21 September 1948

THIS is my first public speech since I took the long and unusual jump from the civil service to politics. I am encouraged in making it – the speech, not the jump – by the knowledge that I am talking to men and women who also have accepted the responsibilities and the opportunities of public service.

The morning after I was honoured by being appointed to the Cabinet, I was asked by an American journalist in Ottawa how long I had been a Liberal. Somewhat to his amazement, I replied, "Since last evening at 5 o'clock, when I was sworn in as a member of the Privy Council." Lest he should misunderstand me, I went on to explain that until the moment I was sworn in, I had been a member of the civil service of Canada for twenty years and that civil servants in Canada had no politics. Of course, the fact that I had joined a Liberal administration may have indicated to him that if I had not been a civil servant, I might possibly have been a Liberal long before that 5 pm hour which I have just mentioned.

It is, I think, a healthy and indeed an essential condition that members of the civil service should be servants of the state and not servants of a party. Without the whole-hearted acceptance of this fact, democratic government cannot be effective, honest, and impartial, or likely to survive. We should do nothing in this country to make such acceptance difficult. In my own career, I have had the honour to serve both Conservative and Liberal administrations, and I don't think I have ever been accused of not giving my best to both while they were responsible for the government of our country. That is the way it should be and that, with very rare exceptions indeed, is the way it is in the civil service in Ottawa. It is one of the strong points in our democratic system.

Because of my own experience and because of my own views on the matter, I have been reading with some interest certain newspaper comments on "politics in the civil service" which my recent change of status has inspired. So far as I am aware, certainly in the department in which I have worked, politics do not enter the civil service. I would regret it very much if my resignation from that service and my entry into the political service should suggest that they do.

The civil service is an honourable and responsible career. If trained and qualified men cannot be attracted to it and remain satisfied in it, good government becomes very difficult indeed. That is why I hope we will not reach a position in Canada, which has been reached in certain other countries, where posts in the civil service are considered as a normal avenue of transition to political or private employment and are accepted for that purpose. In this connection, I heartily support the view expressed in a recent editorial in an Ottawa newspaper, as follows:

The line between the Cabinet and the Civil Servant must be sharp and clear, with the Civil Servant, like Caesar's wife, above suspicion – above suspicion that he is the political ally of the Government. Once blur that line, once give the public or the official opposition the suspicion that the Civil Service may not be neutral, or that some of its members in high places may be using their position to promote political careers, currying flavour with the Government in the process, and may we not then be on the way of risking Civil Service continuity?

That view is, I suggest, very wise. I agree with it, all the more so because I can assert with a clear conscience that I have always tried to act in accordance with it while I was a government official.

Having said so much, however, I am bound to go further and express my own opinion that a civil servant, who is also a citizen, is entitled to the privilege that every other Canadian citizen has, of resigning from his job and attempting to serve his country by entering the House of Commons as an elected representative of the people. I can assure you, from my own experience, that the satisfactions and security of the civil service are such that not many senior officials are likely to yield to this temptation. But I hope when it does happen, and it certainly happens very rarely, that neither the motives of the person concerned, if he has been an honest civil servant, nor the high and impartial standing of the civil service itself will be questioned.

As one official who has taken the plunge, as one who has recently left the ranks of those who are too often referred to as "power-hungry bureaucrats," I can now, without misunderstanding, put in a good word for the members of the bureaucracy, who are so often the victims of criticism which they themselves cannot answer because of their civil service status.

I ought to know something about bureaucrats, because I have been one myself and have seen others in action in a good many countries of the world. There is, of course, always a danger that some official, not responsible to the electorate or answerable directly to Parliament, may overstep the bounds of what should be permitted in a democratic state. The danger is greater in this day of complicated political, economic, and social problems, where the knowledge and experience of the expert is more important than ever before and where the minister cannot hope to be automaticaly informed about all the problems that come up. There might develop a tendency, indeed in some places there *has* developed a tendency, for Parliament and responsible ministries to abdicate in favour of the skilled official. That tendency should, of course, be resisted, or it will mean the end of parliamentary and responsible government. I have never spoken of this matter to any responsible official of the government in Ottawa who has not agreed with me. Indeed, the best protection of the official in the exercise of his proper authority is a healthy, vigorous, and responsible ministry and Parliament, supervising and controlling his actions and laying down the principles and policies which are to govern them. I can, however, understand the impatience and irritation of overworked and underpaid civil servants in Ottawa who, in carrying out to the best of their abilities the instructions of the government of the day, are criticized, even sneered at, and made responsible in the eyes of public opinion for acts over which they have no constitutional responsibility.

There never was a time in history when the expert, the official, on the one hand, and the political representative, the member of Parliament and the Cabinet minister, on the other, should work more closely and more co-operatively together than at present. Only with such close co-operation can democratic government survive ...

In no field of political activity is the necessity for co-operation between the expert officials and the peoples' representatives greater than in that of external affairs. I feel strongly that it is necessary to find and keep the best trained minds we can secure to protect Canada's interests in this field and reconcile these interests with those of other free democratic peoples. It is short-sighted and foolish to think that whereas we need skilled men for building a post office or paving a highway, the business of diplomacy and international relations can be left to anybody. That feeling, where it exists, springs, I think, from the view that whereas a post office or a road has an immediate importance, a conference at Geneva or New York is a matter which has little to do with anybody but the "striped pants boys" who are conducting it. Believe me, such a view is profoundly wrong. For Canada, bruised by two world wars and one world depression, decisions taken in far-away places have a vital importance for the village square. There is no escaping today the results and the obligations that flow from the interdependence of nations ...

I believe also that Canada's external affairs should, to the greatest possible extent, though always subject to the legitimate requirements of responsible parliamentary government, be kept on a non-partisan basis. After all, we are all Canadians, or should be, before we are Liberals, Conservatives, or ccFers, and before we are Quebeckers or Manitobans. So we should aim to face the outside world with a united front. Politics, it has been said by an American leader, should end at the water's edge.

13

THIS is part of my maiden speech in the House of Commons. For many members, certainly for me, the Commons is always a difficult place in which to speak. It is particularly difficult for a first speech even though by tradition all members, including the opposition, are charitable on such occasions to the new and nervous orator. When I sat down, the page boys brought me many of the congratulatory notes customary on such an occasion. I might have had more from my friends on the opposition side if I had not twitted the Conservatives for their hesitation in publicly supporting NATO, something which they did shortly afterwards. It was foolish of me to refer to the undesirability of "playing politics with peace," and a Conservative member was charitable when he referred in his note to these words as simply "an unfortunate lapse."

I made this lapse, I suppose, largely because I was sensitive about being considered by my new Liberal parliamentary colleagues as a mere civil servant who, in his appointment as secretary of state for External Affairs, had been given a "plum" which would normally go to a politician. I may have thought it would help to remove this feeling and convince them that I was a good party man if I included one remark of a partisan nature, likely to offend the opposition.

Later on, it became easier and more appropriate to say things that the opposition – or the government when *I* was in opposition – considered both foolish *and* offensive.

From the Honourable Member for Algoma East

4 February 1949

To deal with more general subjects now, Mr Speaker, I should like for a short time to give the house a review – and it can be only a cursory review at this time – of the international position as I see it. Naturally that position still gives cause for much anxiety. However, the situation should be considered, I suggest, without panic but without illusions. There is no doubt that fear has gripped the world again, fear arising primarily out of the extension of the brutal domination of revolutionary communism, based on the massive and expanding militarism of totalitarian Russia ...

Mr Stalin himself has said that "there is no logic stronger than the logic of facts." That is true, and I think it can be applied to statements which come from Moscow or indeed from any other capital. The leader of the Soviet government also once said to a journalist: "The export of revolution? – that is nonsense." But to his own people he has said in the soviet bible, which is called *Problems of Leninism*: "The goal is to consolidate the dictatorship of the proletariat in one country, using it as a base for the overthrow of imperialism" – that is noncommunism – "in all countries." The people of Czechoslovakia know which of these statements is true ...

Men of good will continually and rightly hope for a basic change in the relations of soviet Russia with the noncommunist world. But easy optimism and self-delusion are disastrous substitutes for cool analysis and consistent policies. The door to real co-operation should always be open but not to admit Trojan horses ...

The foreign policy of this government must be directed to one single end, the avoidance by every means within its power of atomic catastrophe.

How can we do this? By burying our heads in the snow and allowing others to make the decisions, without our participation, which would bind us in spite of ourselves? There is no safety there. Or relying wholly on the United Nations? That to my mind would be clearly unrealistic, because that body, though it must remain the basis of our policy on international co-operation, and we should spare no effort to improve and strengthen it, remains, under present circumstances, quite unable to provide the means by which any country can ensure its security; nor does it, in present circumstances, provide an effective instrument for use in removing the causes of war.

What is the remedy, then? Surely, Mr Speaker, the best way to minimize the possibility of war is for the free nations to stand together on a regional basis, and, by doing so, to make it clear that no aggressor has any possible chance of winning any war which he may be tempted to start. It is necessary to accumulate enough force now to preserve freedom in order that ultimately freedom can be preserved without force. This force must be organized in such a way as to ensure that it will guarantee that the free nations cannot be defeated one by one. This is the policy, sir, which I think would have prevented war in 1914 and in 1939. It is our best hope of preventing war in the years ahead. It is a policy of peace.

In the pursuit of this policy, the government has been for some months now negotiating with other north Atlantic countries who share our democratic ideals a treaty for collective defence, which would strengthen the national security of each of the participants. I hope that these discussions, which have been taking place in Washington on an ambassadorial level, will soon be concluded, and that the representatives who have been participating in them will be able to submit to their governments a complete draft of a north Atlantic treaty, which in its essentials at least can, I hope, be made public at the same time that it is submitted to governments. The next stage will be a careful study by each government, and careful examination by the public opinion of each country, of the principles embodied in this draft. Amendments can be submitted, and then a conference will be held at which I hope the treaty can be signed. It would then be for each government to submit the treaty to its legislature, in the democratic way, for approval or rejection.

What has been said about this proposed Atlantic pact in the present debate, Mr Speaker? The leader of the CCF party (Mr Coldwell) has declared that his party agrees that Canada should support and join such a north Atlantic pact. Similarly the hon. member for Peace River (Mr Low) said the other night: "We of the Social Credit organization favour the Atlantic pact and support it."

There is, however, Mr Speaker, a serious omission in the unanimity with which this matter is otherwise regarded in the house in that no single Progressive Conservative member has so much as mentioned the pact. I think I am not strictly accurate in that statement, because the hon. member for Vancouver South (Mr Green) did mention it. He said that he thought we were busy on it. The hon. member for Carleton (Mr Drew), the leader of the official opposition, went back two thousand years and talked about the Achaean league, which he seemed to think was a federal state, but he had not a word to say about the Atlantic league of 1949. In his opening speech, all that the leader of the Conservative party had to say about international affairs was: "No one will disagree with the fact that the first concern of this and every other government and every other parliamentary body is to do everything humanly possible to preserve the peace and to protect the people in the country which it serves."

That of course is quite true and very well said; but why this omission? Why no reference of any kind to this very important measure which is forecast in the speech from the throne? Is this Parliament not united in the objectives that we are seeking through this pact? Or are any of us playing politics with peace at this time?

MR SMITH (Calgary West) Would the hon. member permit one question?

MR GRAYDON The first speech and he plays politics.

MR SMITH (Calgary West) Will the minister permit one question? In view of the fact that foreign policy has been a matter of co-operation of all parties, does the minister think he is doing any good now by making this a political issue?

MR GRAYDON We expected more of him than this.

MR ABBOTT Suppose you listen to the answer.

MR PEARSON It is because I think and hope that the foreign policy of this country can be the foreign policy of all parties in this house and of all sections of opinion in this country that I am so disappointed that no reference to this important aspect of foreign policy was mentioned in any speech from the other side of the house. I agree that foreign policy should be as nonpartisan as is consistent with responsible government and I hope it will continue that way.

MR GRAYDON That is a poor way to start.

MR FLEMING Why did the government cut off the debate?

MR SPEAKER Order. May I remind hon. members that the hon. member who has the floor should not be interrupted without his permission.

MR GRAYDON That is bargain-counter politics; that is all.

MR SINCLAIR The big foreign affairs expert.

MR SMITH (Calgary West) Cheap playing with the nation's future.

MR PEARSON The reason I mentioned this particular matter, and this important omission, is that it seemed to me that I have been reading about and hearing about speeches on foreign policy made in other parts of this country which are far removed indeed from some of the statements that have been made in this house. That is why I express the hope once again that we will not play politics with peace in this house.

MR GRAYDON Hear, hear; give us an example of that. The Minister had better set the example on that.

MR PEARSON I have known the hon. member for Peel for a long time, and I do not think he believes for a minute that he is going to be able to intimidate me or throw me off my balance.

MR GRAYDON He won't show you how to play politics.

MR PEARSON He used to be so effective, Mr Speaker, in our college debating society. May I return to the main stream of my remarks? May I mention to the house certain principles which have guided the Washington discussions about which I have just spoken, and which will be embodied in the resulting treaty? In the first place, this pact will be a regional agreement, if it is concluded, under the United Nations charter. It should be subject to the provisions of the charter and it should be registered with the United Nations, which it is designed not to replace but to supplement. Indeed, if by some chance the Security Council of the United Nations should become an effective body for the preservation of peace, then our Atlantic pact would be unnecessary and it could be allowed to disappear.

We should also make sure that the Atlantic pact does not become merely a screen for narrow nationalist suspicions and fears; an instrument of unimaginative militarism or an agency of power politics or imperialistic ambitions of any of its members. In this respect I agree entirely with what was said the other evening by the hon. member for Rosetown-Biggar (Mr Coldwell). I feel strongly, as he does and as I am sure all hon. members do, that this regional association must be far more than a military alliance. It must make a collective contribution to the social and economic betterment of the peoples of its member states.

In the past, alliances and leagues have always been formed to meet emergencies and have dissolved as the emergencies vanished. It must not be so this time. Our Atlantic union must have a deeper meaning and deeper roots. It must create the conditions for a kind of co-operation which goes beyond the immediate emergency. Threats to peace may bring our Atlantic pact into existence. Its contribution to welfare and progress may determine how long it is to survive. The Canadian government, therefore, attaches great importance to the part which the pact may play in the encouragement of peacetime co-operation between the signatories in the economic, social, and cultural fields.

There is another point and it is for us an important one. The Parliament of Canada, when the time comes, must be in a position to take its decision, in regard to this proposed security pact, deliberately and in full knowledge of what it means. The nature of the obligations which we undertake must be clear. Further, our own constitutional processes by which we call these obligations into action must be preserved. There must be mutual confidence and mutual trust in the will and ability of each member of the league to discharge its responsibilities. This mutual confidence is something which we do not now find in the United Nations, and it is a fatal defect in that organization at the present time. In our Atlantic league we can hope that the situation will be different.

Canada's obligations under this pact, however, must be within the measure of our resources and as part of the plans agreed to by all and by which each member of the group does the job for which it is best qualified. If I were asked now what precisely those obligations will be, what they will involve, I would have to reply that I am not at the moment in a position to answer. But I can say this: the pact will be a group insurance policy and group insurance is cheaper and more effective than any individual policy.

Finally, every member of the group must share in all the decisions of the group even though we may recognize that the greater responsibility of some in carrying out these decisions must give their views special weight in reaching them. The treaty must therefore establish a constitutional basis by which that which concerns all is decided by all. Canada is no satellite of any country and would not be one in this association. If Canada is to be asked to share the obligations of the group, it must also share in the responsibility for determining how those obligations shall be met. On no other basis could Canada, or indeed any self-respecting state, sign such a pact ...

There is nothing inevitable about war; there is nothing unchangeable about evil. If we of the free world can pursue the firm and constructive policies of resistance to communism that are now in train, refusing to be dazzled by the delusions of appeasement or stampeded by the rash counsels of panicky men, we may emerge from this wasteland of our postwar world into greener fields.

I feel certain that the people of Canada will support this Atlantic pact because it can lead us just in that direction. They will support it, not primarily because under it they can successfully wage war but because it will help them successfully to wage peace ...

14

THE signing of the NATO Pact was an impressive occasion. Those of us privileged to take part felt that we were indeed participants in a historic ceremony. Each signatory was asked to say a few words, and most of us were moved to rhetoric.

The atmosphere of dignified ceremonial, before and after the signing, was heightened by the band of the US Marines playing soft music in the background. Their selections, however, were a shade discouraging: they concentrated on pieces from *Porgy and Bess*, including "It Ain't Necessarily So" and "I Got Plenty of Nothin'." I told my friend, Dean Acheson, who was in charge as US secretary of state, that for once his impeccable sense of occasion and of diplomatic timing had deserted him. Or had it? He was always a bit of a cynic – or, as he would put it, a realist.

If I had been tempted to feel a little *exalté* at my participation in this historic event, I was brought back to normal by an experience on my return. I was visiting my constituency and holding forth at a village store on Manitoulin Island to a few of the local inhabitants on the Washington ceremony and all it might mean for peace. An old man who had been listening thoughtfully and, I felt, approvingly, reminded me when I finished that I was their member of Parliament and only secondarily secretary of state for External Affairs by remarking: "Well, that was a fine thing you did down there in Washington, Mr Pearson, signing that there treaty, but it won't help you much around here if you don't give us a new post office."

I tried not to forget that good advice during the rest of my political career: take care of the village post office as well as the United Nations!

On Signing the North Atlantic Treaty

4 April 1949

LAST week the Parliament of Canada, with only two dissenting voices, endorsed the treaty which we sign here today. This virtual unanimity reflected the views of the Canadian people who feel deeply and instinctively that this treaty is not a pact for war, but a pledge for peace and progress.

The North Atlantic Treaty was born out of fear and frustration; fear of the aggressive and subversive policies of communism and the effect of those policies on our own peace, security, and well-being; frustration over the obstinate obstruction by communist states of our efforts to make the United Nations function effectively as a universal security system. This treaty, though born of this fear and frustration, must, however, lead to positive social, economic, and political achievements if it is to live; achievements which will extend beyond the time of emergency which gave it birth, or the geographical area which it now includes.

This treaty does not, of itself, ensure peace. It does, however, give us the promise of far greater security and stability than we possess today. By our combined efforts, we must convert this promise into performance or the treaty will remain no more than yet another expression of high but unattained ideals. That will not happen to our North Atlantic pact if each of us accepts the challenge it proclaims; if each of us, with trust in the goodwill and peaceful policies of the others, will strive to make it something more than words. We know that we can do this. If it were not so, we would not today be giving this pledge to stand together in danger and to work together in peace.

We, in this North Atlantic community, the structure of which we now consolidate, must jealously guard the defensive and progressive nature of our league. There can be no place in this group for power politics or imperialist ambitions on the part of any of its members. This is more than a treaty for defence. We must, of course, defend ourselves, and that is the first purpose of our pact; but, in doing so, we must never forget that we are now organizing force for peace so that peace can one day be preserved without force.

We are a North Atlantic community of twelve nations and three hundred and fifty million people. We are strong in our lands and resources, in our industry and manpower. We are strong above all in our common tradition of liberty, in our common belief in the dignity of the individual, in our common heritage of social and political thought, and in our resolve to defend our freedoms together. Security and progress, however, like peace and war, are indivisible. So there must be nothing narrow or exclusive about our league; no slackening of our interest in the welfare and security of all friendly people.

The North Atlantic community is part of the world community and as we grow stronger to preserve the peace, all free men grow stronger with us. The world today is too small, too interdependent, for even regional isolation.

This treaty is a forward move in man's progress from the wasteland of his postwar world, to better, safer ground. But as we reach distant pastures, we see greener ones far on. As we reach the summit of a lofty peak, higher ones loom up beyond. We are forever climbing the ever mounting slope and must not rest until we reach the last objective of a sane and moral world.

Our treaty is no mere Maginot Line against annihilation, no mere foxhole from fear, but the point from which we start for yet one more attack on all those evil forces that would block our way to justice and peace.

In that spirit, and with great pride, I sign this treaty as the delegate and the servant of my country.

15

FOR many years the Canadian Institute of Public Affairs has held a summer conference at Lake Couchiching, north of Toronto, where papers are read and views exchanged by the participants as they spend a few restful and enjoyable days characterized by "plain living and high thinking." This was the first time I had been asked to talk to the conference and I took advantage of the occasion to outline my "middle of the road" philosophy of politics and government. The middle is a rational, if often unheroic, place to be, but only if you are not stuck there, and providing you realize that you are in danger of being hit by the traffic on either side of you, right or left.

This was also the first chance I had had to give expression to my views, as a minister of the crown, on a balanced federalism – an application of the middle of the road concept to Canada's federal-provincial problems. The plea I made on this occasion I was often to make later: that if we are to overcome our federal-provincial difficulties, inherent in any federal system, we must recognize and resolve sectional and minority differences while insisting that these differences should not be permitted to prevent the development of a Canada which would be greater than its parts.

The Implications of a Free Society

13 August 1949

THE essential lubricant for a free society is tolerance. This, however, does not necessarily apply to *all* societies. There are obvious examples of states which are held together without the least regard for tolerance. It does apply, however, to all states where there is government by consent. Canada, where various groups live and work together within the boundaries of a national state, is a good example of this principle in operation. This country exists on the assumption that, as far as is humanly possible, the interests of no group – racial, geographic, economic, religious, or political – will prevail at the expense of any other group. We have committed ourselves to the principle that by compromise and adjustment we can work out some sort of balance of interests which will make it possible for the members of all groups to live side by side without any one of them arbitrarily imposing its will on any other. It is my belief that this is the only basis upon which Canada can possibly exist as a nation, and that any attempt to govern the country on any other basis would destroy it. In these circumstances, the basic quality of tolerance in our national character is of the first importance.

Of almost equal importance for our national welfare, and indeed arising out of the practice of tolerance, is the avoidance of extreme policies. This is often called walking in the middle of the road. This of course is not so easy as people usually think. It imposes both self-restraint and discipline, even when we assume that the traffic is all going in the one direction. Anyone who chooses to travel in the middle of the road must not deny the use of either side of it to persons who prefer to walk there. He condemns himself, therefore, to accept during the journey the constant jostling of companions on either side. This middle ground is, I think, becoming more and more difficult to maintain, and the temptation to abandon it is constantly increasing, especially in the face of the road blocks thrown up by unfriendly fellow travellers. I do not wish here to criticize those who choose other ground upon which to walk, or to question the basis of their choice. I wish only to make a strong plea for the preservation of this middle position in our national life. Paradoxically, it is only in this way that the existence of many of those on each side can also be preserved. If the middle group is eliminated, less tolerant elements fall under the irresistible temptation to try to capture the whole roadway. When the middle of the road is no longer occupied firmly by stable and progressive groups in the community, it is turned into a parade ground for those extremist forces who would substitute goose-stepping for walking. All others are driven to hide, disconsolate and powerless, in the hedges, ditches, and culverts.

How can the meaning of the middle way in our free society be described in a few words? What principle does it stand for? Where does it lead in practice? Is it merely the political line of least resistance along which drift those without the courage of their convictions, or simply without convictions? It is, or should be, far more than that. The central quality of this approach is the stress which it always lays on human values, the integrity and worth of the individual in society. It stands for the emancipation of the mind as well as for personal freedom and well-being. It is irrevocably opposed to the shackling limitations of rigid political dogma, to political oppression of, and to economic exploitation by, any part of the community. It detests the abuse of power either by the state or by private individuals and groups. It respects first of all a person for what he is, not who he is. It stands for his right to manage his own affairs, when they *are* his own; to hold his own convictions and speak his own mind. It aims at equality of opportunity. It maintains that effort and reward should not be separated and it values highly initiative and originality. It does not believe in lopping off the tallest ears of corn in the interests of comfortable conformity.

The middle way presents no panacea for the easy attainment of general welfare, but it accepts the responsibility of government to assist in protecting and raising the living standards of all, and, if necessary, to take bold and well-planned action to help maintain economic activity for that purpose.

The middle way, unlike extremism in political doctrine, has positive faith in the good will and common sense of most people in most circumstances. It relies on their intelligence, their will to co-operate, and their sense of justice. From its practitioners, it requires determination and patience, tolerance and restraint, the discipline of the mind rather than the jackboot, and the underlying belief that human problems, vast and complicated though they may be, are capable of solution. This, I believe, is the political philosophy which best preserves the free society which you will be discussing at this conference, and which indeed gives to that free society many of its most important characteristics.

It is not enough, of course, merely to keep to the middle ground. It is necessary to go somewhere. The history of politics is full of the obituaries of groups in society who stood firm, but motionless, in the middle of the road; or who, like the old Duke of York, merely marched up and down the hill. For this reason, the parties of moderation and tolerance in a progressive society must continually chart new country, overhaul and modernize the administrative machine in which they travel through that new country, adapting it to the demands of new conditions. They must move with the times, so that they do not collapse simply through inaction. They must also test the validity of the principles by which they chart their course, checking their philosophical and political roadmaps against the signboards which are provided by the practical day-to-day problems of government.

In this move forward, one of our most immediate problems is the protection of our free society against those who wish deliberately to destroy it. We must be constantly vigilant lest our free political institutions are used for this destructive purpose. We know from experience what happens when a resolute minority which does not believe in government by consent gains power. It uses our free institutions for its own arbitrary purposes and it does its best to see that no one else uses them. The communists, for example, will, if they can, use your town council for the destructive purposes of their own political doctrines, though they will conceal these purposes behind a propaganda smoke-screen of humanitarian proposals. They will also do their best to prevent you from using the same council to give effect to some sensible and practicable scheme of which they do not happen to approve. If, through democratic processes, they gain control of any agency of government, they will do their best to prevent anyone replacing them through the same process. We know how tactics of this kind can corrode and destroy the fabric of a democratic state. We saw the Nazis do it in Weimar Germany. We have seen the communists do it more recently in Czechoslovakia. We have also seen a great international organization like the United Nations brought on occasions to a complete standstill when its communist members used their democratic privileges to frustrate its will ...

At the same time, we must remember that we help the enemies of freedom if we take unnecessary short cuts to deal with them, for by so doing we ourselves may weaken the very political institutions which we are seeking to preserve. I am sure, therefore, that we should continue in our national life to maintain and promote fundamental freedoms within the laws of the land, and to have confidence that an alert and intelligent public will deny power and influence to those who misuse these freedoms. In doing so, I hope we can avoid in the future, as we have in the past, the kind of hysteria that sometimes does more harm than the evil that provokes it. Communist or fascist treachery is admittedly difficult to uproot, because those who practise it successfully are masters of deception. But they will accomplish a large part of their purpose if they spread illfounded suspicions in the community, if they make us think that our universities should be purged or trammelled, if they make us uneasy in our minds about the loyalty of our public servants, if they infect us generally with the wasting fevers of distrust. Let us by all means remove traitors from positions of trust and, if necessary, strengthen our criminal code in order to deal with the enemies of the state. But in doing so, I hope we may never succumb to the black madness of the witch hunt.

The best defence, however, against totalitarianism in any form is to prevent or remove the conditions upon which it feeds. As far as the economic life of the nation is concerned, this means that the government may have to accept a large measure of responsibility for direction, and even for control. Indeed, whether it desires it or not, that role is being forced on the state by insistent and increasing demands for services and assistance, many of which are made by those who subsequently complain of the interference by government in their affairs which is made inevitable by the effort to satisfy their demands. It is, in fact, becoming increasingly difficult to reconcile the satisfaction of such demands with the maintenance of that spirit of self-reliance and competitive achievement which is one of the foundations of our free society.

This problem is one of the most compelling which governments have now to meet. In facing it they must accept the fact that the words "direction" and "control," as applied to state action, arouse intense animosity in certain quarters and conjure up in the minds of many people the worst evils of bureaucratic interference. Those who hold such feelings do not, I think, believe that we should return to the freedom which "big business" once enjoyed. Indeed big business itself would not desire a return to the old era, for it knows full well that its welfare depends not only on its ability to manufacture its product, but also on the capacity of the great mass of the people to buy that product. In their own interests, therefore, the huge enterprises of modern industry look to government for that economic and political stability which, among other things, is essential to the maintenance of purchasing power. In return, most of them – certainly the sensible and enlightened ones – are prepared to adapt their plans to those required for the economic welfare of the nation as a whole. Nor do they claim to be the sole judges of what that welfare is or to identify it exclusively with their own balance sheets. They realize, as we all do, that the real wealth of a nation lies in its collective capacity to produce and to consume. Certain advocates of financial reform have exploited this simple truth for the purpose of persuading people that some sort of monetary magic will make it possible for them to use what they produce. But the problem of maintaining purchasing power is not so easily solved as all that. It is solved by many procedures – as simple as family allowances and old age pensions and as complex as establishing a rate of international exchange. It is a responsibility of modern government to act with as little interference with the private individual as possible, but nevertheless to act so that the resources and productive capacity of a nation may be made available to all the citizens on an equitable basis. Anyone who dislikes or distrusts the way government discharges this responsibility may seek to influence or change the administration in office. But we don't very often hear the claim now that we would be better off if we went back to the days of laissez-faire ...

Another problem in our Canadian society which we must face is the relationship between federal and provincial governments. The people of Canada quite sensibly have refused to regard this question as a contest between federal and provincial authorities, which one or other of them must win. Over the years, they have made it quite clear that they will never give authority in federal affairs to men who advocate a limitation or restriction of the powers which properly belong to the federal government. They have made it equally clear that they will not choose a provincial government which wishes to give away provincial rights, or permits this to happen.

In any case, the idea of a contest in Canada between federal and provincial authorities is misleading and dangerous. It is high time that this sinister concept of inevitable conflict were dispelled. It would, I think, be helpful if the federal and provincial governments could be given an opportunity to join in some declaration which would assist in clearing the air of these dangerous views. The central and local governments together provide the citizen of Canada with the functions of government which he requires, and there is no reason why Canadians should quarrel amongst themselves as to which of these agencies of government should serve their needs in particular cases. If there is overlapping, or if it is not quite clear where responsibility lies, it should not be difficult to work out a satisfactory arrangement to meet any special circumstance. The valuable technique of the dominion-provincial conference, for example, has been and can be used for this purpose. We have, in fact, been making arrangements of this kind for over eighty years, and a surprising variety of techniques and procedures for co-operation between federal and provincial governments has been devised. At no time during this period has the integrity of the provinces within their own fields of responsibility been in any serious or continued danger, in spite of the shrill protestations to the contrary of men who would exploit such a danger to their own ends. Yet, our experience in the past makes it quite clear that the Canadian people do not intend that the deliberate decision made in this country many years ago to accept a federal system of government should make it impossible or even difficult to provide effective national administration in the circumstances of the present.

We should, I think, tidy up our constitutional structure, by establishing the final judicial authority of our own courts of appeal, and by providing ourselves with a more rational and appropriate means of amending our federal constitution than we have at present. We should then go on as we have in the past, adjusting the differences between federal and provincial governments by negotiation and agreement, by judicial decision, by agreed conclusions of dominion-provincial conferences, and by the development of administrative methods for co-operation between federal and provincial governments; if necessary, by constitutional amendment. In doing so, we shall be acting in accordance with the clear intention of those who established confederation, that a genuine balance between federal and provincial governments should be maintained. The growth of our country since 1867 enforces the validity of this intention. Quite apart from the special problem of relations between French- and English-speaking people in Canada, the size and complexity of Canada justify our federal system of government. If the provinces are to play their proper role within this system, they must continue to have real and effective responsibility for the important spheres of government which have been assigned to them. They must continue to attract capable men to their legislatures. They have a vital contribution to make to the life and welfare of the people, and they must continue to be in a position to make it. Equally, the federal government must be capable of giving leadership and assuming responsibility in matters of national concern. When it lacks the authority necessary to perform this purely national function, it must take the initiative in making arrangements to secure it, without, of course, and I emphasize this, interfering with any of those provincial or minority rights which are at the very basis of our national structure.

We cannot achieve the proper balance between federal and provincial governments by any single definition of responsibility which will be valid for all time. If all the provinces, together with the federal government, are to play their full and proper part, there must be a continual process of adjustment between federal and provincial governments, conducted on the basis of a desire on all sides to contribute to the welfare of the Canadian people as a whole. Above all, we must repudiate the untrue and dangerous doctrine that there is some difference between a Canadian who is represented in Ottawa and one represented in a provincial capital.

The establishment of this nation was a great act of faith on the part of men who believed that the ingenuity and resourcefulness of our people could overcome the cultural, political, and physical barriers which impeded our unity. We have found it a bigger task than even the Fathers of Confederation realized to build a state from the Atlantic to the Pacific, and along the northern boundaries of the United States; to populate its hinterland, to develop its resources, and to maintain its unity against the strains and stresses of the modern world. In seeking to accomplish this task we have had to face and overcome problems that the Fathers of Confederation never dreamed of. If we have met success, it has been because national policies have represented a careful and considered balancing of political and economic forces; because we have recognized and understood sectional and minority differences and yet have insisted that these differences should not be permitted to prevent the development of a Canada which would be greater than its parts.

16

THE cold war had been raging at the UN and Mr Vishinsky had been making vicious and vituperative speeches against the NATO countries.

If we did not reply in kind we often felt it necessary to reply with vigour. This selection is from one of my contributions to such unproductive but unavoidable debate, this time in the First Political Committee of the General Assembly. If the language now seems strong in spots, it was mild compared with that of some others. Those were verbally violent cold-war days at the UN.

Vishinsky was the most gifted, energetic, articulate, and unscrupulous of the communist polemicists. He would stop at nothing in the flow of his bitter oratorical assault, and sometimes it seemed as if nothing would stop the flow either; he carried on for hours, without pause. Yet "off duty" he was a cultivated, amusing, and agreeable person; and he could impress you as such, unless you recalled his conduct during the Moscow purges. He flattered me one day by stating that he listened to my speeches at the UN with particular care as I was usually more frank than "the others."

Once I was seated beside him at a dinner after he had spoken for four or five hours during that day, consigning to the nether regions all of us from the West, sparing neither our characters nor our capacity. But he was all smiles, and lively with engaging conversation about literature and life. I suggested that he must be exhausted after talking so vehemently most of the day. "Not at all," he replied smiling. "It is only diversions that are exhausting and I am too old to have any." Personally, I prefer my "villains" to be more easily recognized as such when off duty.

In Reply to a USSR Peace Resolution

30 October 1950

WE are now nearing the end of what is becoming an annual occurrence at the Assembly – a general debate on the essentials of peace. I doubt whether these debates contribute much, if anything, to peace; or the resolutions which emerge from them and which will inevitably tend to repeat themselves, from year to year. It may in fact be argued that these discussions, by underlining and exaggerating differences, by the violence of the language used, create an atmosphere which makes peace more difficult. Headline diplomacy is not the best way to settle differences, especially when the headlines reproduce such Soviet phrases as "unbridled slanders," "dirty insinuations," "nonsensical babbling," "maddened yelps of warmongers." I have my own peace proposal to make. It is a two-year moratorium on bellicose and violent speeches about peace at the United Nations; and a two-year attempt to *do* something effectively about peace.

The Soviet resolution contains an appeal to the permanent members of the Security Council to work for peace and to conclude a pact. While we must be, of course, in favour of renewed effort to reach agreement by every form of consultation, we should not forget that peace lies not primarily in pacts, but in the hearts of men and the policies of states.

In this matter of consultation as in other matters, we should come down out of the clouds and face certain hard facts. What kind of consultations are envisaged? Experience has shown that some forms may accomplish nothing. Indeed, they may do more harm than good by raising hopes that are later dashed and by creating despair out of failure of great expectations. If international discussions on political problems are not carefully prepared, and the preliminary diplomatic work not thoroughly done, they may merely underline and exacerbate disagreement and leave the position afterwards worse than before ... The prerequisite for fruitful consultation is some action which would increase international confidence, something that would make the international climate a little less frigid, so that this delicate peace plant may have a chance to grow. Otherwise, we would be wasting our time over talks. If this debate has shown nothing else, it has shown that. It has also shown how tragically wide is the gulf that divides the two worlds, and how deep the fear that prevents that gulf being bridged.

Mr Vishinsky, speaking the other day, if I may adopt a favourite expression of his, "on behalf of the ruling circles" of the Soviet Union, pins the responsibility for all this fear and division on the United States, the leader of what he calls the Anglo-American bloc. To support this charge, again to use some of his own adjectives, "this monstrous, slanderous" charge, he produced the usual newspaper and magazine reports of speeches and statements by Americans. This device has long since ceased to be convincing. Just as much of the historical and political evidence adduced in these debates by Mr Vishinsky and his friends is, again to use his words, "a crude distortion and falsification of fact," so also their press clippings and magazine articles give a grossly distorted impression of the people and policies of this country. This is a free country, and if some person makes a fool of himself in a university, or even in Congress, there are a thousand to tell him so in language that is almost as strong as Mr Vishinsky's. It is, of course, difficult for persons brought up in a totalitarian police state, where dissent is heresy to be liquidated at any price, to understand this simple but basic fact.

The truth is that the nations of the world outside the Soviet bloc know that the power of the United States will not be used for purposes of aggressive war. They know that the policies of the United States – though we may not always support them, or even approve them – are not designed to lead to war. If they were, they would soon isolate this country from the rest of the free world. We judge the United States as it would wish to be judged, not by Mr Vishinsky's press clippings, but by its actions; as indeed we will judge the policy of the USSR by its reaction when the United States withdraws its victorious forces from Korea as soon as peace has been restored. Will Mr Vishinsky accept this fact as at least one piece of evidence that America is not trying to dominate the world?

We in Canada know this country and its people well. We know them as good neighbours who respect the rights of others, who don't ask for or get automatic support from smaller countries through pressure or threats or promises. We know that they accept the fact that co-operation between large and smaller countries can only exist on a basis of mutual confidence and mutual respect. If the Soviet government would permit its people to learn the truth about the United States instead of filling them with information only about the worst features of its life and culture, they would make a real contribution to the removal of that fear, which is at present being instilled, directly and deliberately, in the minds and hearts of the Soviet people. Mr Vishinsky asks, "Have we no right to criticize western culture?" and says, "We ask only the right to base our education on love for our own national culture and national dignity, the same as others. Slavish worship of other countries is not admissible." No one takes any exception to that, but slavish vilification of other countries is also not admissible, and we have much evidence that this is the foundation of Soviet education; it is one of the things that makes us fear Soviet policy most; it is one of the worst forms of war-mongering, this implanting of fear and hatred of one people in the minds of another. Has the citizen of any communist state the opportunity to get an unbiased picture of the western world, of its way of life, of what it tried to do in the defeat of Nazism, and what it tried to do in the relief and reconstruction of devastated areas after the war? Just one small example of what I mean, given because Mr Vishinsky complained on Saturday that our evidence was old or out of date.

The Polish delegation circulated a handsome illustrated booklet last week on the reconstruction and rebuilding of Warsaw, an achievement which is a magnificent tribute to the energy, zeal, and devotion of the Polish people. This booklet, in its foreword, saw fit to mention what Russia had contributed to this rebuilding, but could not find room for one word about UNRRA, which had done so much fine work in Poland, made possible, largely, by the characteristic generosity of the American people. Incidentally, the booklet also referred to the Polish government-in-exile in London during the war, which had under its authority those gallant Polish soldiers who fought so heroically alongside Canadians in Italy and in Western Europe, as "that criminal band of Polish reactionaries." This is only a minor example, but a very recent one, of the kind of vilification and distortion which brings despair to those who realize that there can be no peace as long as a great gulf of misunderstanding and suspicion exists between the two worlds. All that this kind of thing can do is widen the gulf and bring fear to those on our side of it, fear that this animosity which is being encouraged can only result in conflict. That fear is increased when we read that a primary school textbook used in the USSR has this to say – to children – about those who live under our system: "Under capitalism where the relationship is built on the principle of wolf to wolf, venality, hypocrisy, lying, deceit, cunning, treachery, bigotry ... are the characteristics of the bourgeois representative." What a foundation for good understanding! Possibly Mr Vishinsky would put the author of that textbook – who presumably wrote it under orders from the Soviet government – in the same category of mad persons to which on Saturday he consigned the president of Tampa University.

But Mr Vishinsky says we have nothing to fear from Soviet policy; that facts have proven its unswerving adherence to the cause of peace and international co-operation over the years; that we have nothing to fear from communist ideology, which rests on not only the possibility, but the necessity, of the peaceful co-existence of the capitalist and communist systems. Because of this, Mr Vishinsky argues that we should not be rearming. Therefore, as we insist on doing this, *ipso facto*, we have war-like aggressive aims. It's a simple thesis, but a completely false one. When Mr Vishinsky talks about the peaceful aims of communism and Soviet policy, we remain sceptical, and we find most of his evidence to support his case false and misleading. On our side, we have much concrete evidence to support the other view, of the aggressive, expansionist, war-like aims of Soviet and international communist policy.

But let the facts speak for themselves. Let the map of Eastern Europe speak, let the thousands of exiles from countries that have lost their freedom speak; certainly those that are dead and in Siberia cannot speak. Let the 170 Soviet divisions and 30,000 tanks speak, confronted as they are by a few half-armed divisions in Western Europe. Let Yugoslavia, which knows something of Soviet policy, methods, and peace appeals, speak. There is no point in recapitulating here the evidence which, as we see it, disproves the legend of the peaceful, lamb-like character of Soviet foreign policy. I can assure the representatives of the communist states that this policy has inspired a genuine and terrible fear of war in the people of non-communist states throughout the world. If something can be done to remove that fear, or to prove by deeds, not by words, that it is unfounded, then a great and crushing weight of dread will have been lifted from our hearts and minds. Then and only then can we begin to beat our tanks into television sets, something that every taxpayer in every country is only too anxious to do.

Mr Vishinsky also pours scorn on the idea, which we hold, that international communism could hold any danger for the rest of us. I hope he is right, but here again the balance of evidence is against him ... We will await with eagerness, if with some caution, not words, but actions which will prove in the days ahead that communism on the one hand and capitalism or democratic socialism on the other can, like the lion and the lamb, lie down together, and rise later without one being inside the other.

Meanwhile, the free democracies are determined not to be deflected from their resolve to become stronger, not for aggressive purposes, not in order to force, at the point of the atom bomb, diplomatic decisions on the Soviet Union, but because they fear aggression and wish to put collective force behind their will for peace in order to deter and prevent it; because negotiations for peace have a better chance of succeeding if the parties, not accepting each other's views, respect at least each other's strength. Permanent peace can, of course, never be ensured by power alone; but power on both sides, not merely on one, may give a breathing space in which to pause, reflect, and improve relations. This course will be attacked as power politics, but power politics are often merely the politics of not being overpowered. So it is in this case ...

17

My speech to the Empire and Canadian Clubs of Toronto in 1951 created much controversy at the time. Little notice was taken of those parts dealing with Canadian policy in the cold war, the UN, and collective security. But the last part, which touched on our relations with the USA, got some critical attention, as indeed I thought it might because Canadians have a continuing and what seems at times to be almost an obsessive concern with this topic. This is, of course, understandable in view of the overwhelming importance to us of our relations with our neighbour, but I thought that this address had dealt with these relations in a balanced and objective way, without minimizing their inherent difficulties, as well as their advantages, for us.

The reaction, however, to my statement that "the days of relatively easy and automatic political relations with our neighbour are, I think, over" was vigorous and often critical. What seemed to me to be obvious was a shock to others. This may have been largely due to the fact that the headlines – the only part of a political report most people read – concentrated on words like "Pearson criticizes Americans – says easy relations with them are over."

This was in 1951. To be accused of anti-Americanism now seems strange in the light of subsequent charges that I was "selling out Canada to the Americans" and that I was the "chore-boy of Washington." To repeat, in the middle of the road you are in danger of being hit by traffic on both sides.

Canadian Foreign Policy in a Two-Power World

10 April 1951

I SUPPOSE there never has been a time when the conduct of foreign policy has been more complicated and difficult than at present; or one when the consequences of a mistake could be more disastrous; or indeed when even the wrong kind of speech could make more mischief. One reason is obvious: our scientific achievements have so far out-stripped our social and moral development that while we, in Toronto, can learn in a few minutes of what has happened in Peking, or in Timbuctu, we are not always able to assess the knowledge with objectivity and act on it with mature intelligence. Indeed, too much of our intelligence seems to be devoted to the discovery and perfection of the techniques which bring the news to us, and not enough to the problem of what to do about it.

The formulation of foreign policy has special difficulties for a country like Canada, which has enough responsibility and power in the world to prevent its isolation from the consequences of international collective decisions, but not enough to ensure that its voice will be effective in making those decisions.

Today, furthermore, foreign policy must be made in a world in arms and in conflict. In this conflict there are two sides whose composition cuts across national and even community boundaries. The issues have by now been pretty clearly drawn and, at the risk of over-simplification, can be described as freedom versus slavery. Moreover, the two powerful leaders of these opposed sides have emerged: the United States of America and the USSR.

The struggle has not yet become a shooting war, except in Korea, but is still one of policy. It goes on in the field of economics, finance, and public opinion, and extends far beyond any military or even political operation. It is the more terrifying because, if its breaks into fighting, science will be harnessed to its prosecution as never before, with results almost too horrible to contemplate. Our defence in this conflict must mean increasing and then maintaining our strength, while always keeping open the channels of negotiation and diplomacy. Arms must go hand in hand with policy. Strength, however, cannot now be interpreted in military terms alone, but has also its economic, financial, and moral aspects. We must not forget that, while we are now building up this kind of strength so that armed force may not be necessary in the future for the protection of our society, the situation which faces us may erupt into an explosion at any time. We have to face that fact as a possibility, though not, of course, an inevitability. It may be a deliberate and controlled explosion brought about by the calculated policy of the despots in the Kremlin, men hungry for power and world domination. Or, more likely, it may be an accidental one. In either case, it will result in world war III, with all its infinitely horrible consequences. It is essential, indeed it is elementary common sense, to make ourselves ready to deal with this dread possibility.

On the other hand, and many think that this is the more probable development, the present situation of war without warfare may continue for years. This will confront us with just about the most difficult political and economic problem that has ever faced a democratic society. It is unprecedented, and we have little to go on as we try to work our way through the jungle of the difficulties and dangers of what the London *Economist* calls "three-quarters peace." Certainly we have to become collectively strong in a military sense to meet the shock of a sudden attack; or, and this is more important, to make such an attack unlikely by convincing anyone who contemplates aggression that he has no hope for victory. At the same time we have to be careful, in this country and in other countries, not to organize our resources for military defence in such a way or to such an extent that we sap and weaken our economic and social strength and morale.

The potential enemy may have decided, and at the moment *he* has the initiative in this decision, that this war will be one of long drawn-out attrition and he may hope that we will weaken ourselves for its continuing tests by panic measures and an unbalanced defence. To put it another way, he may decide that this race is not a sprint, but a middle- or even a long-distance contest. We may have to adapt *our* tactics accordingly. This will require steadiness and control, a sense of pace, a refusal to be thrown off balance, but, at the same time, a determination to take the necessary steps to cut down the lead which our opponent now has. The present conflict is, in fact, a dual one, and requires dual policies: short-term and long-term policies, military and civil, which should be complementary and not contradictory.

We are faced now with a situation similar in some respects to that which confronted our forefathers in early colonial days, when they ploughed the land with a rifle slung on the shoulder. If they stuck to the plough and left the rifle at home, they would have been easy victims for any savages lurking in the woods. If they had concentrated on the rifle and forgot about the ploughing, the colony would have scattered or died. The same combination is required today, though it is far more difficult to bring about. We must keep on ploughing, harder than ever, while we arm. We will hardly achieve that double objective by government as usual, by business as usual, or by life as usual. These are all generalities, and you have heard them many times before. More important are the practical problems they present to us, one or two of which I would like to mention.

In domestic policy, one of our main problems is to decide what proportion of our resources should be devoted to our own defence, whether that defence takes the form of national action at home or collective action with our friends abroad. This time there should be no distinction between them. We should accept without reservation the view that the Canadian who fires his rifle in Korea or on the Elbe is defending his home as surely as if he were firing it on his own soil.

There is not likely, certainly, to be unanimous agreement on this question of how much should be done for defence. Some will say that we are actually and completely at war now; that we should base all our policy on that fact; that our military defence efforts should be the same as if the enemy were actually attacking our country; that our economic policy should be based on the same considerations, with complete control of prices and wages and, above all, of manpower for industry or for the armed services. There are others, and the government shares this view, who feel that any such all-out interference with the mechanism of our economic and political society, at the present time, would weaken, rather than strengthen us; might, indeed, even play into the enemy's hands by making it harder for us to maintain our unity, our morale, and our strength over the long pull ahead.

The same division of opinion exists in regard to our proper part in

collective international action. There are those who say that we have not
so far pulled our weight here, except possibly our oratorical weight.
There are others who complain that we are doing too much, especially
as the big decisions which will decide the course of events will not be
made primarily by us but by others. It is of course comforting for one who
has some responsibility in these matters to conclude that if you are attacked from both sides, you have a fairly good chance of being right. But
I certainly would not wish to carry that analogy too far. It may mean
merely that you are doubly wrong! We all agree, however, that we must
play our proper part, no less and no more, in the collective strengthening
and collective action of the free world, without which we cannot hope
to get through the dangerous days ahead. But how do we decide what
that proper part is, having regard to Canada's political, economic, and
geographical situation? It is certainly not one which can be determined
by fixing a mathematical proportion of what some other country is doing.
As long as we live in a world of sovereign states Canada's part has to be
determined by Canada, but this should be done only after consultation
with and, if possible, in agreement with our friends and allies. We must
be the judge of our international obligations and we must decide how
they can best be carried out. But we have no right to make these decisions
in isolation from our friends.

The North Atlantic Treaty Organization is, I think, a good example
of what I mean. The Council of this organization is meeting almost continuously; mainly, at the present time, for the planning of collective defence. The recommendations – they are only recommendations – made
through this collective process are then sent to the separate governments
for decision. But no government is likely to reject them without very
good reasons indeed. The military tasks for the separate members under
the North Atlantic Treaty Organization have been worked out collectively in detail. Those allotted to Canada, which were considered by all
the members of the group to be fair and proper, have been accepted by
the Canadian government and will be carried out once Parliament ap-
proves them.

There is another aspect to this problem. What should our role be in
the United Nations? ... We must be sure, so far as we can ever be sure,
that the United Nations remains the instrument of the collective policy
of all its members, for the preservation of peace and the prevention or
defeat of aggression; that it does not become too much the instrument
of any one country. I am not suggesting that this has happened or is
going to happen, but it is something that we should guard against. If,
however, the United Nations is to be a genuine international organization in this sense, all of its members, except the Soviet communist bloc
who have no interest in it except as an agency for advancing their own
aggressive purposes, must play a part in deed as well as in word. We must
be careful not to be stampeded into rash decisions which cannot be car-

ried out, but we must *all* contribute to the implementation of decisions
freely and responsibly made. I do not think that we in Canada have any
reason to apologize for the part that we have played in this regard. Our
record in the United Nations is a worthy one.

However, I do not think that we should be asked, in the United Nations or elsewhere, to support automatically policies which are proposed
by others if we have serious doubts about their wisdom. We must reserve
the right, for instance, to criticize even the policy of our great friend, the
United States, if we feel it necessary to do so. There are, however, two
qualifications to this. First, we must recognize and pay tribute to the
leadership being given and the efforts being made by the United States
in the struggle against communist imperialism, and realize that if this
leadership were not given we would have little chance of success in this
common struggle. Secondly, we must never forget that our enemy glee-
fully welcomes every division in the democratic ranks and that there will
be times, therefore, when we should abandon our position if it is more
important to maintain unity in the face of the common foe. This reconciliation of our right to differ and the necessity for unity is a tough
problem for anyone charged with responsibility for foreign policy decisions in this, or, indeed, in any free country.

This brings me squarely up against a matter which is very much in
my mind, as I know it is in yours; the question of Canadian-American
relations in this two-power world of conflict. It is, I think, one of the
most difficult and delicate problems of foreign policy that has yet faced
the Canadian people, their Parliament, and their government. It will
require those qualities of good sense, restraint, and self-reliance which
the Canadian people have shown in the past.

It was not so long ago that Canada's foreign relations were of importance only within the commonwealth, more particularly in respect
of our relations with the United Kingdom. These Canadian-common-
wealth problems seem to me to have been now pretty well solved. At
least the right principles have been established and accepted which
makes the solution of problems fairly easy. We have in the commonwealth reached independence without sacrificing co-operation. We stand
on our own feet, but we try to walk together. There is little of the
touchiness on our part, which once complicated relations with Downing
Street. There is now certainly none of the desire to dominate which we
used to detect in Whitehall. We have got beyond this in Canada-UK
relations. We deal with each other now on a basis of confidence and
friendship, as junior and senior partners in a joint and going concern. In
our relations with the United Kingdom we have come of age and have
abandoned the sensitiveness of the debutante. This has been made easier
because any worry we once may have had, and we had it, that British
imperialism or continentalism might pull us into far away wars not of
our own making or choosing, has passed. We now accept wholeheartedly

the Commonwealth of Nations as a valuable and proven instrument for international co-operation, as a great agency for social and economic progress, and, at the present time possibly most important of all, as a vital and almost the only bridge between the free West and the free East. I think also that in the postwar years we have come to appreciate, as possibly never before, the wisdom, tolerance, and far-sighted steadiness of vision of the British people. As their material power has decreased, at least temporarily, because of the unparalleled sacrifices they have made in two world wars, our need for these other British qualities in the solution of international difficulties has increased. This, in my mind, has never been shown more clearly than in the events of the last six months at the United Nations or in the Far East.

With the United States our relations grow steadily closer as we recognize that our destinies, economic and political, are inseparable in the Western hemisphere, and that Canada's hope for peace depends largely on the acceptance by the United States of responsibility for world leadership and on how that responsibility is discharged. With this closeness of contact and with, I hope, our growing maturity goes a mutual understanding and a fundamental friendliness. This makes it possible for us to talk with a frankness and confidence to the United States, which is not misunderstood there except possibly by a minority who think that we shouldn't talk at all, or who complain that if we do, our accents are too English!

We need not try to deceive ourselves, however, that because our close relations with our great neighbour are so close, they will always be smooth and easy. There will be difficulties and frictions. These, however, will be easier to settle if the United States realizes that while we are most anxious to work with her and support her in the leadership she is giving to the free world, we are not willing to be merely an echo of somebody else's voice. It would be easier also if it were recognized by the United States at this time that we in Canada have had our own experience of tragedy and suffering and loss in war.

In our turn, we should be careful not to transfer the suspicions and touchiness and hesitations of yesteryear from London to Washington. Nor should we get unduly hot and bothered over all the pronouncements of journalists or generals or politicians which we do not like, though there may be some on which we have a right to express our views, especially when those pronouncements have a direct effect on policy and action which we have undertaken together.

More important, we must convince the United States, by action rather than merely by words, that we are, in fact, pulling our weight in this international team. But this does not mean that we should be told that until we do one-twelfth or one-sixteenth, or some other fraction as much as they are doing in any particular enterprise, we are defaulting. It would also help if the United States took more notice of what we *do* do and, indeed, occasionally of what we *say*. It is disconcerting, for instance, that about the only time the American people seem to be aware of our existence, in contrast say to the existence of a Latin American republic, is when we do something that they do not like, or do not do something which they *would* like.

I can explain what I mean by an illustration. The United States would certainly have resented it, and rightly so, if we in Canada had called her a reluctant contributor to reconstruction in 1946 because her loan to the United Kingdom was only three times as large as ours, while her national income was seventeen or eighteen times as large. In our turn, most of us resent being called, by certain people in the United States, a reluctant friend because Canada, a smaller power with special problems of her own, ten years at war out of the last thirty, on the threshold of a great and essential pioneer development, and with half a continent to administer, was not able to match, even proportionately, the steps taken by the United States last June, and subsequently, which were required by United Nations decisions about Korea; decisions which, I admit, caught us by surprise.

The leadership then given by the United States rightly won our admiration, and the steps that she has taken to implement them since deserve our deep gratitude. The rest of the world naturally, however, took some time to adjust itself to a somewhat unexpected state of affairs. Canada, in my view at least, in not making the adjustment more quickly, should surely not be criticized more than, say, Argentina, or Egypt, or Sweden.

There may be other ripples on the surface of our friendship in the days ahead, but we should do everything we can in Canada, and this applies especially to the government, and in the government particularly to the Department of External Affairs, to prevent these ripples becoming angry waves which may weaken the foundation of our friendship. I do not think that this will happen. It will certainly be less likely to happen, however, if we face the problems, frankly and openly, of our mutual relationship. That relationship, as I see it, means marching with the United States in the pursuit of the objectives which we share. It does *not* mean being pulled along, or loitering behind.

Nevertheless, the days of relatively easy and automatic political relations with our neighbour are, I think, over. They are over because, on our side, we are more important in the continental and international scheme of things, and we loom more largely now as an important element in United States and in free world plans for defence and development. They are over also because the United States is now the dominating world power on the side of freedom. Our preoccupation is no longer *whether* the United States will discharge her international responsibilities, but how she will do it and whether the rest of us will be involved. You may recall that it was not many years ago that Colonel Lindbergh suggested that Canada should be detached from membership in the British Commonwealth of Nations because that international affiliation of ours might get the United States into trouble by involving the larger half of North America in European wars. That seems a long time ago. There are certain people in Canada (I am not one of them) who think that the shoe, if not already on the other foot, is now being transferred to the other foot.

From what I have said, and I have only touched on the subject, you will appreciate that the days have gone when the problems of Canadian foreign policy can be left to a part-time minister; to a small group of officials; to a couple of hours' desultory and empty debate each session in Parliament; and to the casual attention of public opinion when it can turn from more important matters such as the Stanley Cup or the stock market.

Foreign affairs are now the business of every Canadian family and the responsibility of every Canadian citizen. That includes you and also the minister for External Affairs. I hope that we will together be able to bring to these problems, so complicated and so exacting, good judgment, calm objectivity, and a sense of deep responsibility.

18

THIS was a very sentimental occasion for me, my installation as chancellor of Victoria University (as it now was generally known since the addition of Emmanuel College). My wife and I, my daughter and brothers, had all graduated from Victoria, my father and

grandfather were Methodist ministers, and "Vic" was the Methodist college of the University of Toronto. My mother's first cousin had been chancellor in earlier years, and there were many of the Bowles clan among its graduates over the years.

My Installation Address naturally reflects my feelings: it is both personal and local, though I do indulge in some educational and moral philosophy and express my worries about the "isms" which haunt us in these days "from the cradle to the grave."

On My Installation as Chancellor of Victoria College

4 February 1952

IT is not easy for me to give adequate expression to my feelings on this occasion, when an honour is being conferred on me that I prize more than I can possibly say.

You will not be surprised if, at such a moment, I yield to the temptation to reminisce, or that my reflections should be concerned with Victoria: what her mission can be and should be in the confused and disturbed time in which we live. It is even tempting to speculate on ways and means by which Victoria's resources may be increased so that she may more effectively carry out that mission. This latter temptation, however, I shall firmly resist. I have not been chancellor long enough to have an authoritative opinion on that subject!

My reflections are also, of course, bound to be partly personal; on what Victoria has meant to my family and to myself. I have strong and enduring links with the college, both as a Pearson and as a Bowles, the most enduring and most cherished of which is: I found my wife at Annesley Hall. Those links make the new one which is being given to me today all the more precious.

My mind goes back to the time, as a small boy, when I learned from parents and other relatives about the joys and even the tribulations of life, the somewhat mysterious life, of Victoria and of Toronto. Wasn't "the Chancellor" my mother's first cousin? Didn't I have a cousin and later a brother of my own there, who used to talk to me about glamorous and exciting, but somewhat shadowy doings; of "Bobs," initiations, football games, proms and lits and glee clubs? Wasn't my own grandfather so passionately loyal to the Old Ontario Strand – now only a memory and a song – that he removed his son, my father, from the college when it moved to Queen's Park? Then, of course, I think of 1914, those years of long agony and sacrifice and glory when the life that we had known ended for all of us, and when life itself ended for so many whose memory is still green in the hearts of those of us who came back. There followed the postwar years of adjustment, progress, growing. Later there came the depression, a dreary and perplexing time, but during which we were becoming increasingly aware of the social purpose of education.

Then in 1939 we had to take up once again the torch that had not shown the way to peace in 1918. The sons of those who marched in '14–18 did not do less than their fathers, but there was a deeper questioning, I think, of the situation which made this second sacrifice necessary; as there was a deeper sense of privilege and obligation felt by those who came back to college for the second postwar period. The trumpets that sent us off thirty-five years ago had not blown in '39, and the easy sense of fulfilment and triumph of 1918 was not, and we should give thanks for this, repeated in '45.

Now, once again we face, in college and out of it, an uncertain and confused future. Once again the problems of peace and security to which we put our hands after victory remain unsolved. Nor can there be much confidence that they ever will be solved, unless those who must make the attempt are properly educated. Education is the mission of our university. But education for what? to what social or spiritual or personal end?

There is an Oxford tradition which recalls that in the fifteenth century a scholar – an absent-minded one, I have no doubt – was walking in the woods reading Virgil, when he was confronted by a wolf. With great presence of mind, he thrust his Virgil down the beast's throat and so escaped unharmed. The lesson of this little legend is that there are practical uses for sound learning outside the classroom in moments of crisis and danger.

Today, we live in such a time of crisis and danger, in a world which gives no grounds for complacency. It is, however, also a world where youth is facing with resilience but with realism, with courage but without vainglory, the challenge of stern trials. The countries which are the heirs of Christian traditions are confronted today both by military danger and by the menace of false doctrines. The situation which we face often seems to us entirely without parallel. And, to be sure, in some ways it is; especially in the hideous gap between scientific advance and social progress. But it would be wrong to think that men in other ages have not faced situations which seemed to them equally menacing, equally desperate. When the great arch of the Roman empire began to crack and when those who had lived under its protection fell back from the assaults of the barbarian invaders, there was a feeling, deeper, I think, and more widespread even than now, that the day of wrath was approaching. History is indeed full of turbulence and terror. But throughout the ages wise and brave men have been able to find within themselves the resources to keep that terror at arms length, and the courage to keep their spirits unclouded and their integrity intact.

I have no doubt that such courage is still alive among us today. It will be needed, for there are pressures at work to which individuals in other ages were not subjected, pressures which work to strip man of his independence and dignity and weaken his spiritual foundations. They operate openly and even flamboyantly, but also insidiously and more compellingly than we often realize ...

I am not sure whether at any time in the world's history it was possible to steer by an automatic pilot. Certainly it is impossible today. What are needed are strong and sensitive hands which take account of all the local storms without forgetting the destination to which we are travelling. Direction finding and safety in these matters lies in ourselves; in our maturity of mind, in our moral integrity, in our acceptance of spiritual values as the foundation of conduct. If our university does not help us get this security, which is far deeper than the material security we so often talk about, it is failing in its mission.

The more experience I acquire of political affairs, the more convinced I become that there is no substitute for individual judgment based on high principle applied to each new situation as it presents itself. And this is true, I think, not only of politics but of all other fields of human endeavour. How, then, can we preserve honest and clear-eyed judgment amidst all the confusion of voices in the community, and in the world, in which we live?

That question is so difficult that I am hesitant about attempting an answer. Yet, in spite of the pitfalls, I will venture to make a few tentative suggestions, recognizing, as I do, that my moralizing may be neither novel nor profound; recognizing also that if these suggestions *are* of any value, it is by education through institutions such as ours that they can be made effective.

In the first place, it is well, I think, to try consciously to free oneself, occasionally at least, from the tensions of the present. My historical apparatus by now is certainly rusty. But I retain a strong conviction that if current opinions are not to impose themselves with relentless force on our minds, we must judge them in the light of historical knowledge and historical experience. To stand imaginatively for a while in another age is one of the best ways of assessing the problems of the present. In saying this, however, I do not forget that historical insight, as Denis Brogan has reminded us, is often no more than betting on a horse that has already won.

In the press of daily activity, we will also want, I hope, to refresh our acquaintance from time to time with those great creations of the human mind and spirit in which there is room to move about, room in which to appreciate the resources that man has within himself. Where can this habit be more surely developed than at our colleges?

It is easy to forget how incredibly varied and great these human resources are. It is also easy to let them lie dormant. It is tempting, for instance, to avoid the effort to use our own minds and to take our opinions on political and social matters, ready-made – off the hook, as it were – and handed to us without even a fitting; a process which is often accompanied by a good deal of prejudiced sales-talk, designed to dull the critical faculties and promote easy acceptance of anything offered. The times are too dangerous to indulge in these escapist practices. If the problems which confront us today are to be solved, we will all have to depend less and less on prefabricated ideas, slogans, and headlines, and more and more on a clear understanding of existing situations and on straight and honest thinking about them. But as Montesquieu once said: "Whereas every citizen is under an obligation to die for his country, no one is under any obligation to think for it."

This counsel of straight and honest thinking is particularly important, I think, in considering what should be our attitude to the various "isms" that haunt us these days "from the cradle to the grave."

The most dangerous of these "isms," both because of the evil and reactionary power behind them and because of their ease of abuse and misuse, are fascism and communism. In truth, the coinage of these words has become so debased that very often they now merely signify the beliefs of anyone, on the right or on the left, who disagrees with you ...

It would be a mistake to believe that we can or should attempt to defeat communism by force. Among other things, communism is an idea. No idea, however perilous or noxious, as communism is, can be killed by bayonets or even by an atomic bomb. As an idea, it must be resisted by intellectual and spiritual weapons, and also by removing the conditions of poverty and misery and injustice in which it grows. To the idea of communism and submission, we must oppose freedom and responsibility. But freedom alone is not enough, if it is merely the right to live and work and have our being with a minimum of interference. It must include the obligation to be socially useful, and to take part in the struggle against evil and injustice. Only on that concept of freedom can a free and secure society be based.

Such a society is not created by governments. They have, of course, an indispensable task in protecting freedom when it is threatened and they can do much to foster the conditions in which freedom can be preserved and developed. But we know very well that a free society is made, not by governments, but by free individuals and by the free institutions which have been formed through their association. Among the most important of these are our colleges and universities. Over the centuries they have added to the store of freedom by helping men to break the bonds of ignorance that have imprisoned them. At universities men have been at least exposed to a rich social and intellectual experience. No man dies from that kind of exposure, but from it men have been able to live better.

I cherish the hope that those who are exposed to the truth at Victoria will gain much by that experience. This will undoubtedly be the case if our university continues to cling to the things that are righteous; if it teaches that our society is not only humane, but moral; and that in it man's intellectual potential can be developed far beyond the boundaries of science. Let us give the student a faith, a sense of mission, an understanding of social and moral values. This will never be found in any single "ism" of today, in socialism or profitism or materialism. It will never be found in developing and training a man's faculties merely for his own service. Nor will it be found in encouraging him to find a niche in a state system which will provide for all his wants and weaken and crush his own being in the process. Above all, education, especially at a university such as ours, must be based on a belief in something deeper and higher than oneself, whatever it may be called; on Christian morality, as a basis for the individual and for society.

To communism's dialectical materialism we must oppose spiritual faith that makes no pretence at knowing all the answers, but knows *one*, with an unshakeable conviction, that man is more than physiological and that any system of society which rests on that material foundation alone will perish.

To the conformity of communism let us counter not the conformity of mere anti-communism, but the inspiration of enquiry and even dissent; of search and rescue, if you will. To the orthodoxy that provides and imposes all the political and economic answers, let us reply in this university with a humble but a determined questioning of any doctrine which is merely popular and is not proven.

May Victoria and our other universities and colleges stand firmly on this ground in days ahead when the urge to move towards one side or the other will be hard to resist. Refusal to follow every so-called progressive move – however phony – will be called reaction or obstruction. Refusal to yield to mass hysteria or prejudice or to abandon the right of the individual to be mistaken or to be different, will be labelled treason or subversion. Let us not worry too much about these false labels.

All of us, I imagine, can think of individuals whose eyes seem to look into a particularly clear atmosphere, individuals who have so mastered themselves, so integrated their own personalities that wherever they go they elevate others and create a feeling of goodness and well-being and hope. In the last analysis, our future depends on such individuals. Victoria has produced its share of this select and saving company who have breathed their own spirit into it and into us; men like Gerry Riddell and Ken Wilson, whose premature loss we grievously lament. Victoria could accomplish no greater mission than to add and keep adding others to this company.

The other day I read a deeply moving account of the last moments of Jan Masaryk – a great stateman and a good man, one whose friendship I was privileged to enjoy. This tale was brought out from behind the iron curtain by his private secretary, who is now free to tell about Masaryk's last hours. Before the darkness of violent death closed in on him, and as almost his last act, he opened the family bible at Galatians v, and in pencil underlined each word in the twenty-second and twenty-third verses. These were: "But the fruit of the Spirit is love, joy, peace, long suffering, gentleness, goodness, faith. Meekness, temperance: against such there is no law." Jan Masaryk got solace from these words in the agony of his last moments on earth. We who serve Victoria can take inspiration from them as our Alma Mater faces the challenging days ahead.

It only remains for me to thank you once again for the great distinction you have conferred on me and to give you the assurance of my desire to serve Victoria to the best of my ability in this honourable post. This has been a great day for me. As it ends may I express my feelings in a few lines translated from the Chinese by Arthur Waley. In them the poet Li Po describes how one may pass a winter's night with friends, and he ends: " ... and after the guest has gone, watch him make his way into the distance. If he leaves just at daybreak, this is very agreeable, particularly if he plays upon his flute as he goes."

I shall leave before daybreak, I fear, to return to another world in Ottawa, but I shall certainly be playing upon my flute as I go.

19

WHEN I was president of the General Assembly of the United Nations in 1952-3, I had a good deal of extra-curricular activity thrust on me, including many speaking engagements. At times it was hard work, but not on this occasion when I was the guest of the UN correspondents with many of whom I had established warm and friendly relations. They were a cosmopolitan group and they certainly knew how to entertain. This was a very cheerful evening and my speech was a light-hearted one. I doubt whether my hosts would have tolerated any other kind.

The work of the president of the Assembly is arduous and delicate. Presiding over the sessions is, itself, an exercise both in endurance and in diplomcy. It requires a detailed knowledge of rules and procedures, as well as some ability to deal with situations where rules are no help. Public personages, in any country, are often sensitive about their rights and privileges. When they are also the spokesmen for and the guardians of the good name of their countries, they can be very touchy indeed on matters of personal prerogative allied to national pride. So as president I had ample opportunity to put to work any diplomatic or international skills that I might have acquired.

I was elected by a very large majority to the presidency. By that time elections were beginning to be settled in advance "by consensus," which often meant by "agreement." It now has, of course, reached the point where the formal election is almost meaningless. But it wasn't so automatic in 1952. So I was pleased at getting a large affirmative vote.

My pride in this achievement received a quick and rude shock. As soon as I took the chair, a wrangle began over some procedural matter. I had had lots of experience of this, and I knew that points of order could be debated for hours. I was determined to try to stop this kind of thing at the very beginning of my presidency. I let the discussion go on for about twenty minutes and then, ignoring the clamour from those who still wanted to speak, made a ruling, which could be challenged but not debated. It couldn't have been a very good one for, within an hour of my overwhelming victory in the election, I was overruled in my first decision as president by almost as overwhelming a vote. But it settled the matter; the majority decision had to be accepted and so we got on with our business.

Some Latin American friends conveyed their deep sympathy to me in this blow to my personal prestige and hoped I wouldn't resign. I didn't, and I found that my prestige had not suffered, but long procedural wrangles had. That was what I had in mind in making a ruling quickly, even if it was voted to be a wrong one.

To the United Nations Correspondents' Association

11 November 1952

I MUST thank you in the first place, Mr Chairman, for asking me to be your guest this evening on this very happy occasion. Your introduction was a model of brevity which I wish could be followed by other chairmen. You did, however, state in the six words or so which you used, that I was president of the United Nations General Assembly. That position is one of great honour and I am, of course, proud to be holding it. I am exalted by my election, but feel at times exalted like a workman high up in the scaffolding of a skyscraper under construction. The position is high but also risky and slippery and heady.

In this position I am doing my best, I am sure without complete success, to live up to a motto which I am told President Truman keeps on his desk in Washington and which reads: "Always do right – this will please some people and astonish the rest."

I am very much impressed that my audience tonight includes so many members of the trade union of foreign ministers. We are here in company with our business agents, those men of the press who work in our United Nations glass house and do their best to refrain from throwing stones irresponsibly.

Your Chairman warned me that I would be expected tonight to "sing for my supper," but after the dinner which we have just had, not Ezio Pinza himself would be able to hit the high registers with clarity and resonance on this enchanted evening and across this crowded room. I confess, however, that in one respect I am disappointed. I am not being televised. We delegates of the United Nations, you must realize, no longer like to waste our words, or our appearance, on a mere few hundred privileged spectators.

Recently I have been speculating on the effect of radio and television on international conferences. The result seems to me to be fourfold. First, it keeps the delegates awake and forces them to look interested in what is going on. Second, it requires that they should be very careful about their "doodling" now that we have those special television cameras that pick you up in detail at long range without the victim knowing anything about it. I recall that when television was first introduced in the General Assembly at Lake Success a couple of years ago, one of my colleagues who was viewing our proceedings from the set in the delegates' lounge sent a message to me, as I sat in the First Committee, of a somewhat panicky character which read: "A camera is on your hands. Be careful about your 'doodling.' Stick to those geometric patterns." Third, television has caused a noticeable sartorial improvement among the delegates, in their grooming and in their appearance. I am told that it has even improved mine from the days when a female columnist once wrote about me: "His clothes seem to say: if you are coming out with me, hang on." Incidentally, I resented that charge more bitterly than any attack that has ever been made on my ideas about foreign policy.

Finally, these mechanical publicity devices have widened and deepened the language of diplomacy. In the days of Talleyrand and Metternich (they would now undoubtedly be described as "Tally" and "Met"), diplomats were limited to such mild expressions as "démarche," "détente," or, if the negotiations were successful, "rapprochement." Those were the spacious, happy, and easy days of diplomacy; of the quill pen; the two-thousand circulation newspaper; the courier with important messages, who travelled on a slow boat with sails; days when aristocratic envoys, with red sashes covering the spots on their gleaming white shirt fronts, danced very slow waltzes under crystal chandeliers with beautiful women, while the blue hussars stood on guard. Those were the days and nights when working behind the scenes must have been rewarding and exhilarating! They undoubtedly had their advantages over our own kind of dungaree diplomacy with adjectives used which were once limited to the fish market. On the other hand, it is only fair to add that the glittering uniform of old often concealed a black heart and crooked mind, and the courtly phrase a fell purpose. We are at least franker now; frank to the point of ferocity.

The new language of diplomacy has, I am sure, been very greatly influenced as a result of our radio and television activities. Certainly today no international vocabulary is complete without an easy familiarity with such expressions as: pan left; dolly in; fade it; dissolve; centre it; kill it; wrap it up; I'll buy it; and give him head room. So, if you should see Mr Acheson and Mr Eden and Mr Schuman huddled together in a United Nations corridor these days they might well be saying: Mr Acheson – pan left; then Mr Eden – ok, wrap it up; Mr Schuman – Alors, I'll dissolve and fade.

I suggest to you that now almost the first qualification for the presidency of the Assembly is that the candidate should be a good subject for television. The Assembly should remember this the next time it promotes a member to the podium. That word "podium" which has recently entered into my life has intrigued me. The other day I asked one of the more classically informed members of our delegation what it meant. He replied: "podium" is from the Latin word "podium" which means podium.

The second qualification for a good president is that he should be a good listener. He must curb the natural and human inclination to succumb to the siren sound of his own voice. Relaxed, yet tense with interest and with as expectant an expression as he can muster, he must listen to long speeches in what is often described as the "cut and thrust of debate." I hope you will pardon me if I say that I have already learnt that if the president talks too much from the podium, he is sure to get nothing but odium!

There are, of course, compensations for silence. While listening, the president can think great thoughts. He can decide important problems, such as whether freedom of speech is more important than freedom from speeches; or which are the most important underdeveloped areas – those of the mind or the map. Or he can let his fancy play on the interpretation of the design and decoration of the Assembly Hall, particularly on the meaning of those murals produced by what I can only describe as the result of a brilliant stroke of "legerdemain." Eventually, however, his mind will return to more serious matters, especially to the differences and difficulties confronting us at this Assembly. So may I tonight return to those serious matters for just a moment.

I hear much these days, and read much in the press, about those difficulties and differences. Indeed, United Nations delegates have been described to me as "the men who came to differ." However, we are all agreed, and I am certainly including the press in this, that the Seventh Session of the United Nations General Assembly faces an agenda as crowded, as complex, and as explosive as ever faced any similar body ... Anxiety and uncertainty have indeed been the dominant notes in the symphony of comment that heralded the opening of Trygve Lie's seventh but not, I hope, his last United Nations concerto.

When I was elected therefore to the presidency of the Seventh Session I was under no illusion that it would be anything but a tough session, nor did I pretend that I had been assigned anything but a difficult task. I said then that the issues which confronted us might impose as severe tests on our world organization as any it had faced in recent years. Four weeks of our session confirm the validity of that easy but depressing diagnosis.

There are two main problems. First, there is Korea. The problem here has been narrowed down to the reconciliation of the right of repatriation of prisoners of war, as provided for in international agreements, with the exercise of that right in a way which would reject the use of force against any individual either for repatriation or retention. With good will and a genuine desire for an armistice on all sides, this reconciliation should be possible; indeed, even easy.

The other major problem arises from colonial and racial issues. The problem here is the reconciliation of the domestic jurisdiction of sovereign states, and the responsibility of some of them for the administration of dependent peoples in their progress toward self-government, with the legitimate interest of the United Nations in human rights, racial discrimination, and freedom for all peoples. Here again, this reconciliation should be possible if a sense of moderation and responsibility is shown and if the inevitability of historical development is recognized not only in theory but in practice.

If the Assembly fails to make these two reconcilations, much more than this Assembly will fail. The United Nations itself will be in jeopardy. The stakes at issue are no less than that. In that sense, delegates have indeed – in the words of one of the founders of the United Nations – a rendezvous with destiny. Will we meet this test? I do not know. But the difficulties ahead are no excuse for not trying. They are a challenge to greater effort.

It may be that, despite all our efforts, we will fail. But is there anyone in this room who does not believe that it is better to have tried and failed than never to have tried at all? Even if the odds against success are great, even if the chance of finding a solution is small, we must persist at this Seventh Session and beyond it in trying to achieve our objective of peace and security in this world. Is there any other course than that for the United Nations, of patient negotiation and compromise, in private meetings and in public debate? Is there any other course that we can or should follow?

In this process of creating peace through international confidence and understanding – a process which must be painstaking, which must be gradual – the press, radio, and television, so well represented here to-night, have a very great role to play. It is your task to translate the fact of world interdependence into terms which have meaning and significance for men and women everywhere. In your work you are called upon to grasp the arguments, to present the issues, to explain the forces and factors involved in those issues to "the peoples of the United Nations." We who are on the official side know something of the problems you face in your interpretation of events. We sometimes add to them!

You, in your turn, know something of our difficulties as we search for answers to questions which do not often admit a categorical "yes" or "no"; as we search – to vary the metaphor – for an appropriate shade of gray, not too black to one side, or too white to the other. Sometimes it is a good gray and occasionally rather dirty. Of this, however, I am sure, that we both recognize – press and officialdom alike – that the long and hard task of achieving the purposes of the United Nations – dignity and decency and security for all men – is a combined operation.

Thirty-four years ago today on 11 November 1918 – a day that some of us here will never forget – dazed men, almost unbelieving in the ecstasy of salvation from sudden death, crawled in their millions out of their trenches. The days of horror were over. The days of happiness had begun. They had not. Instead, there were the wastelands of the years between the wars, the revived and sharpened slaughter of World War II; and now the fears and hatreds of a postwar period which could slide into a prewar one. We are faced once again with the possibility of a third catastrophe. If we go down the third time, we may stay down, and we will deserve to.

20

THIS speech was made at a partisan gathering, so naturally it is partisan, but not, I hope, extravagantly so. In any event, I never was much good at making what are called "fighting party speeches" which are often more emotional than educational, more rhetorical than rational.

I was handicapped in this respect by some difficulty in sacrificing the factual for the merely picturesque; and, having been in the civil service for so many years, I confess that I couldn't lose the habit of seeing more than one side of a question. A party leader, traditionally, should only recognize two colours – white, his; and black, the opposition's. Even with this in mind, I did not stick as exclusively to the "white" as I might have done on such an occasion, and I allowed political science to mingle with politics.

To the Ontario Liberal Association

16 May 1953

WE are approaching the "open season," if, indeed, we are not in it, when, to borrow and adapt a good Western phrase, politicians go around "shooting from the lip." This is much safer, though just about as noisy, as "shooting from the hip." It may bore, but does not bore *through* the victims. I do not want to indulge, at least to excess, in this aimless pastime. If I did, you would rightly consider that my judgment had been impaired. And you know what they do with "impaired" people these days!

But this is a Liberal gathering, and elections, as well as spring, are in the air. You would expect me, and I am filled with the desire, to say something about the Liberal party and the Liberal principles under which Canada has grown into a free, strong, united, and progressive nation; a nation which has won the respect, admiration, and even envy of every other free nation in the world. As minister of External Affairs, who has to spend so much time on duty abroad, I have had more chance than most Canadians to secure convincing evidence of this fact. Our position in the world should make us proud. It should also make us sober and even humble, as we face, nationally and internationally, the stirring and testing days that lie ahead.

The architects and builders of Canada's high position in the world today are its people. Their achievements in peace and in war have made Canada what it is. Liberalism is not, in spite of the desperate charges of its opponents, either vain or arrogant. It does not arrogate to itself the credit for Canada's achievements. But Liberals have the right to recall that the policies, domestic and international, which Liberal governments in Ottawa have put into effect have created the climate and helped to establish the conditions in which the efforts of Canadians could produce the best results. If those policies had failed at home or in our relations with other countries, you may be sure that those who now depreciate what we have done would be the first to blame all the failures on the government at Ottawa. There is no cause for boasting in all this, nor should we ever be smug or satisfied. But we can take real pride and satisfaction in what our party has done to serve our country since 1935.

This, however, is not a time for looking back, however good the picture may be, but for looking forward. When we do so, we can see difficult problems of government ahead, both domestic and external. In making the contribution to their solution, which is now expected of us, the Liberal party will have to stand fast by those principles which in the past have served Canada so well.

What are those principles?

The first is service to Canada – not service to any part or any section or any class, but to *all* the people of Canada. Liberalism has always been a Canadian party – a national party, not a class party, or a sectional party, or a colonial party. Let others make different appeals to different sections. We can say the same thing at the same time to every Canadian. Let others appeal to special economic groups, our only group should be the Canadian people.

The second principle flows from the first. It is dedication to national unity. It has been the privilege of the Liberal party to play an important part in moulding the diverse elements that make up the Canadian nation into a unified whole. We have, also, always insisted that this should be done without sacrificing or weakening the federal principle on which our nation is founded; with full acknowledgement of the fact that there are two basic races in Canada, English- and French-speaking.

I said not so long ago in Quebec, and I would like to repeat it in Toronto:

We now recognize in Canada, in a way and to an extent not considered possible in earlier days, that it is not only necessary to base our national existence and our national development on two peoples, two cultures, two languages, but that we are fortunate beyond others in this hemisphere in being able to do so. Our country's growth is made solid and secure because it is so deeply rooted in the great traditions of French Canada and our national unity is strengthened and given a richer meaning by diversity. No Canadian who is proud of his country can help but be grateful for the heritage of New France which does so much to justify that pride.

Liberalism has also welcomed, as adding even greater strength and variety to the national fabric, the new Canadians from other lands who join us. We need more of them for the destiny that awaits Canada. Out of all these strains we are building a united nation. The Liberal party must fight any tendency to weaken this national unity, any move that would set class against class, section against section, province against province.

The opposition, of course, try to portray us as despots, autocrats, riding roughshod over the rights of people and Parliament. That is a travesty of the truth. It is denied by the record of Canadian Liberalism for a hundred years. Its absurdity is apparent in the light of the personality and character of the unselfish, modest, Christian gentleman who is our leader. Throughout all its history, Liberalism has fought for the rights of individuals and minorities, while Toryism is irresistibly attracted towards authority and control. And so it is today, even though the immensely complicated problems of modern government, and the increasing demands made by people on their government, have made necessary here, and in every free country, a delegation of power by Parliament if the public business is to be conducted efficiently. In every such delegation by the government in Ottawa, the rights of the individual under the law have been protected.

As for the rights of the minority in Parliament, the picture that the Tories give of legislation being railroaded by a tyrannical government over a persecuted but defiant little group of defenders of the people, is a caricature. The fact is that no opposition in Parliament's history has ever been treated with such fairness and even generosity as that in Ottawa today. That is in the best tradition of Liberalism and it is in accord with the character of our Prime Minister. The result? We take weeks to get the simplest legislation through, because the opposition talk, and wrangle, and delay, and we have been careful not to give them a chance to pose as martyrs by tightening the rules of procedure. That price is not high, of course, to pay for democracy and parliamentary freedom, but it could be much lower if the members of the opposition would occasionally rise above the temptation to listen to the siren sound of their own voices. Their motto seems to be "repetition is reputation."

I recall a speech made last summer by Mr Adlai Stevenson in which he said:

I yield to no man, if I may borrow that majestic parliamentary phrase, in my belief in the principle of free debate, inside or outside the halls of Congress. The sound of tireless voices is the price we pay for the right to hear the music of our own opinions. But there is also a moment at which democracy must prove its capacity to act. Every man has a right to be heard; but no man has the right to strangle democracy with a single set of vocal chords.

Liberalism, because it has always believed in and fought for freedom, stands for another principle of vital importance today: moderation, tolerance, and the rejection of extreme courses, whether they come from the right or the left; whether they express themselves in demands that the state should do *everything* for the individual, and possibly destroy him in the process, or in demands that the state should do *nothing* except stand aside and let unrestricted competition weed out all but the rough, big fellows; that we should rely on the survival of the fit under the law of the jungle.

Liberalism must continue to have nothing to do with these left or right extremes which, in fact, at times are hard to distinguish. In simple terms, this means that we accept reasonable social security, but we reject socialism; we accept individualism and free enterprise, but we reject economic anarchy; we accept humanitarianism, but we reject paternalism.

Liberalism is the middle way between extremes. But while we are in the middle of the road, we don't stand still. We move – and in the right direction – and I hope we will never slide into the ditches on either side.

This course, furthermore, is not and must not become merely a line of least resistance. There is nothing static or negative about it. It represents dynamic and progressive movement. The record of Liberalism in Canada proves it. So does the frantic effort of the Tories to adopt our policies and principles – usually about ten years after we have acted on them ...

This middle way, the liberal way, has positive faith in the common sense of the great majority of the people. It relies on their intelligence, their will to co-operate, and their sense of justice. Its strength is that of tolerance and restraint. It rests on the discipline of mind rather than muscle, and on the belief that human problems, vast and complicated though they may be, are capable of solution. This, I believe, is the political philosophy which can best preserve a free society in Canada ...

21

A PUBLIC Relations Society dinner seemed to me to be a good occasion to strike a blow for "quiet diplomacy." No one could accuse me on this occasion in Montreal of seeking out an audience which would be automatically on my side. I was also at some pains to insist – and I had experience to back it up – that diplomacy was not a "striped pants and cocktail-party" profession, certainly not in the Canadian service; but one of hard, practical work, performed by men who were dedicated to the service of their country. Canada can be very proud of her civil servants who have served and are serving her abroad in this essential occupation.

International Public Relations

5 January 1954

THIS is the first week of a new year, a time for resolution, retrospection, and speculation.

As for the first, I gave up making new years' resolutions many years ago, deciding about 1923 that I shouldn't add to my burden of resolutions until I had succeeded in disposing of some of those solemnly taken previously. I am still trying to do that, but it may be that by 1960, say, I can conscientiously feel that the statute of limitations has come into operation, and that my inability to carry out old resolves should not prevent me from making and breaking new ones.

So far as retrospection is concerned, as I look back on 1953, my personal prayer is that never again will there be a year when I have to carry out the duties of foreign minister, as well as those of president of the United Nations Assembly, and also engage in the somewhat feverish activities that flow from participation in a Canadian general election.

Though 1953 was, for me, a little too crowded for comfort, it was one which, in international affairs, gave cause for some sober satisfaction, if none for jubilation or complacency ...

Very far-reaching developments may be taking place behind the iron curtain. If so, we should keep an open mind and a clear head about them. These developments may make it possible to advance the policy of peaceful co-operation between states to which we of the free world are committed. On the other hand, words of peace and goodwill which come now from the communist camp may represent merely an orthodox and normal shift in party tactics, designed to disarm and deceive us ...

There never was much doubt that the really serious strain on the Western coalition would begin when the menace of immediate aggression seemed to recede. We are in that period now, with new problems and difficulties – and also new possibilities. This is certainly no time to weaken the common front by dissension or doubts or indifference. It is no time to lower our guard, or start wrangling among ourselves.

In negotiating with the communist states and keeping the coalition together in the face of what may seem, or be made to seem, diminishing dangers, diplomacy should, I think, play a greater part than in recent years. By diplomacy I mean something more than monologues at international gatherings, or public press conferences, or calculated leaks to frighten potential adversaries or "put the heat on" reluctant friends, or even political quiz programmes before the microphone or camera. There should be more room for and greater reliance on quiet and confidential negotiation ... If Moscow, by the crudity of communist diplomatic methods, and by its incessant and direct appeal to peoples over the heads of governments, makes this procedure difficult or even impossible, we should keep on trying to restore it. In any event, we need not follow these communist tactics of propaganda diplomacy in conferences and negotiations between friends.

There are, of course, important situations in which the most effective instruments of diplomacy are open conferences with a maximum of publicity. The General Assembly of the United Nations, and the Economic and Social Council, have accomplished a great deal through the opportunities they provide in public sessions for the clarification and mobilization of international public opinion. The Security Council, too, has often found its ability to marshal the pressure of world opinion on particular issues a strong instrument for peace.

But there are also situations – and they are sometimes the most difficult and most important ones – where highly publicized meetings offer the least promising method of negotiating. An atmosphere of drama is inevitably generated when the eyes of the world are focused on a single meeting. Too much drama is not always good for discussion or decision. It may neutralize the value of talks and even doom them in advance to futility. Where public expectations are over-stimulated, deliberation is apt to be confused with dullness, and compromise with capitulation. The purpose of negotiation is, necessarily, to seek agreement through mutual adjustments. But adjustments are not made easier, and may well be made impossible, when the negotiators fear that any concession or compromise is, within the hour, going to be printed, pictured, or broadcast as a capitulation.

There is another difficulty which you will appreciate. Quiet and constructive achievement often has no one to write or speak its praise. But conflict is its own publicity agent. A clash looks more exciting than a slow edging towards compromise. It is, therefore, more likely to get the front page. But when it reaches the front page, the honour and pride of peoples and politicians become engaged. Headlines harden convictions, without clarifying them. As I have said more than once, there is nothing more difficult for a political negotiator to retreat from than a bold, black headline!

Please do not misunderstand me. I do not advocate secret deals around green baize tables in a dim light with all curtains drawn. No genuinely democratic state can or should countenance commitments secretly entered into; or adopt policies or make engagements without the people knowing about them and Parliament passing on them.

But full publicity for objectives and policies and results does not mean, or at least should not mean, that negotiation must always be conducted, step by step, in public. Certainly no private business, not even a public relations business, could be operated successfully by such methods. And government is the most important business of all.

Diplomacy is simply the agency for the conduct of official business with other states. As such it involves the application of intelligent public relations procedures to the conduct of foreign affairs. There are times when I think we might be well advised to leave more of it to the diplomats. They are trained for the job and they are usually happy to conduct a negotiation without issuing a progress report after each twenty minute period.

I hope that I won't be considered as disloyal to my trade union of political negotiators if I suggest that there are certain things that ambassadors and officials can do better than foreign or other ministers, especially in the early stages of negotiation. If governments fail to reach agreement through official diplomatic channels, they can go on trying or, at worst, fail without fury. But when foreign ministers or, even more, when heads of governments meet, with their inevitable retinue of press, radio, and television companions, with experts, advisers, and advisers to advisers, things become more complicated and often more difficult.

There is always the danger that if agreement cannot be reached at meetings on which so much public hope and expectation have been centred, this will inevitably be interpreted as conclusive evidence that agreement never will be possible. The reaction to this may become, in its turn, unnecessarily despairing and pessimistic. Consequently, there is the strong temptation to conceal or deny the fact of disagreement or to concentrate on blaming the other person or persons for it. In this latter technique the communists are past masters. Their participation at international conferences is, in fact, often for propaganda purposes only. Their tactics to this end are worked out long before the conference opens, and their exploitation of failure by attributing it to others continues long after the conference ends.

One reason why there is a reluctance to revert more often to normal methods of diplomacy, using what we call "official channels" rather than political conferences, is that diplomacy as a profession still has a somewhat dubious reputation. This is a "hang-over" from the days when professional diplomats were the agents of autocratic rulers, carrying out policies that had little or nothing to do with the welfare of people, or little concern for their interests. In its origin and in its practice until recent years, diplomacy has tended to remain aloof and exclusive. Its spirit and appeal have often been more dynastic than democratic. With a faint aura of wickedness still about it, this calling is considered by many to be full of trickery and skulduggery, practised by sinister, if distinguished looking gentlemen, who have replaced the knee breeches of the eighteenth century by the striped pants of today.

This is, of course, unwarranted and unfair. No doubt it could be corrected if a good public relations firm was retained to convince the public that the striped pants are really overalls. Striped pants, in any event, are not a garment but a state of mind. That state of mind, I hope and believe, does not exist in the Canadian External Affairs department or in its foreign service. Striped pants and bow ties do not go well together!

Unfortunately, also, the failures of diplomacy have often been charged with responsibility for resulting wars which men have had to fight after the diplomat has asked for his passports. Diplomatic failures – as is the case with other failures – linger in memory and persist in history long after successes and achievements are forgotten.

In the past, diplomacy has suffered from bad public relations or, even worse, from no public relations at all. It is important to alter this in the future because the public relations aspect of international politics, and hence diplomacy, is now so important as at times to be decisive. The main reason for this is, of course, the inescapable necessity in a democracy of basing foreign policy and its conduct on public opinion, which is now determined by all, not merely a few of the citizens. It is essential, therefore, that public opinion should be kept fully and honestly informed; not, as I have argued, of every step in negotiation, but of every principle of policy, which is something different. Public opinion must also be convinced that, even if its representatives in government are to be given – as I think they should – room to manœuvre in negotiation, they will not abandon any principle that has been laid down to guide such negotiation.

This is no easy task, especially in dealing with communist states. Our fear of communism is understandably so great that if in negotiation we make a concession on any point of detail, and this becomes public as it nearly always does, we may be accused of deserting a principle or of being "soft." This, in fact, can be carried to such a point that fear, both of the communist *and* the critic, can freeze diplomacy completely so that no progress of any kind can be made. I hope that we can avoid this purely static position in the coming year just as I hope we can avoid clutching at every proposal as bound to mean peace ...

We should also be wise to follow the advice of a distinguished United States delegate to the United Nations, Senator Warren Austin, when he said: "Always leave your enemy room to retreat." That seems to me to make sense, if not in war, at least in negotiation, even with communists. Equally good advice would be not to allow yourself to be manœuvred into a blind alley.

Finally, we should resist the Anglo-Saxon failing of making a moral issue of every separate political problem. There are some problems that can be dealt with on the basis of political expediency; others only on the basis of moral principle. It is desirable, though often difficult, to recognize the distinction.

To the communists, of course, there is no such difficulty, because there is no such thing as a moral issue. This may seem to give them a short-run advantage. But in the long run, a foreign policy which has a sound moral basis will prevail over one which has not, providing we build on that base a structure of strength with freedom ...

22

THIS address is as near as I ever came to giving what might be called a religious message, or, if not exactly that, one dealing primarily with moral and spiritual values. Naturally, over the years, I spoke occasionally at gatherings where it was appropriate, indeed expected, that the speaker would strike such a note. Such occasions included my acknowledgment of an Honorary Degree of Doctor of Sacred Letters (I certainly didn't earn *that* one); the temporary occupation of pulpits from which my father or grandfather had once preached; and this particular address in Boston to the National Council of the Churches of Christ in America.

Christian Foundations for World Order

2 December 1954

SOME centuries before the Christian era, a Greek philosopher proclaimed to all who would listen that "Man is the measure of all things." In this age of gadgets and geophysics, that wise observation is worth recalling. The recognition of the individual man as the fundamental criterion of all things temporal has been one of the great liberating forces of history. Among its monuments in Western civilization are the achievements of the Renaissance, of the great humanist movements, and of liberal democracy.

Today, however, too often government, and particularly totalitarian government, has taken the measure of man and reduced him in the process to the level of a machine. Man, of course, must bear some share of the responsibility for this when he measures himself by any but the highest standards. The besetting danger of democratic societies has always been that men may, like the prodigal son, sell themselves "short." It is all too easy to accept the shoddy and second-rate in place of that which is first-class; to be satisfied with counterfeits, so long as they promise to pass muster with a majority; and then to seek to evade the inevitable emptiness which these things produce by ingenious escapisms. There is a world of difference between tolerance and indifference. "I couldn't care less" is the slogan of the voluntarily disinherited who in art seek the contemporary in place of the timeless, and in politics seek the safe in place of the enduring.

When men lower their sights and reduce their standards in this way, they become increasingly forgetful of their true nature and unaware of their full possibilities. This makes it easier for them to be treated as pawns to be used merely for the achievement of some ulterior political purpose.

It is sobering to recognize how frequently, today, in democracies as well as elsewhere, the very vocabulary used to describe and analyse man's political actions is taken from fields whose subject-matter, far from being warm and human, is cold and inanimate. If politicians are praised or blamed, as they often are, more for being architects of social institutions than for anything else, they may come to regard the preparation of blue-prints as their most important function. We should be sceptical of such blueprints. The work of the politician or diplomat or social scientist should be more like that of a gardener than a draftsman; for he is dealing with living things, and at best is only preparing the ground for their growth. As Professor Butterfield has recently remarked:

The makers of blueprints are sometimes like the child who, on seeing the sunset, said: "Do it again Daddy," or the child who thought that it was the gardener who actually made things grow. We seek too great a sovereignty over our history. It is wiser to imagine ourselves as rather preparing the ground where many of the most important things in life will grow of themselves.

Among other things, the gardener knows the value of patience, the absence of which is so dangerous in international politics. Patience is not weakness, and should not be lost if in today's difficult and complex diplomatic problems we are unable to achieve spectacular victories, or sudden and clear-cut solutions; the kind for which we have a passion because decisiveness has been the keystone of so much material advance on this continent. To the extent that this need for patience is inadequately understood, public opinion in democracies may tend to make self-defeating demands on its own political servants and force them into rash and unwise actions.

Moreover, it is worth considering whether sensational diplomatic victories are always desirable, even when they are possible. Serious, constructive diplomacy should always have its eye on long-term results. Diplomatic conversations are often likely to be more permanently successful when designed to convince the other government rather than to satisfy the immediate emotions of the spokesman's own people. In a democracy, this demands not only courage on the part of public men, but maturity and generous understanding on the part of public opinion.

Two weeks ago I noticed in an editorial, aptly entitled "Brickbat Corner" in the London *Economist*, the following sentence: "Independent journalism serves no useful purpose unless editors are prepared to use their immunity from popular wrath to say things that would lose millions of votes if said by politicians or start a strike if uttered by the heads of a corporation." Serving such a purpose can be a valuable and vital function, not only of independent journalism, but also of those who preach and those who are political servants of the state ...

This subjection and submergence of the individual by the totalitarian planners and the architects of grandiose social and political structures emanates basically from a belief in and employment of the doctrine of historical determinism. The more I see of the policies and processes of government, the more remarkable it seems to me that serious and intelligent men could ever have brought themselves to propound, or to accept, such a doctrine: that we are slaves of fate and playthings of destiny. Such a view is only comprehensible when the human intellect loses or surrenders touch with its spiritual bearings.

Such a surrender is, of course, the essence of all theories of determinism. It not only blurs but blots out the whole question. For precisely what gives significance to life and history and politics is the possibility which men and nations always possess – though they by no means always use it – of acting creatively in their environment, rather than merely reacting to it. To some extent, of course, all men transmit to the future impulses determined by the conditioning of the past, or respond almost mechanically to impulses from outside. But men can do more than this. If they will, they can always, in some degree at least, transform a situation in which they find themselves. They can take creative action which, while tailor-made as it were to fit the environment, is in no sense merely a product of it.

The whole of our belief in the possibility of constructive action, whether by men or nations, is, of course, based on the assumption that man and his mind are more than merely products of heredity and environment; that he does have this possibility of contact with the realm of the spirit. Public opinion and political judgment, therefore, are bound to reflect among other things the level of a people's moral insight and spiritual stature. This is as true in international as in domestic affairs ...

An arrogant Pharisaism and smug satisfaction with one's own superior righteousness, in a person or in a nation, are not only unamiable qualities but are not conducive to clear the political judgment. He whose humility and moral sensitivity is least highly developed is most likely to confuse principle with questions of fact or expediency, and to make an easy subconscious identification of his own viewpoint with the cause of right. Furthermore, self-righteousness in international affairs is likely to lead to rigidity of thought and intolerance of other views. This often prevents a wise understanding of complex and changing situations, and tends to make diplomacy captive and inflexible.

There has, for example, been a tendency in recent years for public conferences between governments, at least those where the USSR or its satellites participate, to be regarded less as opportunities for the negotiation of differences than as arenas of conflict between right and wrong;

where popularity with press and radio and television audiences goes less to the searcher for a solution than to him who emerges as the stoutest, or at least the most vociferous and violent, champion of the "right."

This tendency for diplomacy to degenerate into popular appeal, resulting in adulation or denunciation (the two often follow each other in quick succession) is largely the result of communist tactics. Such tactics were laid down and built into a system by Trotsky as long ago as 1918 at the Brest-Litovsk negotiations, when he tried to appeal to the people over the heads of the government with whom he was supposed to be negotiating. But the fact that the primary fault is communist does not make it any wiser for national representatives of free states to treat international conferences chiefly as opportunities to make resounding speeches which are designed primarily to go down well with the audiences back home. Vigorous replies to false and vicious communist charges are, of course, often essential. In the face of some propaganda attacks silence could be interpreted as acquiescence. But let us not deceive ourselves that such diplomacy is other than a deplorable necessity. To be merely anti-communist is not enough. If it were, Hitler would be on a very high pedestal in history ...

It is, I think, not inconceivable that the recent improvement in atmosphere, and in diplomatic habits and manners which these two developments illustrate, may contribute to a gradual but genuine easing of tensions. This may give later and more important negotiations on substantive questions a better chance of success. We realize, of course, that these United Nations development are in line with the current Soviet "peace offensive." That offensive may only be a tactical move in a strategy which remains threatening and unchanged. But tactics may have their effect on habits and attitudes and, ultimately, even on policies. We cannot base our plans on the probability of such a good result but we can and should be ready to take advantage of it, if and when it occurs. To that end we have some ground for encouragement though none for complacency or wishful thinking, in the somewhat better international climate of today ...

President Eisenhower put it well and succinctly the other day when he said that we should keep our feet on the ground and our heads in the stars. It is not easy, however, to keep one's feet on the ground without getting stuck in the mud, or to keep one's head in the stars without drifting aimlessly in the stratosphere.

From the earliest days of the Christian church, the insight of theologians has recognized prudence among the seven cardinal virtues. So today, while exploring every possible step towards a genuine peace, we must be careful that we do not in the process prematurely weaken our defensive strength or weary in that vigilance which is still an essential part of the price of liberty. In his Easter message last year, Pope Pius said, "The danger of today is the weariness that afflicts the good." The world is still an unsafe place for the weary – as well as for the weak and unwary.

Nevertheless, prudence without vision would be a sterile and unrewarding thing. To the Christian, educated in the rich tradition of our religious heritage, it should be a truism that the real driving force behind every important political and social movement has been vision. As the Hebrew prophet pointed out long ago, where there is no vision the people perish. We are far too apt to pigeonhole this in our minds merely as a moral exhortation, rather than to recognize it for the hardheaded political observation that it is.

Patience, strength, prudence, and vision are, then, four qualities which should guide our policies and our diplomacy as we move forward, steadily and relentlessly, in the search for a peace which will rest on something firmer and more lasting than force.

The penalty of failure in this search is not pleasant to contemplate, for it would be a war beside which all others would pale into insignificance. It would be a war from which no one could escape; a war which would bring home to us in awesome and terrible fashion something that has long been evident to religious insight – the oneness of all men. It is a significant feature of this age that interdependence, which has always been there on the spiritual plane, has become a fact also on the physical and political levels. Its most graphic and awe-inspiring expression is a hydrogen bomb ...

Faced with this fact, to debate such a question as whether co-existence is desirable or not, seems an idle occupation. There may be only one answer, either co-existence or no existence. This dread and chilling fact of hydrogen warfare is reason not for panic but for ensuring that we do everything that we possibly can do to convert a co-existence which we cannot escape into a co-operation which will be more than a propaganda slogan and something better than the co-operation between Jonah and the whale.

Since the beginning of history, each individual man and woman has had the capacity for suicide. As individuals, we have learned to live with this capacity, almost to ignore it. We have now reached that stage in history when what has always been true on the individual and spiritual levels has become true also on a world-wide social and political plane.

To survive, we must accept and put into practice the organizational or political implications of these facts. The first step in doing so is clearly to realize the dimensions of the situation, and then to act on that realization through policies which will often have to be a supranational in inspiration and result ...

I would like to conclude these remarks by returning to where I began – to the individual man and his own responsibility.

Today, it is true, we live in fear and tension and under the awful shadow of a nuclear cloud. But if each of us remains true to those

Christian ideals and Christian principles, which provide an answer to every question, a solution to every problem, we have no cause for despair. Professor Arnold Toynbee has suggested that no great society is ever defeated by outside pressures or attack, unless it first defeats itself by disintegration of its own moral standards. If this is true, and I think it is, then the real issues, which will in the long run determine the political future and fate of our society must be faced and fought out within the minds and wills of each one of us. There is no escape from our individual responsibility and no other road to reach our goal.

A great and wise and venerable American jurist and citizen, Judge Learned Hand, once wrote:

You may build your Towers of Babel to the clouds; you may contrive ingeniously to circumvent nature by devices beyond even the understanding of all but a handful; you may provide endless distractions to escape the tedium of your barren lives; you may rummage the whole planet for your ease and comfort. It shall avail you nothing; the more you struggle, the more deeply you will be enmeshed. Not until you have the courage to meet yourselves face to face; to take true account of what you find, to respect the sum of that account for itself and not for what it may bring you; deeply to believe that each of you is a holy vessel unique and irreplaceable; only then will you have taken the first steps along the path of Wisdom. Be content with nothing less; let not the heathen beguile you to their temples or the Sirens with their songs. Lay up your Treasure in the Heaven of your hearts, where moth and rust do not corrupt and thieves cannot break through and steal.

If we all lived our lives and conducted our affairs in the spirit of those words, then, indeed, would we have found a sure and Christian foundation for world order.

23

I WAS invited by Mr Molotov in June 1955 to pay an official visit to the Soviet Union. I accepted and arrived in Moscow on 5 October. I was, I think, the first NATO foreign minister to be their guest. It was a visit I am not likely to forget. It was a proud moment for my wife and me when the Canadian flag was run up inside the Bolshoi Theatre as we entered the box of honour and were given a standing ovation as the representatives of Canada. I remember also, and especially, the weekend I spent with Mr Khrushchev and Mr Bulganin at the former's "palace" on the Black Sea. The hospitality was full to overflowing and our reception warm and friendly, even though our talks were very frank and argumentative.

The official discussions in Moscow resulted in the conclusion of our first wheat agreement and, I hope, in more knowledge, if not greater approval, by each side of the policies of the other. If we had doubts about the essentially pacific nature of much of Soviet policy, they remained. But if we had doubts about the power behind that policy, they were certainly removed, along with any illusions we might have had that the source and purpose of that power was likely to change in the foreseeable future.

On my return to Canada, I made an official report to Parliament, a private one to the Prime Minister and the Cabinet, as well as this off-the-cuff speech to the Women's Canadian Club of Ottawa.

Impressions of the Russians
and Their Leaders

5 December 1955

I MUST thank you, Madam President, for your kind introduction, for your discriminating and flattering recital of facts about my career. I need hardly say that I am very happy to be with you on this occasion, to tell you something about my impressions of the visit which I have been recently privileged to make to the Soviet Union. We visited not only Russia but also, and for the greater part of our time, countries in South-East Asia. Yet I find on my return that nobody wants me to talk about anything but the Soviet Union. Everyone wants to know what the Soviet Union is like, and I feel quite incapable of answering that question.

I am not sure that in the verdict of history, and we won't get that for a good many generations, it will not be found that of the two great revolutions of our time – the communist revolution of 1917 and that now taking place in Asia where hundreds of millions of people are emerging from the sleep of centuries – that of the two, the latter one, whose results we do not yet see, will ultimately have more far-reaching consequences for the world. The people of Asia have now become aware of modern material progress and they are determined to do better for themselves than has been done for them over the past 150 years, both in the search for political freedom and for better standards of life.

It was a real privilege to see what had happened in that part of the world since I was there last, as well as to take part in the Ministerial Meeting of the Colombo Plan. I was inspired by what I heard and saw there and by the way the Colombo Plan is working out. We, in Canada, have, I think, made a respectable contribution to that plan and I assure you that it is appreciated by countries like India and Pakistan and Ceylon, where it is in operation. It is not only a matter of material aid to these countries, helping them to help themselves reach better material standards of life; it is not only that which they appreciate, but the understanding, the sympathy, and the co-operation which we, who are privileged to participate in this plan, are showing.

So far as the Russian part of our trip was concerned I should say at once, as I have already said since I returned, that we were given a magnificent reception. We were shown every kindness by a people who are naturally kind and generous. Of course the official "red carpet" was out, and of course the people who looked after us officially had been told to make us welcome, and to be kind to us, and to give us everything possible to eat and to drink! But even allowing for the fact that we were official guests, I had the impression that those who were told to look after us got a great deal of genuine pleasure from carrying out their instructions.

This reinforced my feeling that if only we could somehow get through to the people of this country, so many of our problems could be solved. But that "if" is a very big word indeed. There is always a gap between such people and their government. I hope it is a narrower one in the free democracies than in a totalitarian society. Therefore the kindness and generosity of people in a country like Soviet Russia has only a quali-fied political significance.

I am often asked by my friends what other impressions did I get apart from that of kindness, generosity, and great hospitality. It is not an easy question to answer because we were there only eight days. Though eight days in Russia may be long enough to write a book, it is not long enough to get to know a country. Someone once wrote a book about the Russian revolution which was entitled *Ten Days That Shook the World.* If I ever do write one about my visit to Russia it will be called the "Eight Days That Shook the Pearsons."

Well, of course, we got impressions. But impressions based on a short, official visit are not very sound foundations for conclusions and judgments. I think, however, that they are of value for a person in my position because it gives him an opportunity to check from first-hand evidence some of the judgments and conclusions previously reached on the basis of official information received and of study made. Also our impressions were possibly a little more valuable than they otherwise would have been because of the fact that we were on an official visit and therefore were also able to see and talk with the leaders of the Soviet state. That was a privilege, indeed, in the sense that it made it a little easier to understand the sources of Soviet power and the nature of that power. The result was not always reassuring but it was valuable.

My abiding impression was one of massive power on the part of the state, of great collective strength, and of inflexible purpose. It is a socialist society, of course, and because of that it starts from the collective and works down to the individual. That was dramatized for me when I visited Stalingrad, a city which suffered terribly in the war and the bravery of whose people and of the soldiers who defended it has become legendary. This city has shown almost as much courage in recovery and reconstruction as it did in war. But the reconstruction began with collective enterprises – schools, theatres, parks, offices, and all that kind of thing – even at a time when the people were living in deplorable conditions. Only afterwards did the authorities move from the collective to the individual and begin to take care of his problems, such as housing. In our society, and rightly so, we start from the individual and work to the collective. But I think we might gain something from their approach by emphasizing more the collective side of our society, though not at the expense of the individual.

I also got the impression, as every visitor does, of total control on the part of the government; of the omnipotence and omnipresence of the state. May we be saved from that in this country, from the complete subordination of the individual. It would be stifling and crushing to us but it does not seem to be so to them. Also we should not forget that the deprivations which Soviet individuals accept as a matter of course would seem very difficult to us who are accustomed to a high standard of material living, where the luxuries of today become the necessities of tomorrow. What would be serious deprivations to us are not such to the Russian, because he has no other standard of comparison than the life which he experienced in the past. By that basis of comparison his condition is improving. He has also no other standard of political comparison than with the conditions which existed previously in his country. Comparison with our kind of freedom is not possible, so he may not feel the loss of rights that mean so much to us.

One certainly does not, however, get the impression that they are a beaten, servile, lifeless people. One does not even feel that they miss freedoms that we take for granted. Indeed, they have their own kind

of freedom. If you obey the dictates of the state you are free to do everything you wish within those limits. As somebody has put it, I think it was
Mr Attlee, we have the freedom to make decisions which govern our
lives. They have freedom from the necessity of making decisions. There
are people, I fear, who get as much comfort out of one kind of freedom
as the other.

Another impression I got was that, in large part because of state control of all the media of propaganda and communication and because
they are cut off from outside, the people not only take great pride in the
accomplishments of their socialist state but that it gives them a sense
of superiority over the effete capitalists. This feeling is something which
we are often inclined to ignore, but its existence was driven in on us
during our visit ...

When in Moscow I expressed a wish to go to a Protestant church service. It was only necessary to express that wish to have it met. So we
were taken on Sunday evening to the Baptist church. That church was
almost as crowded as this room; indeed even more so because there were
so many people they could not all sit down. I could not flatter myself
that it was due to my presence, as they did not know that any visitors
from the West were coming. But when I was led into the church, not
through the front door because we couldn't get in that way, but through
the back door, I was put on the platform with the minister. When we
entered, the congregation were singing a hymn, and when they had
stopped the minister began to speak. Our Ambassador who was with me
and who speaks Russian very well said, "He is introducing you." There
was a certain flutter of excitement among the congregation. Then
the Ambassador said, "Do you know what he is saying now?" I replied,
"How should I know?" Mr Watkins said, "He is telling them you are
going to preach to them." "Well," I said, "you had better tell them that
I am not." He replied, "You will have to say something because he has
told them that you would preach and it would be very disappointing if
you did not." I wondered if it would not be even *more* disappointing if
I did. However, my father was a minister and my grandfather also, so I
ought to be able to produce a sermon, quite apart from the fact that I
am a politician. I felt I should try to do something about it. I had also
this advantage – I would say a few words and then they had to be translated into Russian. This gave me time to think what the next few words
would be.

Looking into the faces of these people, strong, patient, good faces,
mostly of elderly people, I thought that a safe text to use in talking to the
congregation would be "Blessed is the Peacemaker." I assure you it was
a safe and satisfactory text. After I finished my few remarks they spon-
taneously broke into a hymn, the tune of which I knew very well. They
sang it in Russian but the words, when translated, still meant "Rescue
the Perishing." I am not sure therefore whether my sermon had been a
success or not!

When you see and hear people like that, when you listen to those in the cities of Stalingrad and Leningrad who have suffered so horribly from war, listen to them talk about their passion for peace, it is very difficult not to believe in their sincerity.

But I do not get very much comfort out of that because a passion for peace among the people (the people in all countries want peace) is not very important unless it can express itself in political action on the part of those who govern the people. Therefore, it is far more important to try to answer a more difficult question. Do the small closely-knit group (at least closely-knit at present) who govern these 175 million people, do they want peace? If so, are they trying to put into effect policies that make for peace? It is a question that means so much, and they also have a right to ask it of us. Indeed they asked it of me several times.

When officials talked about peace and tried to tell me it was their only desire, I was not as convinced as I was about the feeling for peace I sensed among the people themselves. Yet I think it is probably true that they do desire peace (I am talking of the rulers now), or at least a peaceful interlude. I have come to that conclusion because of two factors. One is that when the two men who are ruling Russia now (they say all are equal in the Russian politburo, but the two who are "more equal" than the others are Mr Khrushchev and Mr Bulganin) claim their devotion to peace, they may undoubtedly want a peaceful interlude. They are hard, realistic men, not suicidal fanatics like Hitler, and they know that the alternative to peace if it takes the form of World War III is extermination. They have the hydrogen bomb. They told me about it. They know the effect of their hydrogen bomb. They know the Americans could create the same effect from their bombs. So I suspect they do not want that kind of alternative to peace.

The other reason is, as Mr Khrushchev said to me on more than one occasion: "We want peace because we can win the conflict between the two systems, your system and our system, without war. So if the communist system will prevail without war, we would be very stupid to go to war." If they feel that way, if they have that confidence (and they make great profession of that confidence), it is up to us to show them that it is not justified: that in this struggle of competitive co-existence which we are facing, their system will *not* prevail. *We* know our system is stronger. *We* know it deep down in our hearts – because it is based on the free man. But they say *they* will prevail because our freedom in the Western world is degenerating into licence and luxury and laziness. Their system, based on total control and 100 per cent discipline, produces a people who are patient, strong, and willing to accept sacrifices for the state, for their society.

There was another word which we heard a lot in Russia – fear. We talk a lot, and with reason, about our fear of communist imperialism. We have good reason to fear it from the record of the last ten years. They talk equally and emphatically of their fear, not only their fear of war but specifically their fear of the North Atlantic Treaty Organization which they claim to be an aggressive anti-Soviet bloc; even more, their fear of the United States of America using this organization for its own aggressive purposes.

Their fear seems concentrated on our neighbour to the south. It may well be that this fear is genuine, even among the people. They have no other source of information than that which is fed to them by the state in order to secure a particular result. Because they have no way of checking the truth of the information they get, it would be surprising if, being exposed to that kind of propaganda, they did not fear the United States. Their ignorance of the Western world, and especially of North America, is total and dangerous. If somehow we could remove that ignorance, as I said earlier, and get into contact with the people through honest, genuine exchanges of information, things would be a lot better.

The leaders, however, who do not have to believe their own propaganda, claim that they also fear the United States. Every time I got into an argument with one of them on this score, and it was one of our favourite subjects for argument, he would pull out of his pocket some press clipping which would be based on a Tass despatch from the United States or Canada and which stated that somebody over here had said that we are going to do something very unpleasant to the Russians. These despatches would be edited and circulated in the USSR, and the effect they could create among the people would be bad. Even the leaders might be impressed by certain talk in the States and in other Western countries. It is just possible therefore, though not probable, that even their leaders' fears might be genuine. You see, it is very difficult for a Soviet communist to believe that anything that appears in a newspaper on our side is not from an official source and inspired by the government of the country. It is also just possible that, by a process of auto-intoxication, they may have come to believe their own propaganda which is devoted to creating fear of the United States. Or it may be that these people are merely trying to rationalize and justify their own aggressive policies by trotting out this fear bogey of the Western world. But whatever the reason is, their ignorance, genuine or calculated, is one of the most dangerous factors in the present situation ...

To sum it all up, we came back to Canada feeling that so far as the Soviet Union was concerned, the likelihood of a military attack was not great if we retain enough military strength in the West – in NATO and in other places – to remove the temptation provided by the hope of easy victory. If we remain strong militarily, there is not likely to be all-out aggression. But that does not mean there is not going to be conflict. We are, indeed, in a new kind of conflict. We have been in it for some time. We are just beginning to appreciate its importance and its significance: political conflict, short of all-out war.

It is one thing to prepare for a military aggression. It is more difficult but just as important to prepare to meet political aggression. For that purpose, in the free world we not only have to be politically and socially and economically strong; we have to be united. Above all, we have to be united in NATO, the annual Council meeting of which I am attending at the beginning of next week. One way of being politically strong is not to be lulled into a sense of false security by blandishments; not to allow relaxation of tension, which we welcome whenever and wherever it occurs, to lead into relaxation of effort.

Another way to be politically strong is to use all the resources of diplomacy whenever there is a real opportunity to negotiate. Our strength is, after all, only a means to an end and that end is the peaceful solution of the problems which at present divide the world.

24

A FOREIGN minister of an English-speaking country will undoubtedly find himself at some time or other the guest of one or both of those two bastions of Anglo-Saxon fraternity and co-operation – the English Speaking Union and the Pilgrims' Society. Their existence, and their hospitality, is above political or any other kind of controversy. Perhaps that is why I have a specially vivid recollection of one dinner in New York given by the Pilgrims when I was preceded on the list of speakers by a distinguished American who made some very pungent political observations about the current US administration which had temporarily made his own services redundant. The shocked hush that crept over the "white tie and decorations" assembly could not have been exceeded if he had risen and sung "The Red Flag."

In this particular speech which I gave before the English Speaking Union in London, I had something to say about the requirements of interdependence, with special reference to the commonwealth, as well as about European unity and the Atlantic community – three subjects of abiding importance to me.

The Atlantic Community

30 April 1956

IT has long been an agreeable and innocent diversion to the student of history to observe man's curious blindness to important and even revolutionary events in the contemporary scene. Almost any age – certainly including our own – provides numerous examples of that common pleasure known as wisdom after the event.

At the very moment when Aristotle was designing the best possible constitution for the city-state, his most renowned student, through his conquest of the civilized world, was making the city-state obsolete. Long after the time when the introduction of gunpowder had completely changed the facts of war, moated castles continued to be built throughout Europe, even though they had become more picturesque than strategic. Early in the nineteenth century, there were grave misgivings in England concerning the increasingly acute shortage of boxwood, with which alone the hubs of stage-coach wheels could be satisfactorily made; this at the time when a network of railways was beginning to spread throughout the country. You will remember, too, that as late as 1917 in the First World War, the Allied Command kept in readiness a division or so of cavalry for the break-through to Berlin. Yet one would have thought that by 1917 it would have been evident that cavalry, although continuing to give "an air of distinction to what would otherwise have been disorderly brawl," had largely gone the way of the crossbow and the muzzle-loader. In our own day, it is probable that none of us can fully apprehend the implications for war or peace of the release of atomic energy. A century or so hence, historians – if there are any left – may wonder at our astonishing shortsightedness.

The fact is that man's inherently conservative nature, and his tendency to think in wishful terms, not infrequently blinds him to developments which are bound to bring about the most profound and unsettling transformations to his familiar world. That is one reason why it is so hard to bring political action into line with those developments. Today, for instance, we may not have fully realized the changes that have occurred which render obsolete many of our old concepts of national sovereignty and which make essential the growth and acceptance of the idea of supranational association: changes which require that we give priority to interdependence over independence.

Security, peace, and ordered progress call for action on a wider basis than that of the national community. This does not mean, however, that we should move at once into world government, or some form of Atlantic union or broad political federation, with a central legislature and executive, a common citizenship, currency, and budget, a single foreign policy, and a defence establishment under central control; in short, with all the institutions of a federal state.

Those who advocate such schemes of federation do so from the highest of motives. They perform, I think, a good and useful service in preparing public opinion for the political changes which will undoubtedly be called for in the future to promote international co-operation. As a practising and, I hope, practical politician, as well as a quondam student of political science, I confess that I sometimes find some of the blueprints of the brave new international world so far removed from the possibilities of the present that it is difficult to consider them in realistic terms. Our ultimate destiny – to safeguard our very existence – may well require some form of federalism on a regional or even a wider basis. But meanwhile we have to work with the institutions which exist today and attempt to adapt them for the efficient and equitable solution of our current problems. This is, I suggest, a necessary and practicable task, and the insistent demand for something more far-reaching to be achieved immediately may at times be an obstacle to its accomplishment. In any event, the formal surrender of sovereignty, in its old form, is not now so decisive an issue as the provision of a new assurance, through adequate international measures, that power, traditionally the main attribute of sovereignty, will not be used for wrong purposes and against the general interest. The decisive factors, therefore, are those which determine policy, those, above all, which bring about a sound and sensible public opinion which alone makes it possible for democratic governments to adopt sound and sensible policies: or should the sequence be reversed?

Power, in the sense of capacity to wage nuclear war against another nuclear state, or to abandon the rest of the world and retire into complete isolation without disastrous economic consequences, is now, in practice, limited to two or three states. Even with those, the consequences of nuclear victory would be about as disastrous as those of nuclear defeat. Realization of this fact has put an effective curb upon the freedom of choice and, therefore, the sovereignty of even the superstates. The concept of power-balance has given way to the doctrine of nuclear deterrent. Even the Soviet Union, rather belatedly, seems to have realized that it is not entirely free to throw its atomic weight around and, making a virtue out of necessity, is offering us "peaceful co-existence."

If the great have been limited in this way, how much less freedom of choice remains for smaller states. Indeed, whatever power these states now have can perhaps be most effectively used by the influence they may exert, either alone or even more in association with others, on the policy of the superpower. I suppose, in essence, that – and fear – are the main reasons which now hold a coalition of free states such as NATO together. Smaller and newer states are often more sensitive about their sovereign rights even than larger and older ones. That is understandable. If a smaller power were not jealous of what it has, it soon might not have anything. And it is not surprising if a country which has only recently gained freedom and sovereignty is not as aware as an older state should be of the limitations, as well as the responsibilities, of that freedom.

I do not suggest, of course, that nationalism should not find expression in political freedom until these limitations and responsibilities are sure to be accepted. Nevertheless, if they have any sense of political or economic reality, smaller powers must recognize that isolation or neutralism or whatever they may call it is today not likely to get them very far in controlling their own destinies. It is primarily by working with others that smaller countries can exercise influence on the big decisions by the big powers which so largely determine their own fate. This should strengthen their belief in international co-operation and international organization. It may also make them insistent on a voice and authority within this co-operation and these organizations, in the effort to recapture some of the control over their own fortunes which they may once have possessed but a large part of which, it must be admitted, most of them have now lost. While this is true, the atom bomb has also become itself a leveller even among those states that possess it. It has, for instance, because of its total destructive effects for which there is no adequate defence, made military superiority almost meaningless and armament races irrelevant ...

It surely does not take much hard thinking, then, to come to the conclusion that in their own interest, nation states should work together towards supranational communities. Such communities can grow in different ways and from different sources. Our Commonwealth of Nations, for instance, has evolved from an imperial centre through the transformation of colonial dependencies into free states who have chosen to remain in political association with each other and with the parent state. This evolution without revolution has been of unique value not only to the nations most directly concerned, but to the world at large. That world should not forget what it owes to the United Kingdom for originating and directing this process – which, of course, has not been completed. I can assure you that Canada is happy about its position in the commonwealth and has no desire to see that position weakened. To us it means independence to which something else has been added.

The commonwealth has never been a static association. It has been able to adapt itself to changing conditions and thereby influence those conditions. In recent years its value has increased, and taken on a new significance, by the membership of India, Pakistan, and Ceylon, and by the steady move towards qualification for such membership of other Asian and African political groups. In this way the commonwealth provides a bridge – at a time when there are all too few of them, and when they are desperately needed – a bridge between Asia and the West.

Another impulse to international community development comes from the realization by contiguous nations, with shared political ideas and traditions and interests, that they would be much more adequately equipped to face current political and economic problems, and exploit political and economic possibilities, if they could remove the boundaries and barriers between them: in short, become integrated.

The contemporary illustration of this trend which first springs to mind is, of course, the move toward European unity. It is a move which must surely commend itself first of all to Europeans themselves, who must remember best how much their continent has suffered from disunity; more especially from the tragic feud over the centuries between Gaul and Teuton. The movement will also, I believe, be welcomed by non-Europeans of good will – this certainly includes Canadians – who see in it not merely the strengthening of the shield against aggression from the East, but also a more solid foundation for the prosperity and progress of the united peoples of Western Europe who are such a vital part of the Atlantic community ... We should favour European unity for another reason. Western Europe has great resources of wisdom, strength, and energy which, along with its traditions of freedom and culture, qualify it to play a powerful and constructive part today in world affairs. It can play this part most effectively if the area of united or at least closely co-ordinated political action is enlarged.

This enlargement therefore is something which we should encourage and support, without – and I am talking now about North Americans – being too insistent in our advice as to how it should be done, or becoming too impatient if it is not done overnight. After all, as Mr Bulganin reminded us last week, "Moscow was not built in a day." I do not myself see anything in this move to European unity which should hinder in any way the growth and coming-together of the Atlantic community. Quite the contrary. Nor do I see anything necessarily inconsistent between the closest possible association of the United Kingdom with this European development and the maintenance and even strengthening of its ties with the rest of the commonwealth.

I appreciate, of course, that while Britain is part of Europe – history provides grim as well as glorious reminders of that connection – it has also a wider destiny and wider interests. The world owes much – some states indeed owe their very existence – to the fact that the vision of the British people has ranged across the oceans as well as across the channel. I do not forget this debt when I express the hope that this country, so rich in political sagacity, so steeped in political experience, and which has provided Europe with imaginative leadership more than once in history, will play an active and constructive part in the efforts now being made by European states to adapt themselves to new conditions which require their closer association. Such a part would represent an important contribution to the development of something more important and far-reaching even than European unity itself – namely the Atlantic community.

I see in that community three essential parts; a North America which must not lapse into continentalism; a Europe whose free and democratic countries must achieve the greatest possible unity, both for defence and development and to ensure that no one of them will dominate the others; and finally, the United Kingdom, the bridge between the two, linked to Europe indissolubly by many ties and perhaps, above all, by the complete disappearance of the channel in the air-atomic age; but linked also to North America in a unique way, because that continent – I hope that I will not be misunderstood in putting it this way – is now occupied by two former English-speaking colonies, one of which is proud to retain its political and monarchical association with the "Old Master."

We have now laid the foundations of this Atlantic community in NATO. Indeed that may be the most important thing that we did when we signed in Washington seven years ago the treaty bringing this international organization into being. On the other hand, what we did then may prove to have been as insubstantial and ephemeral as the signatures attached to many an international agreement which at the time seemed a veritable Magna Carta, but whose very name can now be found only in some doctoral thesis. The near future will tell. There is no assurance yet that NATO will survive the emergency that gave it birth. That emergency was itself born of the fear – for which there was sufficient evidence – that unless the Atlantic countries united their resources and their resolve to defend themselves, they might succumb to aggression one by one. It seemed clear when the NATO pact was signed, even to the mightiest power, that national security could not be guaranteed by national action alone. So we built up our collective defences and by our unity and strength have made NATO into a most effective deterrent against aggression. In doing so we have removed the greatest temptation to aggression: disunity and weakness.

If, however, international tension now seems to ease and the threat of direct military attack to recede, the fear which brought NATO into being in the first place will also recede; and the temptation to relax our defence efforts and indulge in the luxury of dissension and division will increase. We may, in fact, be approaching a period – if, indeed, we are not in it – when NATO will lose much of the cohesive force which has hitherto held it together. There are those who are counting on this loss being fatal to the whole concept of NATO and the Atlantic community.

These dangers must be faced. Defence strength and unity must be maintained, yet we may not now have for this purpose the same incentive which we have had before. We must, therefore, develop a stronger bond of unity than a common fear. As the challenge of the communist nations to our free institutions takes new forms, avoiding tactics and policies which risk nuclear devastation, NATO should in its turn, while maintaining whatever collective military defensive strength is necessary, develop new impulses for unity and community.

NATO cannot live on fear alone, nor can it become the source of a real Atlantic community if it remains organized to deal only with the military threat which first brought it into being. A new emphasis, therefore, on the non-military side of NATO's development is essential. It would also be the best answer to the Soviet charge that it is an aggressive, exclusively military agency, aimed against Moscow.

We are now faced by the challenge from the communist bloc of competitive co-existence; or, to put it another way, of all conflict short of full-scale war. This may be an improvement on the imminent possibility of nuclear devastation, but it is a long way from the security of co-operative co-existence and it has not removed the menace of communist domination.

The NATO countries must find the answer to this new challenge by demonstrating the quality and value and sincerity of their co-operation, between themselves, and with all members of the international community. We have here a new opportunity as well as a new challenge, and if we do not take advantage of it, speeches about the Atlantic community will, before long, have as little meaning as those about the lost continent of Atlantis. As the material and technological gap between the NATO countries and the Soviet bloc diminishes, it will be all the more important to maintain the distinctions in other and more important respects, and to ensure that these are more fully understood and valued. This will require closer co-operation – political and economic – within NATO than has been the case; finding new ways by which we can build up and strengthen our own sense of community, and showing others that what we are building is no selfish and exclusive domain.

I hope that the meeting of the NATO Council later this week will find the answers to some of these questions, and begin a serious and practical search for the others. So it should be an important meeting, if not an easy one. At it we may find ourselves discussing policies rather than power, aims rather than arms, division rather than divisions.

NATO, in truth, is now at the crossroads of its existence. If it is to go forward, and in the right direction, it must concentrate on ways and means of bringing its members closer together politically, without weakening its defence unity and strength. For this purpose the Council must become a more effective agency for consultation and co-operation than it has been. It must be given more authority and its meetings, with ministerial attendance, should be more frequent. Through the Council, consultation should be developed into an accepted custom, to the point where no member would think of taking action which affected the others in any substantial way – either politically or economically – without prior discussion with those members in NATO.

For this purpose I do not see the need for any substantial organizational changes or for any amendments to our treaty. Nor do I think that NATO should try to make special economic arrangements between its members or be charged with the duty of removing trade barriers. There are other international agencies which have been specially set up for this purpose – such as GATT and OEEC – and we do not want duplication. I doubt also whether NATO is the agency best equipped actually to provide aid to materially underdeveloped countries. In this matter, the United Nations should, I think, be brought more and more into the picture. I do not mean that the world organization should be the sole or even possibly the major executive agency for international aid or replace practical and successful operations like the Colombo Plan. Its special value would be to provide a forum where all assistance plans could be co-ordinated and policies discussed. I think also that the USSR should be encouraged to participate fully in such United Nations discussions. It would give us a very good opportunity to test the nature and the substance of her participation in this field of international economic assistance.

In political and economic consultation NATO's role, as I see it, is more limited, but more precise and politically more significant in that here discussions are between closely co-operating friends who are trying to bring about not merely the co-ordination, but the closest possible identity, of plans and policies. As the mechanism for this process, NATO can become the foundation for the Atlantic community of the future. It must in fact develop along these lines, or it will drift into futility and may ultimately share the fate of other international agencies which disappeared because their roots were not deep enough for survival and growth.

May I close with a story, substituting only one of two words in the original, to fit this particular occasion:

Making her debut at a NATO gathering, a young matron sat silently through a two-hour discussion of the Atlantic community. Afterwards, she thanked the people to whose spirited pros and cons she had listened. "I'm awfully glad I came," she said, "because I was so terribly confused about the Atlantic community. Of course," she confessed, "I'm still confused, but on a higher plane."

If after my talk you are still confused, as you may well be, I dare to hope that it is at least confusion on a higher plane.

25

THESE are two interventions or, more accurately, two parts of a single intervention made through the Emergency Special Session of the UN General Assembly. They are separated in time, but on a single subject – the Suez crisis of November 1956.

This crisis was, in my view, the nearest we had yet come in the postwar years to a conflict between smaller states escalating into a war between the giants. It was the most dramatic international dispute in which I had ever been involved.

In dealing with it, I felt that the UN must keep two objectives constantly in view. First, to bring the fighting to an end by the intervention of a United Nations force which would separate the Arab-Israeli combatants and provide a good reason for British and French withdrawal. Second, to use the atmosphere of crisis and danger to begin the process of peace-making in the Middle East. The UN failed to achieve the second objective but it succeeded in the first and, in doing so, many have prevented a great international tragedy.

In an effort to help end the fighting, the Canadian government decided to put forward a resolution for an international police force to be organized at once and sent to the area of conflict and danger. The two statements which follow established the basis for our resolution for this purpose. Certainly, if we had voted with the UK and France instead of abstaining on the resolution referred to in the first statement, we would have had no chance of succeeding in the initiative which was made by the second. The statements represented more than two days' uninterrupted activity on my part in Ottawa and New York. Once the resolution was passed, there were forty-eight hours more of continuous work with the Secretary-General and his assistants in order to meet the deadline for reporting back to the Assembly. I shall have something to say in my memoirs about these hectic days and nights.

On the Middle East Crisis

2 November 1956

I RISE not to take part in this debate, because the debate is over. The vote has been taken. But I do wish to explain the abstention of my delegation on that vote.

It is never easy to explain an abstention, and in this case it is particularly difficult because we are in favour of some parts of this resolution, and also because it deals with such a complicated question. Because we favour parts of the resolution, we could not vote against it, especially as, in our opinion, it is a moderate proposal couched in reasonable and objective terms, without unfair or unbalanced condemnation; and also, by referring to violations by both sides to the armistice agreements, it puts, I think, recent action by the United Kingdom and France – and rightly – against the background of those repeated violations and provocations.

We support the effort being made to bring the fighting to an end. We support it, among other reasons, because we regret that force was used in the circumstances that face us at this time. As my delegation sees it, however, this resolution which the General Assembly has adopted is, in its present form – and there was very little chance to alter that form – inadequate to achieve the purposes which we have in mind at this Assembly. These purposes are defined in the resolution of the United Nations under which we are meeting: Resolution 377(v) of 1950, entitled "Uniting for Peace." But peace is far more than ceasing to fire, although it certainly must include that essential factor. This is the first time that action has been taken under the "Uniting for Peace" resolution.

I confess to a feeling of sadness, indeed even distress, at not being able to support the policy now taken by two countries whose ties with my country are and will remain close and intimate; two countries which have contributed so much to man's progress and freedom under law; the two countries which are Canada's mother countries. But, while I regret the use of military force in the circumstances which we have been discussing, I regret also that there was not more time, before a vote had to be taken, for consideration of the best way to bring about the kind of cease-fire which would have enduring and beneficial results. I think that we were entitled to that time, for this is not only a tragic moment for the countries and peoples immediately affected, but it is an equally difficult time for the United Nations itself. I know, of course, that the situation is of special and, indeed, poignant urgency, and that action could not be postponed by dragging-out discussion, as has been done so often in this Assembly. I do feel, however, that had that time, which has always to my knowledge in the past been permitted for adequate examination of even the most critical and urgent resolution, been available on this occasion, the result might have been a better text. Such a short delay would not, I think, have done harm, but, in the long run, would have helped those in the area who need help most at this time.

Why do I say this? In the first place, this resolution, though it has been adopted, is only a recommendation, and its moral effects would have been greater if it could have received a more unanimous vote in this Assembly; which might have been possible if there had been some delay. Secondly, this recommendation which we have adopted cannot be effective without the compliance of those to whom it is addressed and who have to carry it out. I had ventured to hope that, by a short delay and in informal talks, we might have made some headway in securing a favourable response, before the vote was taken, from those delegations whose governments will be responsible for carrying it out.

I consider that there is one great omission from the resolution which has already been pointed out by previous speakers – more particularly by the representative of New Zealand, who has preceded me. The resolution does provide for a cease-fire and I admit that that is of first importance and urgency. But it does not provide for any steps to be taken by the United Nations for a peace settlement, without which a cease-fire will be only of temporary value at best. Surely, we should have used this opportunity to link a cease-fire to the absolute necessity of a political settlement in Palestine and for the Suez. Perhaps we might also have been able to recommend a procedure by which this absolutely essential process might begin.

Today there is a feeling that we are facing an almost desperate crisis for the United Nations and for peace. Surely that feeling might have been harnessed to action; or at the least to a formal resolution to act at long last and do something effective about the underlying causes of this crisis which has brought us to the very edge of a tragedy even greater than that which has already taken place. We should, I think, have recognized the necessity for a political settlement in this resolution and done something about it. I do not think that, if we had done this, it would have postponed action very long on the other clauses. Without such a settlement, which we might have pushed forward under the incentive of fear, our present resolution, as I see it, may not make for a real and enduring peace. We need action, then, not only to end the fighting but to make the peace.

I believe that there is another omission from this resolution, to which attention has also already been directed. The armed forces of Israel and of Egypt are to withdraw to the armistice lines, where presumably, if this is done, they will once again face each other in fear and hatred. What then? What then, six months from now? Are we to go through all this again? Are we to return to the unhappy status quo? Such a return would not be to a position of security or even a tolerable position, but would be a return to terror, bloodshed, strife, incidents, charges and counter-charges, and ultimately another explosion which the United Nations armistice commission would be powerless to prevent and possibly even to investigate.

I therefore would have liked to see a provision in this resolution – this has been mentioned by previous speakers – authorizing the Secretary-General to begin to make arrangements with member governments for a United Nations force large enough to keep these borders at peace while a political settlement is being worked out. I regret exceedingly that time has not been given to follow up this idea, which was mentioned also by the representative of the United Kingdom in his first speech, and I hope that even now, when action on the resolution has been completed, it may not be too late to give consideration to this matter. My own government would be glad to recommend Canadian participation in such a United Nations force, a truly international peace and police force.

We have a duty here. We also have (or should I say, we had?) an opportunity. Our resolution may deal with one aspect of our duty – an urgent, a terrible urgent aspect. But, as I see it, it does nothing to seize an opportunity which might have brought some real peace and a decent existence to the people of that part of the world. There was no time on this occasion and in this resolution for us to seize this opportunity. My delegation therefore felt, because of the inadequacy of the resolution in this respect, that we had no alternative, in the circumstances, but to abstain in the voting.

I hope that our inability to deal with these essential matters at this time will very soon be removed and that we can come to grips with the basic core of the problem.

3 November 1956

THE immediate purpose of our meeting is to bring about as soon as possible a cease-fire and a withdrawal of forces, in the area which we are considering, from contact with each other. Our longer-range purpose, which has already been referred to tonight and which may ultimately in its implications be even more important, is to find solutions for the problems which, because we have left them unsolved over the years, have finally exploded into fighting and conflict.

In regard to this longer-range purpose, important resolutions have been submitted this evening by the United States delegation. We value this initiative, and our delegation will give the resolutions the examination which their importance deserves; we will make detailed comments concerning them later.

So far as the first and immediate purpose is concerned, a short time ago the Assembly passed, by a very large majority, a resolution which is now a recommendation of the United Nations General Assembly. And so we must ask ourselves how the United Nations can assist in securing compliance with the terms of that resolution from those who are most immediately concerned, and whose compliance is essential if the resolution is to be carried out. How can we get from them the support and cooperation which is required, and how can we do this quickly?

The representative of India has just read to us, on behalf of a number of delegations, a very important resolution which deals with this matter. In operative paragraphs 2 and 3, certain specific proposals are made with a view to setting up machinery to facilitate compliance with the resolution.

I ask myself the question whether that machinery is adequate for the complicated and difficult task which is before us. I am not in any way opposing this resolution which we have just heard. I appreciate its importance and the spirit in which it has been put forward. But I do suggest that the Secretary-General be given another and supplementary – not conflicting, but supplementary – responsibility: to work out at once a plan for an international force to bring about and supervise the cease-fire visualized in the Assembly resolution which has already been passed.

For that purpose my delegation would like to submit to the Assembly a very short resolution which I shall read at this time. It is as follows:

The General Assembly, bearing in mind the urgent necessity of facilitating compliance with the Resolution (A/3256) of November 2, requests, as a matter of priority, the Secretary-General to submit to it within forty-eight hours a plan for the setting up, with the consent of the nations concerned, of an emergency international United Nations force to secure and supervise the cessation of hostilities in accordance with the terms of the above resolution.

I would assume that during this short period the Secretary-General would get into touch with, and endeavour to secure co-operation in the carrying out of the earlier resolution from, the parties immediately concerned – whose co-operation, I venture to repeat, is essential – as well as try to secure help and co-operation from any others whom he thinks might assist him in his vitally important task.

This draft resolution which I have just read out, and which will be circulated shortly, has an added purpose of facilitating and making effective compliance with the resolution which we have already passed on the part of those whose compliance is absolutely essential. It has also the purpose of providing for international supervision of that compliance through the United Nations. Finally, it has as its purpose the bringing to an end of the fighting and bloodshed at once, even while the Secretary-General is examining this question and reporting back in forty-eight hours.

If this draft resolution commends itself to the General Assembly – and I suggest that it is not in conflict with the draft resolution which has just been read to us by our Indian colleague – and if it were accepted and accepted quickly, the Secretary-General could at once begin the important task which the draft resolution gives him.

I apologize for adding to his burdens in this way, because they have already been added to in the immediately preceding draft resolution, but we know that he can carry burdens of this kind both unselfishly and efficiently.

Meanwhile, during this period of forty-eight hours, we can get on with our consideration of and decision on the United States and other draft resolutions before the General Assembly which deal with this grave and dangerous situation which confronts us.

26

IT is sometimes forgotten that, in the midst of the drama and excitement of the Suez crisis, there was unfolding the grim and distressing tragedy of the Soviet aggression against Hungary.

In most violent terms the Soviet delegation was condemning Britain and France for their military intervention in the Suez (an intervention which these countries were shortly and voluntarily to bring to an end after the UN had taken action), and at the same time condoning a brutal invasion of Hungary and the shooting down of its citizens who had risen for freedom.

It never seems embarrassing or even difficult for Soviet delegates to try to reconcile the irreconcilable, but this was a particularly savage example of inconsistency and hypocrisy. I tried to express our feelings of shock and outrage in the attached short statement given at a very late hour one night at a meeting of the Emergency Special Session of the Assembly.

The Tragedy in Hungary

3 November 1956

Mr President, notwithstanding the words of the Soviet delegate, we have witnessed in Hungary in the past twenty-four hours one of the greatest and grimmest betrayals in history. This is a sad and desolate moment for all who have been striving for the extension of freedom and justice throughout the world.

It is, first of all, and above all, the people of Hungary who have been betrayed – the students, the peasants, the workers, whom the Soviet Union so frequently professes to champion. For ten years all the resources of a great empire were used to weaken and destroy all feeling for national and personal freedom in Hungary and the other countries of Eastern Europe on whom communist régimes had been imposed after World War II by foreign forces. But events in Hungary, and elsewhere, have dramatically revealed the result of these ten years of suppression and indoctrination to be a failure, often concealed behind a smiling façade of propaganda, but failure. In Hungary the mask of a "people's democracy" has been stripped away; the myth of the monolithic unity of the communist empire has been destroyed. With incredible courage the Hungarian people proved once again that man, once free, will never finally accept oppression and slavery, even though he may be forced to submit to it for long periods. Armed at first only with burning patriotism and a dauntless spirit, the plain people of Hungary rose against the oppressor. And the world watched their struggle hopefully, as the new head of the government, Mr Nagy, promised free elections, the abolition of the secret police, and negotiations for the withdrawal of foreign troops from Hungary. It seemed only a few days ago that the courage and the sacrifice of these men and women would yield them freedom at last, bring them a government of their own choice. It was the dawn of a new day. The people had risen and their will would prevail. Or so it appeared.

Then came the great betrayal. At the very time, we have been told, that negotiations were beginning between Soviet and Hungarian military leaders on a withdrawal of Soviet forces from Hungary, the Soviet Union was moving large new forces into position in that country where they could stamp out the rising flame of freedom and reimpose a ruthless and savage oppression. Or, as the Soviet representative put it, the

Nagy government "fell apart." The Soviet Union's shameless disregard of its obligations under the Charter by its armed intervention has done more than kill Hungarians. It has betrayed the principles and ideals of our United Nations.

We have heard a great deal from the representative of the Soviet Union in the past few days about the iniquities of aggression, the unpardonable sin of force exerted by large countries upon small countries in order to bend them to the "imperialist" will, as he put it. There is no need for me to dwell now on the hypocrisy of the Soviet concern for this other small nation when its own tanks and bombers are compelling an even smaller nation, which had briefly but gloriously raised its head, to put the chains on again.

The Soviet delegate has made the parallel between the situation in Egypt and the situation in Hungary. I would reply first, that the United Nations should judge each situation on its merits; but also, that there is no parallel between the intentions of free democratic nations with a long history of respect for the rights of other nations and those of a dictatorial régime which has not shown the slightest understanding of international collaboration or consideration for the rights of others. That difference is, I think, very clearly revealed in the present situation. The governments of the United Kingdom and of France have stated firmly and publicly that they are prepared to hand over what they claim to be solely a police role to a United Nations force, a force which we are now trying to organize. It is quite true that there remain differences between the British and the French on the one hand, and a majority of this Assembly on the other, on the conditions in which this transfer can take place. Nevertheless, a transfer has been accepted as necessary and desirable. A promise has been given that will be kept.

Will the Soviet Union give us the same promise with respect to their military operations against Hungary? I put this question directly to the Soviet representative. He has told us that his government has intervened in Hungary for a purpose, and that this purpose is ostensibly to protect the interests of the Hungarian people themselves. He wants to protect the Hungarian people, so he says, from a reactionary fascist clique. No one in this Assembly has any desire whatsoever to see the long-suffering Hungarian people delivered from the tyranny of one clique into that of another. All we ask in this resolution which is before us is to let them form the kind of free national government they want. How can this best be done? Surely by an impartial and disinterested international authority which can hold the ring and enable all the Hungarian people, without fear or reprisal, to establish a free and democratic government of their own choice. We have before us a proposal that the Secretary-General investigate the situation. Where else can such an authority come from than the United Nations. Will the Soviet government recognize that? If not, why not?

Yesterday my government proposed the intervention of a United Nations force for peaceful purposes in the Middle East, and that proposal secured the overwhelming support of this Assembly; no single vote was cast against it. Why should we not now establish a United Nations mission or United Nations supervisory machinery of an appropriate kind for the situation in Hungary? I ask the Soviet Union to accept this chance, perhaps this last chance, to prove its good faith to the world. It is not only the Hungarian people who will be the victims of a refusal. It is the Soviet claim, so very often repeated, to be the only true champion of peaceful co-existence, the only real foe of imperialism, the only opponent of colonialism. If they refuse this United Nations investigation and examination into conditions in Hungary, never again will they be able to talk about colonial oppression or imperialism except in terms of the most blatant hypocrisy, recognized by everyone as such.

This is also the last chance of the USSR to show that their collective security system in Eastern Europe is something more than a collection of master and satellites. In this respect, what a contrast it is to an association of free states banded together on a basis of free co-operation, any one of which may withdraw if it wishes. Their system, if they persist in this aggressive intervention, stands exposed for all the world to see, resting on nothing but brute force and despotic control.

Mr President, we owe it to the people of Hungary, we owe it to the United Nations, we owe it to freedom to condemn in the strongest terms what we know has happened and to investigate through the United Nations what is happening now. Surely, Mr President, no single member of this Assembly will refuse to join in that condemnation, and in the request for this investigation. Perhaps at this moment we cannot do more than this, but we surely cannot do less.

PART III

1957–1963

27

A PLEA for personal political support was never an easy one for me to make, especially when I was competing for the leadership of a party against an old friend. This speech, I think, reflects that difficulty.

The decision to enter the race for the Liberal leadership after Mr St. Laurent's retirement was the most difficult one I ever had to make – more difficult than that to enter politics in the first place. The earlier decision, of course, meant a big change for me, but at the time I didn't fully appreciate all its political implications, actual and potential. I felt, in a way, that I was merely taking one more step on the familiar External Affairs ladder from under-secretary to secretary. I knew that I would still be working under a chief I greatly admired and respected and in a field where I was at home. I had confidence also that he would win the forthcoming election and that I would have four or five more years, at least, in External Affairs.

Now I was seeking to take over the leadership of a defeated party at a very low point in its fortunes. Why, then, was I a candidate?

The pressure from my friends was great and made me feel that, having entered the government and politics "at the top," I had no right to refuse to stand for the leadership if my name was put forward, especially in the less than favourable circumstances that faced the party. So I stood. But I remained uneasy about my qualifications or desire for the new role I was called on to play in politics; and in the election of 1958 shortly afterwards, my worst fears seemed to be realized.

I never like to be beaten – at any time and in any contest – but I got some comfort out of the fact that this particular defeat seemed inevitable and there was nothing much I could do about it. But the defeat gave me a strong desire to reverse it; and a resolve, for that purpose, to work as hard and well as I could to help build a new Liberal party on the ruins of the old.

To the National Liberal Convention

15 January 1958

I FEEL both pride and humility as I present myself to you as a candidate for the leadership of our party. No greater honour, and no greater responsibility, could come to any Canadian.

In the last sixty-four years we have had only three leaders – three great Canadian statesmen – Laurier, King, St Laurent. The first two have now become historic figures in our national story. They seem very close and personal tonight on this great and inspiring Liberal occasion.

The third name on this list, The Right Honourable Louis St Laurent, will always have a very special and revered place in my heart and mind. He has been a fearless knight, a knight beyond reproach. He has been my adviser and my friend during many years and I hope he always will be. If I have been able to achieve something in the field of politics, it is due mainly to the constant inspiration and support I have found in his wise and sound judgment. Never will our country forget the disinterested and devoted service it has had from Mr St Laurent, service which he always believed should be above and beyond national, racial, or personal prejudices.

In seeking to follow Mr St Laurent, I can assure you that it is not because of any urge for personal position or political power. I entered public life, as Mr St Laurent and so many other Liberals have done, from a sense of public obligation and duty. That is what a good Liberal should do. That is a basic source of the strength of our party. It is in that spirit and with that resolve that I stand here tonight.

I share this platform with two others, both imbued with the idea of service to Canada through Liberalism. Perhaps I may be permitted to make special mention of one who has been my friend for thirty years and more. I know, as well as anyone, how devotedly and how effectively he has served in government and Parliament over so many years. If I said anything more about Paul Martin it would look as if I were asking you to support him – which is not exactly my purpose at this time.

I ask you, as delegates, to make your choice for the leadership on only one basis. Which of the candidates will be best for the party at this critical time in Canada's and the world's history? Which of the candidates will the people of Canada be readier to choose as their prime minister? This is a free, democratic convention, a Liberal convention. I know that each delegate individually will vote according to his honest judgment of the merits of the candidates and not, as has been suggested, for any other reason. That is true Liberalism and I know that you will be true to Liberalism. I ask nothing else of you.

I intend to say little about myself. You know my record and you can judge me from that record. I have served the state, first as a civil and later as a political servant, for nearly thirty years. During that time I have had a unique opportunity to learn at first hand about Canada's problems.

Since last June domestic problems have taken on a gravity which we had not experienced for many years. Our prosperity is threatened as it has not been since the Tories were last in power during the hungry thirties. Unemployment: there are already three-quarters of a million out of work and little to show that the government realizes what is happening. Trade: the figures are declining and there is a fumbling uncertainty about what to do; only loose talk and threats which prejudice access to our largest market. Agriculture: palliatives and words instead of the price security and fair share of income to which the farmer is entitled. Federal-provincial fiscal relations: a solution based on the equalization of standards and welfare in all provinces which has itself been prejudiced by special deals with the rich, and which has now been postponed to an indefinite date. The nation's balance sheet is blurred by refusing a budget. Meanwhile, every move, every word, is designed primarily to win an election when the country needs vigorous, effective action to save us from grave trouble and restore the confidence in Canada which has been shaken.

Canada now needs a strong and steady Liberal government of the kind that handled such problems in the past and brought Canada out of the depression of the thirties and out of postwar dislocations.

We need a steady and energetic leadership and I will try to give it;

not leadership by domination or rhetoric, or by flamboyance. Leadership through the direction of a team of colleagues who are sincere and vigorous, imaginative and able.

I have heard it said that I have not had much experience as a "practical" politician. But I have learned from one by-election and three general elections that the most important practical political attribute is to get elected yourself and to be useful in helping others get elected. I have had some experience now in both these roles. In my political career I have tried to speak frankly, deal fairly, and think honestly. I consider these things the most important *practical* political qualities. However, I am not, I confess, and I doubt if I ever will be or would want to be, an easy or skilful practitioner of the smoke-filled room, machine-type of politics. I do not think that is what the Canadian people want in the leader of a Canadian party.

I believe that party politics are the very foundation of parliamentary democracy. I know that party and political organization – from the lowest to the highest level of responsibility – is essential to the successful working of a party. We have a lot to do in that regard and we should work hard to bring our party to the people and organize it effectively to that end. We must start at the local level, the main source of strength in any party, and never allow the central offices, important as they are, to become isolated from the feelings and needs of the local organizations.

Above organization, however crucial it is, I put people; those men and women of the Liberal faith who have made our party great in achievement; especially those young men and women who will make it greater, if we give them the chance. The accent should be on youth, on its energy and idealism.

As a Liberal, there is something that I put even above people. It is principle. Unless our principles are sound, our policies and practices will not prevail. National unity is such a principle, an ideal and a policy always defended by our party, still being defended by our party, and which our party must never cease to defend. Our concept of national unity, however, does not include uniformity, but respects provincial rights and minority rights. Liberalism accepts as one of the more important facts of history that Canadian unity must be founded on two peoples, two languages, two cultures, and two traditions. All Canadians should acknowledge such national unity – not as a regrettable necessity but as a national asset of immense value and as a distinctive characteristic which focuses the particular place we have on this continent. If any Canadian at any time wishes to point out how different he is from an American, and naturally how superior he is, all he has to do is address him in French.

There are other principles of Liberalism which I would wish to strengthen and support as leader in any way I could. I have time only to mention one or two of them. First, we must everlastingly insist on the freedom of the individual against the state. We must also recognize the fact that this freedom will be dust and ashes if the individual does not have social security. Liberalism means reform and I hope always to be a reformer. Ours is the party of constructive change; the party, not of privilege and exploitation, but of the common man and his rights. It is the party of full employment and the party that stands for the freest possible trade; for jobs not jobbing; for expansion not restriction.

I wish to mention one other matter: the struggle for peace through international co-operation. If we lose here, we lose everything. For many years now, Liberalism has ensured that a united Canada would play a constructive and significant part in this peace effort. As leader of our party, I could do more for this great cause than I could hope to do in any other capacity. I make no apologies for asking for this new responsibility and this new opportunity.

If you should choose me as leader of our party, I can promise only one thing: I will devote to my new task all the qualities I possess with energy, determination, and honesty of purpose.

This convention has shown that I would be leading a renewed, vigorous, and progressive party; one with not only principles and a programme, one with a fighting and crusading faith. We can be proud – very proud – of the record of our party over many years. We gave Canada for twenty-two consecutive years the kind of government that was the envy of the world. We brought Canada through a depression, a world war, and a period of reconstruction to a state of unexampled prosperity and promise for the future. While we made, of course, some mistakes, there is no need for apology or excuse. But, great though the record has been, the more important thing now is to make new records of which we can be even prouder in the future.

We have started to do that at this convention. We have set our course for the future. We have recaptured our zeal and reaffirmed our unity of purpose. Liberalism is a living faith, and whatever difficulties Canada may face at home or abroad, Liberalism can surmount them and achieve for Canadians the prosperity, the dignity, and the responsibility of free men ...

If you decide to choose me as your leader, I will, with the help and support of each one of you, work with all my power to realize through this great Liberal party a great Canadian destiny.

28

So far as I know, I have no Scots blood in my veins, but I like to go to Scottish functions and I love Scotland and admire its people. So I felt very much at home at this St Andrew's Day dinner in Winnipeg, the kind of joyful affair where Canadian Scots become even more sentimental about Scotland than its own inhabitants are wont to be.

One thing I like particularly about Scotland. Its history has shown that you can have a strong nationalism without a nation state.

St Andrew's Day Address

30 November 1959

We are all Scots tonight: by birth, race, adoption, invitation, participation, or payment. I, for one, am proud to be here by invitation, though somewhat worried about my participation; about my ability to do justice to this toast.

This is the eighty-ninth annual dinner of this venerable and honourable society. You go back almost as far as Winnipeg itself. And you are only one of many such societies which keep alive the love of the land of Scotland.

I have been told that the first St Andrew's Society on this side of the Atlantic was formed in Boston in 1657. The reason was the arrival of a ship, the "John Sara" with two hundred-and-seventy-two Scots prisoners taken by Cromwell at the Battle of Dunbar. Their compatriots in Boston decided to help them and so they formed a Society of Saint Andrew.

They also decided, characteristically, that prudence and planning must go along with sentiment; that their benevolence should look ahead and embrace their own possible misfortunes in the future. So in the language of their constitution, they "did agree and conclude for the releefe of ourselves and any others for which we may cause ... to contribute ... that none give less than twelvepence on first entering and then quarterly to pay sixpence and that this our benevolence is for the releefe of ourselves being Scotsmen, or for any of the Scottish nation whom we may cause to help." Then followed a sentence which I hope did not prevent immediate help to the prisoners, because it provided for the accumulation of capital before any disbursements. "It is agreed that there shall nothing be taken out of the box for the releefe of any for seven years." Prudence and generosity, then, have always characterized Scotsmen!

Your introduction tonight, Mr Chairman, made me feel, almost, that I had a halo over my head. I must remember that a halo, twelve inches farther down, can become a noose.

When my friend, Leonard Brockington, an eloquent master of the English language, was once acknowledging an equally generous introduction at a St Andrew's dinner some years ago in one of those eastern cities which are unable to win the Grey Cup, he thanked the Chairman, not for putting a halo over his head, but for placing a chaplet of Scottish flowers around his undeserving neck. But he too guarded himself against any resulting and unseemly vanity by telling a story of two men who were watching a funeral pass by. Said one, "That looks like the funeral of a very important man; who is it?" Said the other: "I don't know, but I think it is the gentleman underneath the flowers."

In any event, the words of introduction are over, and as the old Scottish song says, "The glen is mine."

I really have no right of race to possess it tonight, or to ask for your patience, as I respond to this hallowed and historic toast. After all, this is a day for Scots to do the talking, to forget their natural modesty, their tendency to self-depreciation, and remind themselves that they are the salt of the earth. I myself, as I have said, have no racial claim to join in this reminder. The sad fact is, while no one could be prouder at having been asked to respond to this toast, that so far as ancestry is concerned I must, in all honesty, but without any apology (Scots don't like apologies anyway, except for some of the stories inflicted on them) admit that three of my grandparents were Irish and the fourth of New England Quaker stock.

In Dublin last August, my wife and I were delightfully entertained at dinner by some of my Irish friends who were glad to find an occasion to meet and talk politics. In the inevitable postprandial "few words," I was boasting of this racial mixture of mine; more particularly of its proportion of three to one in favour of the Green over the Granite. It was the right atmosphere and the right company for such boasting, and I got a very good hearing. Indeed, so stimulating was the occasion, and so happy the subsequent week of wandering through the fairest island on earth, that if I had remained only a few more days I might well have been enticed, in a state of racial emotion, into the Irish Republican Army.

I confess, however, that tonight I could wish that my own mixture contained some Scotch. In the hope that it might, I have lately indulged in some genealogical research to see if, perchance, the name Pearson – my forbears came to Ireland with Cromwell via Yorkshire – might not have been in its North England form a Sassenach corruption of Mac-Pherson. In that happy circumstance, I might be able to claim that I am descended from some members of a Scottish clan who had drifted across the border, as so many Scots have done without changing their names, in pursuit of prey or plenty; or as missionaries to elevate to a higher level of civilization those lesser breeds to the south, improving, naturally, their own financial position in the process.

That literary hammer of the Scots, "Malleus Scotorum," and prejudiced Englishman, Samuel Johnson, once insisted that the noblest prospect which any Scotsman ever sees is the high road to the south; not the road to the Isles? But whatever Samuel Johnson's feeling may have been, I, myself, was deeply disappointed when I could establish no contact between a Pearson and a MacPherson. My racial background will have to remain "unrevised and unrepentant."

I do, however, have in my office a Scot of Scots, from Cape Breton, who has the Gaelic and a passionate fixation about his homeland. So I begged him to write for me something that would be worthy of this occasion, something that would strike the right note of Highland eulogy and eloquence, bring lumps to your throat and tears to your eyes. He refused, because he did not believe that my heart and voice would be able to do justice to his work. He would not produce a Highland record for an Irish-Canadian player to scratch.

In one sense, however, the hard, unhappy fact that I am not a Scot is an advantage. Without favour or prejudice, refusing to be led away by sentiment, or haggis, or heather, I can stand back, survey, and appreciate your virtues; what Scotsmen and Scotland have meant to the world, including that good and glorious part of the world which is Canada.

In the midst of all this Scottish adulation, of praise for Scotia's sons and daughters, you may be in some danger of losing that innate modesty, that sense of balance, which distinguishes Scotsmen from more effervescent races. To protect you from this danger, it would be only kind on my part to remind you that there have been envious and mean-spirited souls in the past who have not succumbed to Scotland's spell, as I have. Lord Byron, whose Scottish reviewers had not done justice to his works – and there is no fury like a writer scorned, unless it be a politician rejected – described the country as a "land of meanness, sophistry, and (shades of John Knox) of lust." Dryden, another tortured English soul, debased and up-ended the finest and deepest of Scottish virtues – loyalty and devotion beyond the call of duty, the loyalty of a Flora Macdonald – by writing of "treacherous Scotland to no interest true."

These are harsh words. But they merely serve to put in bold and glorious relief all the tributes and praise that Scotsmen have accepted, and of course deserved, over the centuries. I hope you will accept in the proper spirit my reason for mentioning this derogatory comment. If you do not, I may expect to have thrown at me a Winnipeg 1959 equivalent of Jenny Geddes' stool to the accompaniment of those immortal words she shouted: "Out, out, false loon."

The toast is "The Day and A' Wha Honour it." The day is that of St Andrew, Scotland's patron saint. Honoured on this day in many other places, perhaps even in Russia where for centuries St Andrew was well beloved and officially recognized, with his cross the badge of bravery. We are told that the pre-eminent qualities of St Andrew were those which Scotsmen are wont to claim, and with some justice, as characteristic of their race: fidelity, courage, and tenacity. There is an old Scottish saying which, while somewhat unkind in two of its four lines, goes:

> The Englishman creeps,
> The Irishman sleeps,
> But the Scotsman
> Gangs till he gets it.

Even a non-Scot, who has *any* feeling, cannot fail but be moved by the romance, the glory, and the greatness of this small country of lochs and lassies; of moors and mountains; cottages and castles; of so few people, who have meant so much in so many places in the world by their quality and achievement; the mother country of so many who have never even seen her, but whose devotion spans the distance of space and time and circumstance.

It is good for a new nation like Canada to have its roots deeply buried in the past; in the legends, the traditions, and the cultures of older people. It adds strength and steadiness to our own national life, colour and variety to the pattern of our national development, when we are part of honoured races over the seas. There is more to national growth than a new oil well, or factory, or superhighway. That is one reason why, in this hopeful land of destiny, we should cherish the ties that give depth, stability, and cohesion to our progress, as we face in unity but not uniformity the difficulties and challenges of a new era.

Narrowness of approach, provincialism in policy, parochialism of outlook, whether within or between countries, is no longer to be tolerated as our national societies grope toward that international unity and solidarity which is now becoming essential for survival in a shrinking nuclear world.

In this search, Scotland can teach us much from its own experience. Scots have been able to reconcile an intense national sentiment, a strong sense of national identity, with participation in a larger political unit of which they are only a part, though of course, a superior, even a dominant part. They have shown the world that strong national feeling can be maintained without formal and separate national sovereignty; that nationality does not always require complete and legal independence. This, indeed, is the path along which humanity itself must move if we are to be saved. Any lesser way will not be good enough to meet the problems that we face.

This feeling of the Scot for his own nation is experienced, though not of course to the same intensity, by those of us who share with Scots membership in a larger association of nations, which we once called an empire, but which now has grown into a commonwealth. Because Scotland is one of the mother countries of our supranational group, we all have a sense of belonging to this envied race. Can this be the reason why, in the British cadet battalion where I was taught to become an officer and temporary gentleman in World War I, so many of my fellow cadets including an O'Toole and even a Levinsky applied for their commissions in Highland regiments? Or am I betraying my own race in the case of O'Toole, and something else in the case of Levinsky, by even suggesting that it could have been anything but the lure of the kilt, of the bagpipes, and the appeal of that martial glory which Highland soldiers have gained in all the battle-fields of history?

I admit, at once, the superiority in martial appeal of the kilt over the khaki, the bagpipes over the bugle, and the Camerons over the Army Service Corps. "Breathes there a man with soul so dead" who has not thrilled to the skirl of the pipes or the rhythmic swish and measured tread of a marching Highland column!

There is one slanderous story that tries to disprove this. I tell it in fear and trembling. A Scottish soldier was wounded in Burma and was evacuated to a military hospital in Calcutta. His condition got worse and he seemed to be dying. The doctors gave up hope and an orderly put a screen around his bed so that his passing would not be seen by the other patients, all of whom were Indian soldiers. He was asked if anything could be done to ease his last hours. He replied that if a piper could play outside the window, he would die happy. A piper was found in a nearby camp and began marching and playing outside. A doctor looked behind the screen to see if Jock had passed on. To his surprise, the patient seemed better, his pulse was stronger, his temperature lower. Other doctors were summoned. They had a consultation and decided the pipes had produced a miracle. The Highlander would recover. Then they moved from behind the screen, looked around, and to their consternation found that all the other patients had died.

My own first visit to the land we honour tonight had a less romantic reason than that inspired by any of the feelings I have tried to express. I was on my first leave from Shorncliffe camp in the spring of 1915 before going, as it turned out, to the Mediterranean. With a friend I had my railway pass made out to Inverness – because it was as far as one could go. But this was the beginning of a deep and permanent attachment. I shall not soon forget the calm and beauty of the glens and lochs; the warm hospitality of strangers who wished to do something for two Canadian soldiers; the deep but proud grief of the people of Oban who had just learned that most of their young men once again had fallen in foreign fields, this time in the bloody, ill-fated landing at the Dardanelles.

Not long after this first visit to Scotland, I stood by the side of a Balkan ditch, in a cold and drizzling rain, and watched a Highland regiment moving back from some bitter days of rearguard fighting. They had been decimated. They were not defeated. They were bloody, but defiant. Some pipers met them, to play the survivors back. The pipes began;

shoulders went back, heads up, the spirit strong again. It might have been the Edinburgh Tattoo.

Whence comes the gallant and unconquerable spirit of men like these? From the testing of battle in many lands, from the tradition of martial triumph handed down from Scottish chiefs? Yes, but also from the proud, fierce will to independence and achievement, of plain men and women in their cottages on the hard and heather-covered hills; from the isles where life is demanding but where the demands are met by effort; in the drab but tidy houses of the industrial towns. It comes from the covenanting fire of a stern faith and from the determined ambition to get ahead, even if it means adventuring in far-off places, in every corner of our globe, far from the lone shieling and the misty isle.

But surely the deepest source of all for the strength of the Scottish spirit is the Scot's passion for education, whatever his material circumstances may be. Far back in history, the King who fell on Flodden Field laid down the policy of "a school in every parish and in every school a master." And that has been Scotland's ideal – the student in the garret room with his bag of oatmeal and his books, drinking deep of the things of the spirit and training his mind to become the disciplined instrument of his energy and ambition.

J. M. Barrie once said to the students of St Andrew's University: "Great are the Universities of Scotland but always remember that there are not four, but five, and the fifth and the greatest is the proud homes from which you come."

Have we that kind of spirit today, with our schools that are palaces, our dormitories that are equipped with television and record players; some of our students with sleek cars to take them and their fur-coated lady class-mates from the lecture hall to the road house? It is all easier now; I hope we don't suffer from it.

I have seen men of Scotland in many far places, doing every kind of constructive work, building up new societies, and helping to make older ones stronger. Wherever they have gone, they have stood out, but not alone, for courage, endurance, and plain good work.

It is not necessary for me to tell you what this has meant to the lengthening story of our own history, every page of which pays such tribute to the contribution of Scotsmen to every phase of our national growth. The record of Canadian discovery and development reads, indeed, like a roll-call of the clans: from the first Scots settlements of Nova Scotia in 1622; the "gentlemen adventurers" who opened up the west, the north-west, and the Pacific coast; Hearne, Simon Fraser, Alexander Mackenzie, Douglas; the Selkirk settlers and those of Glengarry, of Perth, Lanark, Bruce, Huron, and Simcoe – oh, of every part of Canada where work was to be done, settlements to be made, lands to be cleared, frontiers to be pushed west and north. And the Highland soldiers disbanded in Quebec after the battle was won for the crown they had fought against a few years before, now soon to become absorbed as "Frasers" and "MacDonalds" in French by the people among whom they settled. All this has meant so much to Canada that it would be a work of a supererogation to dwell on it – even tonight.

These men brought us much, including Scotland's own two national sports – golf and curling. It is fitting that golf should be a Scottish contribution to civilization – and other things. It is the game that above all demands qualities that the sons of St Andrew claim to be peculiarly their own; sheer unadulterated skill, patience, and a strict control of the emotions; a sense of touch and a requirement to keep in the middle, and out of the rough.

As for curling, I'm not sure but that this is not the greatest glory of all; or that we Canadians will not bless the Scots for sending it to us, even after (please forgive this political heresy) we have forgotten Macdonald except as a name for a Brier Trophy. The special merits of curling, I need not elaborate. I once had to make a speech in Ottawa at a curling dinner, to very largely the same category of people that are here tonight. I decided to see what an encyclopedia of sport had to say about this game which has some connection with politics in that you have to get "into the house" and a "take-out" is easier than a "draw." This is the entry I found:

CURLING: An ancient game, similar in essence to lawn bowling except that it is played on ice. It is certain that it was first played in Scotland before the dawn of recorded history. Authorities agree, that since curling was played in the open, usually during inclement weather, the early Scots found it essential to provide themselves with some means of fortifying themselves against the elements. This they did with typical Scottish thoroughness (See Whisky).

WHISKY: An alcoholic liquid made from a distillation of grain mashes almost certainly first discovered and employed in Scotland at a period too remote for us now to trace. Certain ill-informed authorities maintain that the early Scots invented and perfected whisky as a means of fortifying themselves against the cold while engaged in their favourite game of curling. The truth seems to be that curling was invented only to provide the early Scots with a reasonable pretext for continuing in the open their habitual domestic libations (See Curling).

Now, I do not for one moment suggest that the St Andrew's Society of Winnipeg or of any other place was "invented to provide" Scots and their friends with a "reasonable pretext" for having a pleasant evening together. But it does do that, among more serious purposes, and as one of your guests tonight I am the grateful beneficiary of this subsidiary reason.

I thank you for the honour of responding to this toast to a great race.

29

THIS was a unique and pleasant occasion – three "leaders of the opposition" in the USA, the UK, and Canada speaking at a Washington session of the Annual Conference of American Newspaper Editors. The afternoon was made even more enjoyable for me by the fact that the other two speakers, Adlai Stevenson and Hugh Gaitskell (I am, alas, the only survivor, though the oldest, of the three), were personal friends.

Adlai Stevenson I had known for years. He had one of the most attractive and cultivated personalities I have ever met. He was wise, witty, and brilliantly articulate, and his political speeches in the 1958 campaign for the presidency have seldom been matched for literary and oratorical excellence. His speech on this occasion was one of his very best. I wish it could have been included here.

Politics, Opposition, and the Plight of Democracy

22 April 1960

THIS is a unique occasion: the first time, I think, that the leaders of the opposition, active and titular, of the three countries of the North Atlantic Triangle have gathered together for the same quiz programme. Here we are; three BAs (failed), at least at the last examination; three representatives of teams who did not win the last World Series; three horses who did not win the last Derby, "Darby," or Queen's Plate.

You asked me, I thought, and in any case I propose to do it, to speak not merely about opposition; but opposition in the framework of politics; and about democracy, its perils and its plight.

The plight of democracy has been the subject of concern and alarm ever since there has been democratic government – a relatively short time. Before that the plight of whatever kind of government was in force was also the cause of concern and alarm. Politically, things are always better in earlier days (especially to those who are now in opposition).

Someone dug up not so long ago a Chaldean inscription of several thousand years ago which included these lines:

> We are fallen upon evil times
> and the world has waxed very old and wicked.
> Politics are very corrupt.
> The sons of the people are not so righteous
> as their parents were.

This should help us keep a sense of proportion – and of history.

Of course we have special worries in our own times. We always have had. Ours are greater, however, than formerly because they are now concerned, or should be, with the grim fact of physical survival on a planet on which we can now make life impossible. Fortunately, we are doing this at a time when we are about to discover other planets. I hope that the immigration regulations on these other planets will turn out to be liberal and generous to underdeveloped earth people who may seek admission. Better still, if we could only discover *one* habitable, but uninhabited planet for each aggressive, antagonistic grouping now on earth, I'm sure this kind of interplanetary segregation would meet general approval.

So far as the plight of democracy is concerned, perhaps its most noticeable characteristic today is doubt. This is, in part at least, due to the fact that its processes, its requirements, and its demands are so complicated and yet so insistent that the political leader finds it increasingly difficult to deal with all of them to his own satisfaction. He is therefore bound to transfer some of his own doubts to those who chose him to exercise responsibility.

It also inevitably results in the transfer of more and more of the business of government to a specialized bureaucracy. But, as Henry Kissinger has put it, "specialization encourages administrative and technical skills which are not necessarily related to the vision and creativity needed for leadership." It also makes government more of a mystery, and therefore more aloof from the popular source of its strength.

Inevitably, doubts and difficulties of this kind have led to an increased reliance on the collective making of policy through committees, which were recently and cynically described in a great New York newspaper as consisting of the "unwilling, picked from the unfit, to do the unnecessary." This is too severe. Kissinger was closer to the truth when he said, in the article from which I have already quoted, that "the committee approach to decision making is often less an organizational device than a spiritual necessity."

It is tempting for the democratic leader to take the decision of his committee as his own policy, just as it is tempting for committees to insure themselves against error by associating as many opinions as possible in their decisions. To add to our concern, policies developed this way, with so much inward doubt, tend to become settled and sacrosanct once the verdict has been given.

All this leads to the rigidity which is becoming one of the greatest threats to the democratic policy-making process. Decisions once made after long travail are hard to change. Indeed, any change becomes worrisome and adds to our doubts. This is natural. An elephant is likely to be more anxious about its offspring than a rabbit. It took so much longer to form and produce it.

I could, of course, talk about many other developments which bear on the plight of democracy. But I must turn to the other half of the topic: politics and the role of the opposition in democracy.

My main qualification to speak about this is that I have watched opposition in action from both sides of a Parliament. My views incidentally may have changed slightly with my change of location.

The opposition in a democracy consists of politicians who are applying for a new job and conducting themselves, they hope, so as to acquire it and, more important, so as to be worthy of it. Its first duty, of course, is to oppose, to criticize, to try to change. It customarily "views with alarm" in order to protect the people from the complacency and overconfidence that comes from a government which is continually and exuberantly "pointing with pride." It demands information and it excoriates any abuse of power by governments. Indeed that is almost its major function. As such it is an indispensable part of any healthy democracy.

As Disraeli once put it, perhaps when he was in opposition, "no government can be long secure without a formidable opposition," a view confirmed earlier by Burke's words, "He that wrestles with us strengthens our nerves and sharpens our skill. Our antagonist is our helper." I can agree with that in general without accepting a specific commitment, as an opposition leader, to keep a government either secure or even comfortable.

On the contrary, the insecurity of the government becomes the opportunity of the opposition; to replace it with new and, of course, better government. So we oppose, correct, and criticize. In doing so we cleanse and purify those in office. We are, in fact, the detergents of democracy! ...

While vigour in opposition is desirable, criticism should always be tempered with responsibility. A purely negative, obstructive opposition would be condemned to remain an opposition for a long time. There is also a difference to be observed between vigour and violence. The good opposition leader in a good democracy doesn't go around looking for belts so he may hit below them or looking for parades merely so that he may head them. He will certainly fail if he insists on no bread because he doesn't like half-a-loaf.

Those in opposition are politicians who have confronted electoral misfortune with fortitude and are upheld by that optimism which comes from a knowledge of the fickleness of public opinion and the infinite capacity of those in power for getting into trouble. They know how to

convert the disaster of one year into the success of the next. The wise
politician – and I admit this is easier in opposition – knows also that in
the operation of the democratic process nothing is fixed or final; nothing
is all black or all white. This may work to his benefit. In any event it must
work, or democracy could hardly survive.

As a political reporter for the *New York Times*, W. S. White, put it
some years ago:

Politics, in this or any other free society, settles nothing finally, nothing
arbitrarily, and nothing on the first and most capital totalitarian principle of
either-or. At its infrequent very best, politics makes a sensible and a tolerable
amalgam of the wishes and desires and prejudices of a great many people. At
its very worst politics still distinguishes men from ciphers, men from cogs in a
managerial machine.

When I talk about opposition, I am thinking primarily from my own
experience in a parliamentary democracy ... It is a minor glory, and some
evidence of the maturity of our parliamentary democratic processes,
that the government of Canada each year asks Parliament to appropriate a sum of money to pay a salary to the leader of Her Majesty's
Loyal Opposition so that he will have a more abundant opportunity,
with greater resources, to pursue his efforts to deprive the members of
the government of their salaries by defeating them at the next election.
Mr Gaitskell is also the beneficiary of this mature and democratic behaviour. Mr Stevenson, I believe, is not. His position is different from
ours, for better, even for worse.

The way in which a government accepts an opposition, and in which
an opposition accepts its responsibility, provides one of the best tests of
the maturity of democracy; of whether it is based on a strong and solid
foundation of popular acceptance and support or whether it is merely
a word taken over by those who have no understanding of its reality.
Like "peace," "freedom," "security," and many other words that once
had an honest and clear meaning, the coinage of the word "democracy"
has become debased by the nature and amount of trafficking done in
it. So today we have "controlled" democracy, where the control is despotic; "guided" democracy, where the guidance is one way; "popular
democracy," which functions without any regard to the expression of
the people's will.

This particular test of political democracy, in the confrontation of
authority and opposition, fails when authority degenerates into tyranny
and intolerance, and opposition into faction and fury. The first decline
becomes apparent, and dangerous, when a majority rides roughshod
over the strong views, sincerely held, of a minority; the latter, when a
minority by purely obstructive tactics and by abusing parliamentary
processes, tries to frustrate the will of the majority when that will has
been made clear after adequate debate.

Opposition and authority can best function in their relations with each other when there are two parties, one of which emphasizes reform, with responsibility, and the other conservation, without stagnation. In one party there should be a place for the liberally-minded; in the other, for the conservatively-minded. They tell me that this neat and tidy division of political parties is not too obvious in the United States. Is it, in fact, in any democracy today? There are too many pressures and influences and complicating factors in modern democracy to make this classic political and party division among an electorate easy or even perhaps possible. But the nearer we can approach it, the stronger and more stable a democracy should be. Parties organized along these lines of basic division can be an effective device for containing and modifying extremes on either end of the political spectrum, without preventing that steady change which is the best protection against violent and destructive courses.

While there are differences, there is, however, an important and binding similarity between oppositions in any form of democracy. We all work to throw out the government of the day; to replace it by a more economical and more generous, a more progressive and more cautious, a more responsible, and a more imaginative one: in short, by a better government. In this respect, we are willing to go to great lengths to strengthen democracy in our respective countries. To this end, we plan and produce policies. We also tailor personalities and create images of leadership to fit these policies, or, if necessary, vice versa. The "vice versa" is not so good.

Without the daily and crushing pressure of official duties, oppositions – and particularly their leaders – are supposed to have time to produce ideas which will be as sound as they are captivating. Indeed, opposition leaders constitute, with editors and professors, the thinking element in democratic society. Government leaders, I am told, have no time for anything except decisions, with the space "sign here" already thoughtfully and carefully indicated by those who have, behind the scenes, or in front of them, decided what the decision is to be.

Mr Dean Acheson once wrote, *after* he ceased to be secretary of state, that policy "bubbles up" and does not "trickle down." It was popular and not bureaucratic bubbling that he had in mind. Yet it is one of our dangers that this other bureaucratic bubbling, carefully regulated, is becoming the dominating element in the process. Here an opposition, as I have already ventured to state, can play an important and corrective role; by supplying a continuous, spontaneous, and occasionally hissing contribution to the bubbling-up. In this way it can disturb and impress, and even assist, those responsible for government. It can also irritate and often exhaust them. Perhaps that is also beneficial. Governments, it has been said, more and more tend to secure decisions by exhaustion; inside, in the procedures of officialdom; outside, in those of legislation. Oppositions can make their own effective contribution to this exhaustion – and hence to agreement. Lest in saying this I seem to contradict what I said a few moments ago, may I add that it can be done without filibustering!

Members of the opposition and the government in democratic states, however, have at least one strong bond which normally transcends party differences: they are all members of the One Big Union of Elected Politicians. The fact that this union has received as much abuse as the Teamsters, from more people and over a far longer period of time, tends to draw all its members together. Politicians have always been the victims of undeserved criticism and condemnation. Shakespeare called them "scurvy" and Adam Smith, "insidious and crafty."

This has gone on for a long time, long before politicians were "democratic." Both the criticism, when it is unfair, and the politicians, when the criticism is justified, may constitute a greater threat to democracy than those more direct attacks which are made on it and which seem a greater menace to us. If politics are ignoble, so is democracy which operates through politics and politicians.

Some part of the disdain and disapproval of the politician is due to the bad conscience of those who desert their own civic duties. It is easier to be a critic than a county councillor and it helps to remove one's sense of guilt at evading a tax or avoiding a vote.

The politician, without being corrupt or even shady, can also evoke the disapproval of the fastidious through his aggressive zeal and his vivid imagination in applying those devices and pursuing those courses which are considered necessary to woo voters who are more impressed by singing commercials than monetary policy. These voters, we are told, are in the majority, and it is essential for the politician to secure most of them for himself, if he desires to save his country or even humanity. So if he often wraps himself up in slogans and salestalk, remember he has to get elected. The executive-assistant has to play up to the vice-president, and later to the president if he is ever to end up as chairman of the board, or so I am told.

It is a first rule of politics, which many a good man has forgotten to his public sorrow though perhaps his private gain, that you can't take part in the game unless you remain on the team. In our system, he can only be kept there by the periodic choice of his fellow-citizens, whose motives might not always commend themselves to our contemporary Plato's, but who may be perfectly reasonable in their choice.

In any event, no better method has yet been found to channel the expression of the popular will into political action. Several others have been and are being tried – methods which may even be more suitable to the form of society to which they are being applied. They have even seemed better to some of our own Western democracies, at certain periods, because they made the trains run on time and got the beggars off the streets. But in a society where all men have learned to read, many of them to think, and enough to appreciate, even dimly, the glorious gift of personal freedom in a responsible society, these political "improvements" on our kind of democracy have ended in the crashing of dictators and the destruction and tragedy that followed it.

It is as silly to criticize the politician for not being far ahead of public opinion as it is right to criticize him for being so far behind that he cannot even be pulled into the present, let alone lead into the future.

If the politician yields to unworthy pressures, some of which he may honestly mistake for the compulsions of a public opinion which cannot be denied, he is to be condemned. But equally – or even more – to be condemned are those who apply the pressures and those who create the climate of indifference and complaisant morality which makes the application easy.

I call to witness in my defence of the politician as the pillar, if at times the tarnished pillar of democracy, a professor from Duke University, Dr Mayo, who has recently written the following comforting and, I hope, reasonably accurate words:

The politician is the broker, the adjuster, the reconciler, the arbiter – subject always to the sanction of the next election. He pours oil on the troubled waters of dispute. He is the peace-maker, transforming bitter social struggles into a game with rules. Among the clash of abstract principles he injects the saving doses of sweet expediency. He is the indispensable instrument of democratic politics, through whom grievances are ventilated and tolerable justice done. To every problem there are too many solutions – usually incompatible and often contradictory. The politician thus rightly ignores many of the high-minded but impracticable schemes for the moral reform of humanity. He knows they could not be put into practice except by force and the destruction of liberty. He aims not at ideal justice, but at the right which is attainable, at the feasible and the tolerably good. The conscience of society is not sensitive enough to accept the highest ideal. Politics like salvation is for sinners not saints. Saints would probably not get elected in the first place, and would certainly never be re-elected.

Professor Mayo is right.

There is no greater proportion of rascals or hypocrites among politicians than among lawyers, or farmers, or dentists, or ball-players, or the repairers of television sets. The politician, however, by the very nature of his activity, and his ambitions, is continuously and clearly in the limelight. This rascality, therefore, when it exists, can be, as it should be, easily spotlighted, and even flood-lit.

It is well to keep these editorial spotlights, that TV camera, and the radio microphone, right on the politician. He asks for it; at times he cries for it. And it is good for him if not always to him. If the result is bad for the politician, it should be good for politics, especially if the agency of exposure is honest and objective.

Nevertheless, it is wrong, and can damage democracy, if we despise or even ignore the politician or if we wrap ourselves up in a white sheet of superior, if phony, virtue, because the political servant at times permits his principles to be adjusted to circumstances without being abandoned; because he realizes that the best can be the enemy of the good in the management of human affairs, and that a too intense and intolerant concentration on perfection (a not too common political weakness, I admit) can encourage imperfection.

Above all, I hope that the professional and editorial critic will not sneer at the politician because normally he is not – there are, of course, a few brilliant exceptions – an intellectual; or even one whose mental processes are always as rational as his instinctive reactions ...

Whatever he may do, or say, the politician is, in general, the reflection of those who choose him. So if the reflection is one that invites concern about the plight of democracy, we should blame it on ourselves. If our values are being lowered; if we do not cling, with the assurance of earlier and simpler times, to the things that are righteous; if we are not even sure what they are, because we increasingly mistake the package for the content – then it is our fault, and not that of some congressional committee.

It is not our politics and our politicians that have deteriorated. If there is such deterioration, it is in ourselves. Or perhaps I should put it this way. Politics and politicians have always been deteriorating in the eyes of contemporary observers, a fate which they share with every other kind of human activity. It was always better in grandpa's time.

It should encourage us in this day of confused and worrying democracy, where we are behind in missiles but well ahead in coloured TV and new models, to recall that politics were never so corrupt and inefficient in England as they were from 1732 to 1832 when the politicians were the most aristrocratic and privileged of gentlemen. It was not in 1960, but in 1830, that de Tocqueville commented on the talent among the American people and the lack of it among their governors: "The most able men in the United States," he said, "are very rarely placed at the head of affairs."

How strange that at this moment a hundred and thirty years later – if I may end on a light-hearted note – this is still so demonstrably the case. Perhaps I had better stop there.

30

SINCE I graduated from my own university, I must have given half-a-hundred addresses at other convocations. As the number grew, it became more difficult to avoid platitudes and conventional advice to those graduating. I also became more conscious of the generation gap and more sensitive to the charge made by a cynical French philosopher: "Old men give the young good advice to conceal the fact that they are no longer capable of setting a bad example."

This address at Sir George Williams University is typical of my endeavours to give good advice to students while I was still capable, I insist, of setting a bad example.

Education: The Creation of Finer Human Hungers

27 May 1961

I AM honoured by having been invited to be with you tonight and to speak to the graduates, faculty, and friends of an institution which deserves well of you who have benefited from it, and who have also contributed to it. It is the kind of educational institution whose members appreciate, perhaps more than some university students elsewhere, the value of education; and who from their own experience are able to distinguish between knowledge and wisdom, between the pure and the applied, between the practical and the academic.

In our world today we need, more than ever, both the practical and the academic in education, and the maintenance of a right balance between them. As the President of the Carnegie Corporation in the United States warned us the other day: "We must have respect for both our plumbers and our philosophers, or neither our pipes nor our theories will hold water."

In any event we know and it should keep us humble when we add academic letters after our names, that the unlettered man, the mechanic at his bench, the miner in his pit, by the grace of God and the miracle of brain cells, can be wiser than a PH D or even a full professor.

I think that the greater danger now is that we will concentrate on the pipes at the expense of the philosophy; that we may be panicked into balancing our educational values too much in favour of the practical and the scientific, because a few men in Moscow have decreed that in their country they should concentrate on missiles and rockets rather than on the building of a faster motor car or the achievement of a better detergent. So I hope that we will not yield to contemporary fears and pressures to overhaul our educational system to the point of scrapping scholarship for science; or poetry for electronics.

I remain profoundly sceptical of the value of any exclusive engineering or technical prescription for salvation or even the acceptability of salvation itself on any such basis.

Education, even at a time when Soviet man is in outer space and the red flag has been deposited on the moon, will always be more than test tubes and mathematical formulæ. These things are more important for us now than they have ever been. Our own material progress has made that inevitable. But they should not be allowed to overpower the humanities as we search for survival in a tense and dangerous world ...

The certainty of mutual destruction, which is the source of security based on fear, is also the measure of man's amazing scientific and technical progress which has enabled him to uncover forces of nature before he has learned how to prevent their use for his annihilation. This is the paradox of all paradoxes and it could end life on our planet; a fate which is not, happily, as final as it was, now that man's technical genius has opened up the possibility of other planets to which we might flee.

This paradox was beautifully – is that the right word? – illustrated in a newspaper story I read the other day. A United States naval spokesman on Polaris missiles, as he was called, said that his government now had enough nuclear power "to eliminate everything above the insect level in the world." He agreed, apparently, that the men on the other side of the curtain had similar power because he added that a nuclear war would mean "mutual annihilation, for sure." Thus far, he was speaking sensibly, if a shade depressingly, talking as a scientific and rational being about physical power and its consequences. Then, speaking as the retarded social and political animal which in these matters we all are, to greater or less degree, he added, proudly and confidently, that the USA, his own country, could "survive any sneak attack." He was able to reconcile "mutual annihilation" and "survival" almost in the same sentence.

The grim fact is that moral sense and physical power are now monstrously, and might be fatally, out of proportion. Man can find no secure link between his yearning for peace ... and the all-destroying hydrogen bomb controlled by those who watch each other warily across a curtain of fear and suspicion; a curtain over or through which they cannot communicate in any meaningful and constructive sense though they send to, and receive messages from, a missile millions of miles away in outer space.

Surely this drives home my point that education is more than experiment and discovery in the natural sciences. Increasingly important as this is, education is, above all, and ever has been, the process of learning how to think honestly and straight; to distinguish between the true and false; to appreciate quality and beauty wherever it may be found; and to be able to participate and to desire to participate with intelligence and tolerance in that most important of all forms of free enterprise, the exchange of ideas on every subject under the sun, with a minimum of every restriction, personal, social, or political.

In a word, education means – and this I think is the best definition of it that I have ever discovered – the "creation of finer human hungers."

So the educated person, even in May 1961, will place the desire to put muscle into missiles or into men below the desire to put dignity and decency into living; moral values into action; beauty into words or images. He will put the search for the good life in peace and freedom above every other search, even that into the operation of natural laws.

It must be as exciting as it is important to discover that a molecule or a gas or an insect or an equation can do something or other that no one else had ever realized. I think it must have been even more thrilling for the Chinese poet Li Po to put together these words in a leisurely and contemplative fashion many centuries ago: "The earth has swallowed the snow. Again we see the plum-trees in blossom. The new willow-leaves are gold, the waters of the lake are silver. Now the butterflies powdered with gold lay velvet heads within the hearts of flowers. In his still boat the fisherman pulls up his dripping net, rippling the still water."

Let us never forget, however, that the individual can never develop the qualities that God and his heritage gave him except in freedom, the freedom which too often is the passion only of the unfree. We who live in fortunate lands where we have inherited good things are prone to accept this freedom, the most important of these good things, with an indifference which is the greatest threat to its continuance; a greater threat even than the pressures against it which come from the fear I talked about a moment ago. Yet these pressures from fear are growing.

In war we give, and are willing to give, as much of our fredom as is necessary to preserve it from the results of defeat. In a "cold war" which is caused by and feeds on fear, there is increasing pressure to make the same surrender and for the same reason, survival. If the cold war continues, with the lines drawn by us between our democratic freedom and totalitarian tyranny, can we avoid this self-defeating result without falling a victim to those systems and ideas which would destroy us? This is the supreme test of the strength of our democracy: our ability to protect it without losing, in the process, those things, like freedom, which make it worth protecting ...

We are not truly free, personally or nationally, unless in the interests of society we voluntarily accept reasonable and necessary limitations on our freedom, on our right to exercise our power.

In the international field, such limitation on freedom – that is, on sovereignty – has become absolutely essential by the possibility of atomic power being used for total destruction, if international conflict degenerates into all-out war.

The French writer, Albert Camus, a great and courageous thinker whose premature death was such a tragedy, can argue that this compulsive, atomic necessity makes action easier for our generation. In his last book of essays, he wrote:

Since atomic war would divest any future of its meaning, it gives us complete freedom of action. We have nothing to lose except everything. So let's go ahead.

If we are to fail, it will be better in any case to have stood on the side of those who choose life than on the side of those who are destroying it.

So let's go ahead and be daring in action, with those who choose life – and freedom ...

You have been told, until you must get tired of hearing it, that this is a time for greatness. It is. But every age has been just that – a time for greatness. Today, however, more than at other times, greatness requires qualities of steadiness and balance; a refusal to be stampeded or bullied into the uncritical acceptance of the most strident appeal, the biggest headline, the loudest noise.

These qualities are now so vital because the pace of change is bound to batter our peace of mind and often to confuse our sense of values. After all, so furiously have we moved – in material things – that the bomb which in a few seconds killed some 60,000 at Hiroshima is now almost as old-fashioned as a bayonet; and Jules Verne going around the world in eighty days would now be summoned for holding up traffic.

I'm sure you are not going to hold up any traffic because, as educated human beings, your mission is to direct it. Far from being discouraged about our troubles and difficulties, I know you accept them as an incentive to action. That is the way it should be.

So, let me return – as I finish – to Albert Camus. This is what he said as he received the Nobel Prize, and not long before his death: "My conclusion will be simple. It will consist of saying in the very midst of sound and fury of our history: 'Let us rejoice.' Let us rejoice at being faced with cruel truths. Let us seek the respite where it is – in the very thick of the battle."

So, don't be downhearted in the thick of the battle. It is the place where all good men would wish to be.

31

I ALWAYS found it inspiring to attend gatherings of Canada's "ethnic" communities. These groups never fail to impress me with the importance of their part in our national development, with Canada's good fortune in the colour, strength, and variety of their contribution to that development. We should not forget this as we become more and more preoccupied with the relations between English- and French-speaking Canadians.

The fact that in our earliest years and in our constitution these two groups were the only ones officially recognized – apart from the Indians and Eskimo, the first and indigenous races of this country –

should not obscure the great importance of those other peoples who came across the oceans to help build the Canadian confederation whose unity and strength they so stoutly protect and promote.

Many of them left homelands which had old civilizations and traditions of national freedom which had been overthrown and which were now controlled by external aggressors. These new Canadians retained a passionate belief in the rebirth of freedom in their former homes and a strong desire to do what could be done to bring this about, without prejudice to their loyalty and duty as Canadians.

The dilemma that sometimes resulted from these two sentiments was not made easier by those who hoped to secure political support by holding out false hopes of liberation and hinting at promises for official Canadian action to assist such liberation, promises that couldn't possibly be carried out.

At the Toronto Freedom Festival

14 January 1962

THIS is an inspiring and magnificent occasion – the Festival of Freedom. I congratulate all those responsible for its inception and realization, and all those who have taken part in it. My wife and I are honoured to be your guests. We are as deeply moved by the significance of a festival of this kind as we are thrilled by the beauty and charm of the programme.

Once again we have been reminded, and very delightfully reminded, of the richness and colour and variety of the national cultures that, together, make up our Canadian heritage. How much poorer we would be without them!

We are all Canadians – with the same privileges and the same responsibilities. There should be no discrimination of any kind; no divisions or any feeling of separateness between all the citizens in our country. There should be no first- and second-class citizens. There should be no fact or feeling of distinction between those who were born here; those who came here of their own free will to a land of opportunity and hope; or those who were driven by communist persecution and oppression to seek that freedom outside their national boundaries when it was denied and destroyed at home.

This Canadian unity, however, this emphasis on our all-Canadian identity, need not and must not mean the loss of the traditions, cultures, and arts of the lands from which so many have come ... There is not likely to be drabness or dullness in our national development while we can draw on those rich cultural resources which are being so impressively displayed at this festival.

One thing more. This is a freedom festival in a free country. How can there be any meaningful cultural and artistic expression of the soul of peoples without freedom? Our unity, our growth, our Canadian destiny is inseparable from freedom.

There are many here tonight who know by bitter experience what its loss means; who have experienced the horror and brutality of its forced replacement by communist despotism. We respect them, and appreciate the sacrifices they have made.

Perhaps there could be no better demonstration of the great difference between our free democracy and communist despotism than this great festival itself at which the leader of a parliamentary opposition can speak while, included among his fellow-guests, are friends from the party and the government which it is his duty to oppose. In a communist country the only platform on which a leader of the opposition could stand, if there could be such a person, would be the dock or the scaffold.

Freedom, then, is essential to the kind of unity we cherish. But freedom is necessary also for peace and security, unless it is that of the gaol or concentration camp. There cannot, in fact, be enduring and creative peace in the world until all men and all nations are free. Too often today freedom from oppression is thought of in terms of the experience of Asian and African peoples, some of whom once had a national existence, others of whom did not, and all of whom were once colonies of overseas empires. That kind of colonialism and imperialism is today disappearing fast. It is no longer a serious menace to freedom or to peace.

But the colonialism and imperialism of communist despotism, the kind that has subjugated proud and ancient European nations and destroyed their national existence, this remains the dominant menace to world peace and to world freedom. That menace must one day be removed.

It must also be made clear to those despots who threaten peace and who would dominate the world, that freedom will be defended, that free men will not surrender or yield to the blackmail which would force such surrender. Peace at the price of submission to dictation is no peace at all. To avoid this, not only eternal vigilance, but strength and firmness are essential; strength without provocation, firmness without fear.

The strength and steadiness of free peoples working together will save us, I believe, from the awful choice which some say we will have to make: of submission to communist tyranny, or war and nuclear annihilation ...

Our strength, however, must be more than military. It must be economic and, above all, spiritual. It must be based on those moral values which alone can give a solid foundation for freedom. It must be positive and not merely defensive. We must resolve to fight *for* things – as well as defend ourselves *against* things; fight for the things that make for the better life. Strength must include the resolve to make our own free democracies work for the benefit of *all* the people, not merely for a few or a class.

Freedom, in short, must be creative. This festival has shown how, in the arts, that can be done.

Those who are really dedicated to freedom's preservation will accept its burdens and responsibilities as well as the privileges that go with it. Otherwise, it could be lost without a move being made against it. Freedom will not exist merely of itself.

This, then, is our duty. To defend our freedom, and make any sacrifice necessary to do so, against those who threaten it from outside or inside our borders; and to make it a living, vital force in our own lives and in our own society, and therefore something worth defending to the very end.

32

IN 1959, when I was out of office, I was asked to become chairman of an international organization called the Council on World Tensions. We held conferences from time to time in various parts of the world and examined the cause and cure of tensions in those areas with representatives of governments, universities, and business. The discussions were stimulating and informed and may have had some influence on the politics of the governments concerned.

One of these conferences was in Brazil. I presided over it at the University of Bahia and gave the closing address which dealt with the subject of co-operation and aid for development. There could have been no more appropriate place for this kind of conference than northern Brazil, where the contrast between potential and actual development and between rich and poor was so startling; where aid from the United States to help reduce these contrasts was so greatly needed but where, as in so many parts of Latin America, that aid was often as suspect as it was welcome.

Tensions in the Western Hemisphere

11 August 1962

THIS week we have been discussing tensions in our hemisphere – for the most part, those in its southern half.

Tensions are inevitable and not all are bad. Indeed, within the individual, within the state, or between states, progress without tensions is unachievable. The removal of all tensions is neither possible nor desirable this side of paradise. It would result merely in stagnation.

Equally impractical and contrary to all the lessons of history are those formulæ, neatly packaged as instant cures for undesirable international tensions. Those who press them on us do little good for the cause of peace or progress. They would merely take our minds off the complex day-by-day problems which can be adjusted only with effort and which must be lived with until the adjustment *can* eventually lead to a solution. This process of adjustment to the requirements of democratic development, or of good neighbourhood, can never be easy or simple. There are no patent medicines to cure our troubles after a few doses, though there are many to conceal their symptoms.

We are a long way from achieving an idyllic state of world brotherhood. Meanwhile there will be conflict and competition, tensions, even between men of goodwill. It is not their elimination, but their control that we have been seeking. In the search we must begin with the fact that relations within and between states are changing more rapidly than at any time in history. They will continue to change and the pace will not slacken. We cannot stop this process, even if we wished to. The tensions that inevitably result from such rapid change are not all the work of wicked men, though wicked men can, and do, exploit them.

In our hemisphere – more particularly in the Latin American part of

it – the ardent champions of nationalism, change, equality, or social justice often increase these tensions because they feel more strongly than
less passionate people. It is futile to ask them to be quiet in the name of
peace and order. Those who denounce such people as tension-makers
are quite right. Yet the denouncers have often themselves created, by
their insistence on an established order and a tranquillity based on in-
equality and injustice, those very tensions which they denounce.

Tensions, then, are neither good nor bad in themselves. Moreover,
when they become neurotic and menacing, their removal cannot any
longer be brought about by applying the kind of force and fighting that
could be effective, if only in a temporary sense, even a century ago. The
atom bomb and outer space have changed all this.

There is only one thing to do. Liquidate, or render harmless,
dangerous tensions by pressing toward a world of peace, with freedom,
justice, and a decent life for all. We must seek the establishment and the
general acceptance of processes for political adjustment of disputes and
the levelling up of life as absolutely essential for the easing of tensions
without violence.

The complexities of international relations, economic and political,
on this hemisphere are obvious. They will be unravelled only if the best
minds – in all our countries – work together for this purpose; if we all
give up the futile pleasure of scoring points off each other, rejecting attitudes of superiority on the one hand or suspicion on the other. This will
require a great and sustained effort. We of the industrially developed
countries, the comfortable countries, have some reason to fear that we
may not be equal to the test. Similarly, a feeling of frustration and impatience grips governments and people in the less developed countries
who are determined to catch up, but who are often unable to match their
effort with their desires.

In the face of the agonizing complexities of a situation, the temptation is strong to indulge in self-deception and wishful thinking, in feverish
and aimless movement as an escape from harsh perplexities. By increasing our speed in the familiar political and economic grooves, by shouting
the same old slogans, we seek to reassure ourselves that things will
continue more or less as they have been, though we are aware that this
is impossible. We know that we must make fateful decisions. Yet we are
often quick to denounce each other's view of what those decisions should
be, if only to conceal our inability to make the right ones ourselves.
Indeed, we sometimes doubt whether anyone really knows how we
should act to be saved. We cling to a mystical belief that our democratic
system, in spite of its limitations for emergency action, will show us the
way and give us the means. Yet we are troubled by doubts that we will
not have the sense of purpose, sacrifice, and self-discipline which are
essential to the effective operation of democracy and which alone will
enable us to take the hard and speedy action necessary for progress,
security, and even survival.

There is no assurance today even of survival, let alone security and progress. This is because of two great gaps in our world, two great chasms in which, if they are not bridged or closed, humanity will be lost. The one is the gap between moral and material progress; between man's scientific genius that split the atom and conquered outer space and the idiocy of his social and political behaviour in the face of these revolutionary changes. The other gap is that between the poor and the rich, between the developed and developing countries. We can be lost in this gap too, by the tensions it creates, which could result in the explosions that destroy.

At least we now recognize this gap – and its implications. That is one reason why we are here. Moreover, our nations are pledged to do something about it. It is one pledge we should keep. It attaches to *all* nations, rich or poor, developed or underdeveloped, whatever their circumstances. The obligation, of course, must be discharged in different ways. No nation, however, owes anything to any other nation if that other nation does not discharge the obligation it owes to itself.

In this hemisphere there are great extremes of wealth and poverty, of development and underdevelopment. This applies within and between nations. These are two aspects of the same problem, and the domestic is as important as the international. We may have tended at times to forget this in our discussions this week, which were often concerned more with international than domestic tensions.

It is inadmissible, for instance, that the annual per capita national income of a Latin American country should be less than $200, while that in the United States is over $2000. It is also disturbing to compare, inside a state, the magnificence and the cost of a new factory with the primitiveness of a new primary school; to learn of the amount of electric power available for the factory and that there is not enough of that power in the school to run the film strips that are important in primary education.

Disparities of this kind, within or between nations, are dangerous. Where they exist, there will be tensions of insecurity, instability, impatience. Their continuance, irrespective of their origins and causes, are no longer to be tolerated by civilized men or nations ...

There is so much more than materialism in these tensions between rich and poor nations that they will not be eliminated or may not even be substantially reduced *merely* by reducing the gap between standards of living. The spirit in which help is offered – and received – is as important as the help itself. So there should be a feeling of full participation on the part of all concerned. This may require taking certain risks, even sacrificing some aspects of efficiency, in the interest of full and acknowledged partnership. It will be worth it.

It is well to remember, also, that the positive effort to co-operate for progress, by joint operation of schemes for development, is bound to cause some tensions when so much in the way of material help is coming from outside; from the richest and most powerful country in the world; from a country whose policies in the past have often created fears and resentments too easily kept alive. There will be a feeling of dependence even when the theme song is interdependence. The United States is intervening to help us. That is fine and good. But the word "intervention" has a bad sound even if it is for salvation.

Even in a tolerant, rich, and highly developed industrial nation like Canada, there is some uneasiness that we may be selling our pure Canadian soul for a mess of American potage – in this case, us dollars. If, however, we cannot protect our soul against this kind of financial pressure, it will not be so very pure and we will have only ourselves to blame. Meanwhile, I hope the dollars keep coming and I know that we will put them to good Canadian use for Canadian development.

So, I beg of you, my Latin American friends, be careful; but don't misjudge the Americans. They are a wonderful and generous people, the least imperialistically-minded people that ever had world power thrust on them. They have made lots of mistakes and will make lots more. So have we, the other countries of the hemisphere. If our mistakes are smaller ones, it is only because our countries are smaller ...

More seriously, we should not expect quick and exciting returns from a co-operative effort for hemisphere development. Perhaps an operation like the Alliance for Progress has already created too many illusions of quick and spectacular results. I have heard the opinion expressed this week more than once, that it has been oversold. But that is understandable. It is a political initiative. And some political proposals, to be sold at all, must be oversold – especially to Congress or other legislative assemblies which provide the money.

It is understandable that the leaders and the people of materially underdeveloped nations should be impatient for quick economic returns. There is, however, no way to ensure them, or any magic method by which they can be achieved through foreign aid alone. Even the most generous measure of such aid can only be marginal.

There is another problem that is full of potential tensions. Who qualifies for foreign aid? Must governments be reformist and democratic to qualify for membership in an Alliance for Progress club? Is the alliance to be one for democratic progress, or one merely for progress? Should the dictator not only be denied the embrace, but should the handshake be goodbye? I leave this problem to the oas – in membership of which my country has become increasingly interested – and to the United States of America.

Here again I feel rather sorry for the government of Canada's nearest neighbour. In this matter they are bound to get into trouble, whatever course they follow. You cannot buy friends with aid; nor can you ensure democracy by withdrawing or refusing aid. In any event, this would be a form of American intervention, and that is taboo. But if you help a dictator, are you not betraying democracy? I can only suggest that this problem be treated as a collective one and the solution to each manifestation of it should be taken collectively. There is nothing like a dispersal of responsibility in such cases!

One other very important matter was stressed in our discussions this week: that Western Hemisphere problems and tensions, both political and economic, cannot be separated from those of the rest of the world. Latin America, for instance, cannot escape the consequences of the cold war, or of United States leadership of the free world coalition in that war. Yet this situation should not require – though it may result in – the linking of active collaboration in defence measures against the communist menace with participation in any co-operative effort for development and progress. There is, however, a corollary to this. While you cannot buy friends and allies, or at least sincere friends and reliable allies, nevertheless no country has a *right* to share in the economic benefits of collaboration if it is actively working against that collaboration or working for others who are dedicated to its destruction ...

One other question that was perhaps more in our minds than in our words during the week – though it was mentioned – was whether the system of free and representative democracy would be equal to coping with the tensions that come from development. Certainly the effort to meet the challenge of these tensions within the democratic concept is going to cause some disorder. In the process of achieving the quickened progress now demanded, there may even have to be restrictions and modifications of the democratic system as we know it in some of our comfortable countries. We must never, however, in order to achieve material goals, think in terms of putting the clock back or of looking for alternative forms of rule which history has shown to be in the long run both unstable and unworkable.

Developing countries today, under the furious urge to get ahead, will often tend to be more disciplinarian in practice than those with longer established societies and more stable economies. It is foolish for us to expect such countries to show the economic flexibility and political give-and-take that are possible only after slow and prolonged development. The important thing, the essential thing, that we want to preserve, that we *must* preserve within all our institutions, is a respect for freedom and human rights, adherence to the rule of law, and to that spirit of tolerance and free enquiry which alone makes material progress worth while. Without these, co-operation between states for development will be very difficult.

The Russian communists faced this problem of the political control of forced development with relentless logic and ruthless methods. They decided to shut their people off from other and more prosperous people in the world and to lift themselves up by their own bootstraps, at any price. During this period, no citizen would be allowed to abandon his allocated task in the total, gruelling endeavour. The verdict is not yet final on this experience, but the Russians seem to have shown that harsh methods can be effective in a limited and purely practical sense.

People can be drilled and forced to accept austerity, to forgo the immediate consumer pleasures in order to invest in the future, *provided* all easier alternatives are denied and force is used to make sure that the denial is observed. Free democracy is not the only form of government that gets immediate material results, but the price to be paid for the totalitarian alternative is too high to be acceptable to men who cherish freedom. However, and this is the point of importance, it should not be necessary – it *is* not necessary – to pay that price in terms of political tyranny.

The austerity which the British and some other West European peoples imposed upon themselves in the decade after the last war in order to invest in the future, and the remarkable resurgence of the West European economy after the destruction of war, have shown that parliamentary democracy is capable of the necessary self-discipline when it is required. It has been able to meet challenges and crises without the compulsions of total dictatorship.

There is little wonder, however, that new and underdeveloped countries are often impressed by the Soviet example of forced growth, even if not one of them has yet accepted it voluntarily as a model. The attraction of what seems to have been dramatic material advance, combined with absence of those suspicions and tensions that can come from direct contacts and from historical association, can be a powerful combination. It has undoubtedly had a strong effect, also, on many Latin American people – especially young people. It creates a problem that cannot be solved merely by lashing out against communist subversion but only by showing, not merely by words but by results, that there is a better way for progress.

We have had a good week in beautiful Bahia. I leave this conference grateful for the privilege I have had of listening to, and participating in, an exchange of views on problems of great and growing significance to the security and progress of an important part of our world. I have a far better understanding of those problems than when I arrived. I hope you have also, and that we are now in a better position to utilize any opportunity we may have to do something about them. That is the purpose these conference are designed to serve.

But I leave the conference also profoundly disturbed over what will happen to Latin America if something is not done, and done with all possible speed and effectiveness, to meet the challenge of the "revolution of rising expectations" which dominates the Latin American scene. Time is against us in this effort because the growing consciousness that poverty and degradation is not to be tolerated has produced an angry impatience which is inflammable. It is now a race between evolution and explosion.

Our week together may have made a very modest contribution to the result of this race – on which so much depends – *if* we take back to our homes something of the spirit of our discussions here and, more important, a determination to translate that spirit into whatever constructive action may be open to us.

33

I DO not think I ever made a more important speech in the House of Commons, or one that got more general support, than this plea for better relations between English- and French-speaking Canadians, and, as essential to this end, for the wholehearted acceptance by the majority of the full partnership of the French-speaking minority in confederation.

My views on this subject never changed. I do not see any hope for a strong, enduring, and united Canada if we cannot base our policies and attitudes on the principles outlined in this speech. One concrete proposal I advanced at that time, the setting up of a commission on bilingualism and biculturalism, I was able to implement some months later when I became prime minister.

The Canadian Partnership

17 December 1962

MR Chairman, our country is now preparing to celebrate the centenary of its confederation. We have certain proposals before us which make us conscious of this fact. It should be an occasion for thanksgiving and for hope. And yet, as we prepare for this centennial celebration, we in Canada are anxious, indeed uncertain, about our future. We seem doubtful and confused about our place and our role in a rapidly changing world. Our wealth and our resources, both human and material, are great. Our standard of living is high. But we worry, and in my opinion rightly, about inadequate economic growth and the unemployment which results from that; about our unfavourable international balance of payments; and about other things which may affect our future. We worry also because we are becoming more and more dependent, instead of less and less dependent, upon the United States economically, culturally, and even politically. This leaves us with a feeling of frustration and irritation. Recent events have shown clearly that we are going through another serious crisis of national unity. Not only have we been unable in this country to agree on all the symbols of nationhood long after we have become a nation, but in some quarters the very foundation of our confederation is being questioned. Professor Frank H. Underhill, a perceptive if somewhat astringent commentator on the Canadian scene, said the other day in a speech:

The unpleasant fact is that we seem to be drifting without a compass. We have lost that conviction of positive national purpose which inspired our forefathers in 1867 ... We are fumbling for that sense of impending greatness which once buoyed us up ... What the times demand of us is a higher degree of sustained intellectual effort, a more courageous imagination, a more experimental spirit than has ever been before required in our history.

Confederation was our declaration of faith in the destiny of a united Canada. It was also our declaration of independence from the United States. We would go it on our own on this continent from coast to coast, first as part of the British empire and later as an independent nation of the Commonwealth of Nations. We knew at that time that such a declaration, based on such a faith, would involve an economic price. We were ready then in Canada to pay that price. I hope and believe we are still ready to do so, the price of being Canadian.

Confederation, however, also involved another price which too many of us either forget or do not wish to pay because perhaps it is inconvenient for us to do so. Confederation meant the rejection not only of political and economic annexation by the United States but also of the American melting-pot concept of national unity. Confederation may not have been, technically, a treaty or a compact between states, but it was an understanding or a settlement between the two founding races of Canada made on the basis of an acceptable and equal partnership. That settlement provided that national political unity would be achieved and maintained without the imposition of racial, cultural, or linguistic uniformity.

I sometimes think that the understanding was more academic than actual. Outside Quebec, as Canada grew from coast to coast, this understanding was more often honoured in the breach than in the observance and for reasons which any of us who know about the development of Canada can understand. As a result, there has grown up in this country two different interpretations of confederation. It is this difference in interpretation which has created and is creating today confusion, frustration, and indeed some conflict.

To French-speaking Canadians confederation created a bilingual and bicultural nation. It protected their language and their culture throughout the whole of Canada. It meant partnership, not domination. French-speaking Canadians believed that this partnership meant equal opportunities for both the founding races to share in all phases of Canadian development.

English-speaking Canadians agree, of course, that the confederation arrangements protected the rights of French Canadians in Quebec, in Parliament, and in federal courts. But most felt – I think it is fair to say this – that it did not go beyond those limits. This meant that, for all practical purposes, there would be an English-speaking Canada with a bilingual Quebec. What is called the "French fact" was to be provincial only.

Mr Chairman, this difference over the meaning of confederation was obscured for many years after 1867 by other considerations which I have not time to go into now. However, it is the basic source of present misunderstandings and difficulties in relations between the two founding Canadian races.

The first important clash between those two different interpretations occurred when the school question was raised in Manitoba. Later, during and after World War I, French Canada and indeed English-speaking Canada too – French Canadians and English-speaking Canadians – were perplexed and disheartened by the conflicting interpretation of the obligations of Canada in her participation in that war. French-speaking Canadians increasingly felt they had failed somehow in their attempt to secure the acceptability of their culture in other parts of Canada. Hence they tended to withdraw, with their frustrations, into what has been called at times the Quebec reserve. This tendency to withdraw did not, of course, prevent important changes in Quebec, brought about especially by rapid industrialization.

I think it is fair to say that French Canadians were often slow to adjust themselves to this new industrial environment. Most of their leaders were trained in law, theology, or medicine. They saw Quebec's future in terms of political autonomy, decentralization, and a mainly agricultural economy. There was fear of the new industrialization as something that would break up French Canada's cohesion and weaken its special values, special traditions, and special culture. I believe that fear was increased, as I think the record will show, by the fact that the capital, management, and skilled personnel required for industrial growth were largely imported from English-speaking Canada or from the United States of America. These managers, these financiers, these technicians from outside rightly felt that they were helping to bring wealth and material progress to Quebec. And they were. It was hard for them to realize that, often through no fault of theirs, French-speaking Canadians were being excluded from the direction of and even from satisfactory participation in the economic development of their own province. Changes, then, which brought economic advantages to Quebec suffered from the political disadvantage of being so often imported from outside and of often being alien to the spirit of Quebec.

There was ample room for misunderstanding here. We English-speaking Canadians ought to be able to appreciate this because we often react critically to American financial control and management of industrial growth and resource development in the English-speaking parts of Canada. In the English-speaking provinces the barriers, when they existed, were national, not racial. In Quebec they were primarily racial, but they tended also to become national when the English-speaking Canadian managers, engineers, and technicians made no greater effort to adapt themselves to a Quebec cultural and linguistic environment than did Americans who had come there.

This, Mr Chairman, was bound to bring about political strains and stresses in Quebec's economic progress. In spite of much sincere and conscientious effort on both sides, and I think that effort has increased in recent years, to reduce and remove these strains, "The Two Solitudes" developed side by side in many of the cities and industrial areas in the province of Quebec. In earlier years after confederation, this state, if I may call it that, of bicultural co-existence did not raise many or obvious problems. In those days there were only marginal contacts between the two groups and English had become the language of bilingualism. Even after World War II, when things began to change rapidly in Quebec, the Union Nationale régime helped to hide what was taking place in French Canada from the English-speaking community.

This Quebec industrial revolution was accompanied, as revolutions of this kind nearly always are, by parallel revolutions in other fields. Perhaps it was most apparent in the arts and in literature. But the structure of society was changing in other respects as well. Co-operatives, labour unions, credit unions all grew rapidly in that province. Even more important were the changes taking place in the system of education. Engineering, commerce, the natural sciences, and the social sciences began to attract a greater and greater number of students.

People in English-speaking Canada were aware, of course, that something was happening in Quebec. We were becoming also more conscious than we were before of Quebec's importance as a partner in confederation. We were not lacking in good will and in a desire to understand the special situation of Quebec. But perhaps we needed shock treatment to make us appreciate the full significance of what had happened, of Quebec's social revolution. That shock was given in recent years by separatism; by the agitation in some quarters, which got so much publicity, for what was called political liberation. That was an extreme reaction to what had been going on for at least fifteen years in industrial and social change. Less extreme reactions, however, were perhaps even more significant and quite as sincere as a reflection of Quebec's impatience with her present position in confederation. In any event, for Quebec the period of rural isolationism was over and the prospect of mere survival in confederation was not good enough.

It is now clear to all of us, I think, that French-speaking Canadians are determined to become directors of their economic and cultural destiny in their own changed and changing society. They feel that in doing so they are not being isolationists but that, on the contrary, only in this way can they make their rightful contribution to the true development of Canadian confederation. To this end they also ask for equal and full opportunity to participate in all federal government services, in which their own language will be fully recognized. This right flows from the equal partnership of confederation.

Are these objectives of full participation in the discharge of national responsibilities along with the full enjoyment of rights and opportunities attainable for all French-speaking citizens in our country as it is at present organized in confederation? I submit that the answer depends in part on French-speaking Canadians themselves, on their willingness to continue the effort they have been making, on a large scale since 1960, to develop educational facilities and to ensure that there will be enough qualified French-speaking Canadians to exploit the opportunities and fulfil the responsibilities that develop.

But the answer also depends, and I believe in greater degree, on English-speaking Canadians because we are in the majority. In managerial levels in industry, for instance, and in the federal public services, it is the English-speaking Canadians who must accept the changes which are required to make a reality of full partnership. Are we willing to do it? Are we prepared not only to accept those long-term objectives of partnership but, perhaps more important and more difficult for us, to take immediate and concrete steps to achieve them?

If the answer to these questions is in the affirmative, then we can be confident of the future of our country and we can look forward to a new era of strength and unity which will enable us to overcome any economic, cultural, and political differences and to go forward together as Canadians. But if the answer is negative, not so much in words but in fact, and if we become unaware or careless of the obligations and opportunities of true partnership, we will continue in this country to drift from one difficulty to another until a majority of people on both sides will have had enough of this unique Canadian experience. The final result of that would, indeed, be separatism. I am sure we are all in full agreement that this course would be only a desperate and despairing solution, for it would mean the end of our united country and the betrayal of a great national heritage. It would be a loss, an indescribable loss to us all.

Today, when the greatest need of free men and free nations is to come closer together politically, economically, and culturally; to accept and act on the compulsions and opportunities of interdependence; at this time of all times it would be a tragic thing for Canadians to have to admit their failure to unify their own country in any real and meaningful sense; which means unity without sacrificing special and separate values. No Canadian, surely, could contemplate with anything but bitter regret the weakening, let alone the failure, of confederation, especially when Canada has grown so much in stature and won so much respect in the world.

But we cannot afford to be complacent about this. The world around us shows that nations, when reasonable and acceptable compromises are postponed or are offered too late, will resort to desperate solutions which earlier had appeared to be unthinkable to them and against their own best interests.

So, Mr Chairman, we should be careful not to be complacent about what is happening. We should also be careful not to let emotions created by immediate controversies or special incidents warp our judgment or distort our perspective. We should not assume that cracks mean the wall is falling. On the other hand, we will never restore strength merely by papering over the cracks as they occur. It is a time, Mr Chairman, not for extremists and their passions but for a deep, responsible, and understanding examination of basic situations.

This means, I believe, that we have now reached a stage when we should seriously and collectively in this country review the bicultural and bilingual situation in our country; our experiences in the teaching of English and French, and in the relations existing generally between our two founding racial groups. In this review there should also be, in my view, every opportunity and every encouragement for Canadians, individually or in their associations and organizations, to express their ideas on this situation. If they find it unsatisfactory, they should suggest concrete measures to meet it and to reach a better, more balanced participation of our two founding groups in our national affairs.

Are we ready, for instance, to give to all young Canadians a real opportunity to become truly bilingual? If the answer is yes, as I am sure it would be, what concrete steps should be taken at the different levels of our educational system to bring about this opportunity, having regard to the fact that constitutional responsibility for education is, and must remain, exclusively provincial? What further contribution to this end have we the right to expect from radio, from television, and from films in both languages? How can we encourage more frequent contacts between young Canadians?

Then, there is the question which has already been mentioned in this debate, one of specific and inescapable federal responsibility. What are the reasons why there are relatively so few French-speaking Canadians in the professional and administrative jobs of the federal civil service, including crown corporations and federal agencies? How can that situation be improved as it must be improved? Would it be desirable, for instance, to have a bilingual school of public administration operated by the federal government in Ottawa?

There are a great many more questions that we might ask ourselves. These questions are now very much in the minds of Canadians, more so I believe than ever before in our history. They deserve concrete answers because they are vital to our future as a united country. They should be thoroughly examined and Canadians should be given an opportunity of expressing their views about them. There could not be any better preparation for the celebration of the centenary of confederation than to seek and find these answers. The federal government, as I have already stated and as is obvious to us all, has a special and exclusive responsibility to do something about the federal service and the crown companies. But an inquiry here, Mr Chairman, and even necessary changes, will not in my view go far enough. Many of the most important problems to be solved fall within provincial jurisdiction, especially those arising out of the teaching of both languages. Therefore, if this wider inquiry into the means of developing the bicultural character of Canadian confederation is to be undertaken, the provincial governments would have to be associated with it.

I suggest that to this end the federal government should consult with the provincial governments without delay. If these consultations – I hope this would not happen and I cannot see any reason why it should – do not result in a positive response or if they are delayed, then of course any federal government would have an obligation to go ahead with the inquiry into matters which fall within its own jurisdiction. One addition advantage, Mr Chairman, of the joint inquiry, that is with the provinces, is that it would show the importance of the contribution to our national development made by Canadians other than the founding races, a contribution which has been of special and indeed exciting value since World War II. This contribution of our new Canadians from old races has added strength, colour, and vitality to the pattern of our national life. It has enriched Canadianism by qualities inherited from old and noble traditions and cultures of other lands.

What better way could we prepare for our centenary than by taking effective steps now to deepen and strengthen the reality and the hopes of confederation so that all Canadians, without regard to race or language or cultural backgrounds, may feel with confidence that within this nation they can realize, without discrimination and in full partnership, a good destiny for themselves and for those who follow them. In that spirit of hope and confidence we can all work together and build up a greater and more united Canada.

34

THE proposals made in this speech on nuclear defence policy became a major issue in the election which was called shortly after it was given. It also helped to cause division and disruption in the Conservative government of the day. The position I took was reached only after deep consideration, and I knew that it would produce strong reactions, though I confess I did not expect the false and absurd charge that I had made some kind of "deal" with President Kennedy on this matter.

A few months earlier the Conservative government had confirmed beyond any possibility of doubt their acceptance of the strike-attack role for Canadian air squadrons in the NATO forces in Europe. They did so when those squadrons received planes and equipment which would be useless without nuclear warheads. The die was cast and all possibility was gone of changing, at this time, the role of Canadian forces to one which would not require nuclear weapons. I had advocated such a change.

Canadian forces were now to share with the United States control of the use of nuclear weapons, which were in US custody but at a Canadian base. Yet the government refused to make the decision which would enable the weapons to be used at once, if war broke out. Such a decision was left to be made when the emergency arose. This created an impossible situation of dangerous uncertainty, as the Cuban crisis had just shown. It could prevent either of the two governments from carrying out the role that each government had accepted under collective security arrangements.

I came to the conclusion that this was a humiliating position for Canada, as a member of the NATO coalition. Therefore I proposed that nuclear warheads should be accepted under US custody, but under joint control, and that negotiations should take place with the USA for a later and more acceptable non-nuclear Canadian role when that could be arranged. I knew that this change would take some years to bring about, but I was certain that eventually it could be made.

Meanwhile, I felt we had to discharge the commitments we had formally accepted or withdraw from NATO; and I certainly didn't favour withdrawal, as my address to the York-Scarborough Liberal Association revealed.

On Canadian Defence Policy

12 January 1963

TODAY I want to talk about defence policy. The position I am taking has been reached after careful and long consideration, in the light of the situation as it exists now and of information that is now available. The experience, and the information of recent months, even recent weeks, has influenced that position.

In talking about defence, I am aware that the opposition in Parliament have not all the confidential information available to government. I am also aware that nothing on defence policy has been said for a considerable time by any government spokesman.

This is surprising, especially in view of the shock of the Cuban crisis and of statements made by NATO military leaders and others. The people of Canada should have a statement on defence policy from its government, a clear and frank statement. This is a responsibility which can only be finally discharged by a government, which alone is in possession of all the facts. I have waited – as others have – for a long time for such a statement. It has not come. Perhaps my remarks today will help to produce one.

Defence policy is, of course, one of the most difficult and important problems the government of Canada has to handle. As the Cuban crisis has recently reminded us, it involves awesome decisions for the leaders of the free world. For a few tense days last autumn, the world stood on the brink of thermonuclear war. We owe our escape from catastrophe to a combination – notably in Washington – of skilful diplomacy and adequate deterrent military strength. We will continue to need both in the days ahead.

Today, with nuclear power balanced uneasily between two great blocs, each capable of destroying the other, the only defence is a constructive and enduring peace. You cannot win a nuclear war. Indeed you can't wage a nuclear war in the old sense. Therefore, defence policy must be designed to prevent it, by ensuring that the price of aggression will be too high to be borne by an aggressor. The prevention of war,

however, cannot mean the sacrifice of freedom. We must have both –
peace *and* freedom. The first aim of defence policy therefore is the preservation of peace, the prevention of war.

We defend Canada, and we defend freedom, when we secure and
defend the peace. The means for this are more than military. They are
economic, political, moral, and indeed spiritual. While peace is our
objective and our only sure defence, deterrent and defensive force is
needed to preserve it in the international situation we face today.
Furthermore, every country has an obligation to do what it can, even
in a nuclear age, to defend its own territory. Canada's defence policy
must, therefore, provide for some territorial protection as well as make
a contribution to collective security through international agreements,
in particular, through NATO. These two things, dedication to peace and
acceptance of NATO commitments, will not conflict as long as the NATO
alliance remains a purely defensive one, as it is today – and as it must
stay ...

Today, defence policy is based more on the interdependence than
the independence of nations. No country, not even the most powerful,
can defend itself alone. The only security, especially for a country like
Canada, lies in collective action through a defensive alliance such as
NATO, which rests, or should rest, on a pooling of strength.

Collective defence of this kind is based on treaties; on obligations
undertaken, and on commitments given. These are not treaties, however, merely between governments. The obligations they involve are
between nations. That is why we talk about the foreign policy of France,
the defence arrangements of Germany. In dealing with our friends, we
must assume that a change of government would not normally mean a
sudden and unilateral renunciation of the treaty obligations they have
undertaken. Our friends have the same right to assume that the commitments of Canada are the commitments of the nation; that they
would not automatically disappear with a change of government.

These are the facts of life in the modern world. They demand as
much continuity and as much bipartisanship in defence policy as is
possible. They demand that we act as Canadians first, Liberals and
Conservatives second. They mean also that an opposition has a duty
not to exploit defence for purely partisan reasons. I certainly accept that
obligation for myself.

A government has the same obligation, but an added and special one
to inform and explain. It is only on a basis of frankness and knowledge
that you can have a truly national policy in defence. Partisanship is
inevitable if the facts of defence policy can be discovered only by the
opposition continually pressing the government for information which
it cannot secure ...

To find the best defence policy for Canada would be a difficult
enough problem in any circumstance and for any government. But it

has been complicated and confused by the controversy over one aspect of policy: whether to use nuclear weapons of any kind, or not to use them. This has been made into a moral question. That makes argument and even explanation difficult, because it arouses strong emotions concerned not only with the behaviour, but the very survival, of man.

Whether Canada, in present circumstances, uses nuclear weapons or not cannot be decided on moral grounds, without hypocrisy on our part. As a member of the NATO coalition, we accept the nuclear deterrent in the hands of the United States as essential for defence; and we supply much of the uranium that goes into American nuclear bombs. To say therefore that, on moral grounds, we will not accept the protection of any nuclear weapons in any circumstances is dishonest and hypocritical unless we are at the same time willing to withdraw from NATO and refuse to export, to anyone, uranium for military defence purposes.

The fact is that the argument for or against nuclear weapons for Canada is a political not a moral one. There is, of course, a moral problem, but it is concerned not so much with any particular weapon but with war itself. War is the evil, the immorality. Indeed, by concentrating our emotions on a particular kind of weapon we are in danger of obscuring the real issue, which is disarmament and outlawing war as an instrument of national policy. Also, the search for a sane defence policy is only made more difficult by mixing it up with slogans and emotions. We should be clear on this.

The basic defence question to be answered is a simple one: "How can Canada make her most effective contribution to collective security in order to avoid war?" Before we can answer that question we have to ascertain what our present commitments are. These, as I have said, are commitments not for a government, but for Canada. So what is the situation here, especially as it concerns nuclear weapons? We know more about this than we did a year ago but not by any statement of the Canadian government.

The Canadian government in 1959 agreed that the role of our overseas air division in NATO should be changed to the very important one of strike-reconnaissance. The Liberal opposition in Parliament opposed this new and changed commitment. Nevertheless, it was undertaken for Canada. The aircraft for this role, American "Starfighters," or CF–104s as they are called in the RCAF, are now being delivered to discharge this commitment. For this purpose, they are designed to be armed with nuclear warheads. We know that they cannot effectively do the job in question without such warheads. That's the commitment.

The government, however, after commiting us to expenditures of hundreds of millions of dollars on these planes, has not made up its mind, even yet – or it hadn't this morning – whether to accept the warheads or not. It has not even made the political agreement with the United States which would make the nuclear warheads available if it were decided later to accept them. This agreement will take some time to negotiate, as will the training of our airmen in the use of the weapons; between three and six months, according to the former NATO Commander. But nothing has been done, one way or the other. No decision has been made. The result is a serious gap in the defence arrangements of NATO and of this continent. We said that we would assume a particular responsibility in collective defence. In fact, we are not doing so.

Similarly – though it is less serious – our NATO ground forces are being equipped with "Honest John" artillery designed to carry nuclear warheads. We have taken no decision, however, to secure the warheads, even though we are committed to use them for defence against an attack.

At home, our Bomarc missiles – ground to air – are in the same state of impotence. The government must have decided, back in 1959, that the two Bomarc bases are important links in the continental defence chain. We Liberals at the time thought they were wrong in this, but the decision was made – made for Canada. Yet it is clear that these missiles are useless without nuclear warheads, and that these cannot be secured and used *at once* in an emergency. Plans have to be made in advance; agreements reached with the United States for that purpose. Our Bomarc missiles, for instance, stood useless during the alert in the Cuban crisis. That crisis also showed how absurd it is to think that a decision could be made and quick, effective action taken, *after* the emergency developed.

Similarly, our CF–101 aircraft, the Voodoos, to be effective as interceptor fighters for the continental defence role we have undertaken, require nuclear warheads. It is ridiculous to think we can reserve the decision to get them, and have them ready for use, until the emergency develops.

In short, both in NATO and in continental defence, the Canadian government has accepted commitments for Canada in continental and collective defence which can only be carried out by Canadian forces if nuclear warheads are available. Since then, however, the government has refused to make the decision either to alter the commitments or accept the warheads. Those are the facts about our nuclear defence situation today. If there was any doubt about those facts, that doubt was removed the other day by a man who should know, General Norstad, the man who for many years was supreme NATO commander.

As a Canadian, I am ashamed if we accept commitments and then refuse to discharge them. In acting thus, we deceive ourselves, we let our armed forces down, and betray our allies. As I understand international affairs, and I think it is the understanding of all Canadians, when you make, and continue to accept commitments, you carry them out. If we had not done so in the past, Canada would not have achieved a position of respect and influence in the world.

The important thing now, however, is not to indulge in recriminations over the past, but to decide what it is best to do now. Before we can make that decision, we have to understand the nature of the threat to peace that faces us.

For many years after World War II there was no great change in the fundamentals of defence strategy. Atomic bombs got bigger. Delivery aircraft got faster. But the means of attack and defence against it were, in essentials, unchanged. Then came the missile with a nuclear warhead of supremely destructive power; intercontinental missiles from land bases, or others from submarines and aircraft. One nuclear submarine now carries more destructive force than all the armies on both sides in all the years of World War II.

The greatly increased power and range of nuclear missiles has also, paradoxically, increased the importance of non-nuclear conventional weapons. Cuba showed that. NATO is showing it. Without strong conventional forces, every attack would become a nuclear war. Western military thinking is therefore putting more emphasis on the strengthening of conventional forces. For smaller powers, this is economically the most feasible form of defence. Also, on other grounds, it is desirable to restrict the manufacture or custody of nuclear weapons to those countries now possessing them. Custody and control, however, are not the same thing. Custody of defensive tactical weapons could remain in the hands of the United States while such weapons could be made available to the forces of another country which would share in the control over their use, each country, in fact, having a veto over that use. This joint control over US nuclear weapons has already been provided for through political agreements between the United States and certain NATO members. But it does not make the second country a nuclear power, through manufacture or ownership of nuclear weapons. Ownership, under present American law, must be reserved to the United States. However, control of use can be shared, and that is the most important thing, apart from abolishing nuclear weapons altogether by international agreement which should of course remain our overriding and ultimate objective.

What should the Canadian government do in these circumstances? It should end at once its evasion of responsibility, and put itself in a position to discharge the commitments it has already accepted for Canada. It can only do this by accepting nuclear warheads for those defensive tactical weapons which cannot effectively be used without them, but which we have agreed to use. An agreement with the United States for this purpose would have to be negotiated. This would be similar to those already signed by the US government with the United Kingdom and other NATO countries to provide for joint control of the use of the weapons, if and when they are accepted. In such an agreement, a US finger would be on the trigger; but a Canadian finger would be on the safety catch. Action taken under such an agreement would ensure that the Air Division in NATO or the Bomarc squadrons for continental defence would have these weapons available, would be trained in their use, and would be ready in an emergency to do the job entrusted to them by the Canadian government after agreement with our allies.

The Canadian government should also support any move for genuine collective control of all NATO tactical nuclear weapons – a genuine NATO nuclear deterrent. If this could be brought about, it would be restricting rather than enlarging the nuclear club because the three NATO members now possessing such weapons in NATO forces would have to give up their independent control of them. The Canadian government should support the strengthening of NATO conventional forces so that undue reliance would not have to be placed on nuclear tactical weapons for defence against every attack, even a limited and conventional one.

Canada should not contribute to the strategic, nuclear deterrent. Defence of the West now rests largely on nuclear retaliatory power. This is almost entirely in the hands of the United States. It should be left there. We should oppose any additional independent and national nuclear forces. Canada should, however, continue to take part in early warning systems designed to protect the US strategic deterrent forces by making them secure against sudden attack and thereby ensuring their ability to retaliate against an aggressor.

The government should also re-examine and at once the whole basis of Canadian defence policy. In particular, we should discuss with the United States and with NATO a role for Canada in continental and collective defence which would be more realistic and effective for Canada than the present one. This examination would be concerned, among other things, with the necessity of building up NATO's conventional forces and the part Canada could play in this. However, until the present role is changed, a new Liberal government would put Canada's armed services in the position to discharge fully commitments undertaken for Canada by its predecessor. This would be the only honourable course for any government representing the Canadian people. We would not betray our trust, or weaken Canada's reputation for living up to its word.

In the full re-examination of defence policy, and in which all parties could participate through a defence committee of the House of Commons, a Liberal government would be guided by the following considerations:

1 Defence policy must be a part of our foreign policy, and that of our Allies, which is directed to the establishment of a constructive and enduring peace, based on disarmament, especially nuclear disarmament; on co-operation between all nations; and on the promotion of freedom and human welfare everywhere.

2 It follows that Canada's defence policy must not hinder or minimize

Canada's influence at the United Nations and in the councils of the world in the effort to realize these political objectives. I would be the last man to advocate any policy that could interfere with the realization of this objective: to strengthen Canada's influence for peace at the UN and in international councils.

3 We must take whatever steps are feasible for the protection of our territory, through measures for passive as well as active defence. Defence measures must also be related to our international commitments for collective security. They must be determined by the circumstances of today, not of yesterday. Protection effective only against dangers that have disappeared is merely a waste of money and resources.

4 Canada's defence policy should be geared to its industrial structure. We should not try to do a little of everything. As a member of a coalition which is supposed to operate on the principle of the most efficient and co-ordinated use of our collective defence resources and the standardization of arms and equipment, we should concentrate on doing the things that are strategically, industrially, and politically best and most appropriate for Canada. Our financial resources are limited. Therefore we should be careful to see that our defence dollars are spent sensibly and economically, avoiding commitments which require expensive equipment that is, or soon will be, obsolete; and activities that are, or soon will be, meaningless. Only the United States can afford to try to close *all* the defence gaps and make *all* the frequent changes necessary to keep up with the changing conditions.

5 Canada must continue the closest possible co-operation with the United States and with her friends in NATO. She must do nothing to weaken continental or NATO collective policy and action, while insisting that this requires full and continuous consultation between partners. Otherwise, the defence coalition will not survive and the defence policies of its members will go their separate ways, along with their foreign policies. The Cuban crisis showed up some of the gaps in our partnership.

6 Canada's defence forces, whether stationed in this country or in Europe, should be so organized, trained and equipped as to be able to intervene wherever and whenever required for United Nations, NATO, or Canadian territorial operations. We should, especially, be ready and willing to take part in United Nations peace-preserving operations. This means that it must be a first essential of Canadian defence policy to give our forces maximum mobility, especially through the provision of adequate air transport.

7 The three Canadian defence services should be fully integrated for maximum efficiency and economy, both in operation and administration. The necessary changes should be made at the National Defence Department for this purpose.

8 Canadian defence policy should not become frozen to provide for increasingly meaningless activity. It should be under constant review, not only by a defence committee of the Cabinet, but by a defence committee of the House of Commons.

These then are the principles which will underlie the defence policy of a Liberal government: to put a policy into effect based on present commitments that would be carried out and not evaded, while negotiating future commitments more appropriate for Canada. This will be the challenge which we will have to meet when we are given the responsibility of government.

PART IV

1963–1968

35

I AM including this address in my book partly because it was the first one I gave to a non-political audience in Quebec after I became prime minister and partly because I felt that there should be something here in the French language.

Mes difficultés dans l'utilisation du français, quand je me suis trouvé dans le Québec, ont fait que je ne me suis jamais débarrassé d'un certain sentiment d'humiliation à ne pas pouvoir m'adresser couramment dans leur langue, à des auditoires de langue française ou à mes amis québécois que je rencontrais dans des réunions sociales.

Je pouvais lire le français assez bien et parler à partir d'un texte sans trop de difficulté, même si mon accent, comme on me l'a dit une fois, était "cute, like a Frenchman speaking in Brooklyn English." Et la conversation était toujours laborieuse à moins qu'il ne s'agisse d'une réunion d'intimes où tout le monde se sent détendu.

For this language deficiency, I was inclined to blame those who were responsible for my education. But I blamed myself much more for not overcoming this educational handicap by my own efforts when I was young.

Il est déplorable qu'au Canada chaque enfant d'âge scolaire n'ait pas au moins la possibilité d'apprendre la langue maternelle de près du tiers de notre population. Il est aussi regrettable que, dans les régions de notre pays où les deux groupes ethniques vivent côte à côte, le bilinguisme ne soit pas accepté comme normal et nécessaire et qu'on ne prenne pas les moyens pour qu'il en soit ainsi. Nous sommes chanceux au Canada que nos deux langues officielles soient l'anglais et le français, utilisées à travers le monde, et il est inconcevable, nationalement et culturellement parlant, qu'on n'en ait pas tiré profit.

It is hard for me to believe now that in high school I had a choice between French, German, and Spanish. I took German – I hate to admit it – because I was told that the examination was much easier as the teacher was a mild and kindly person. This was long ago. I hope it couldn't happen now.

J'ai aussi inclus ce discours parce que les remarques que je faisais en français dans le Québec sur l'unité nationale dans la diversité sont telles que je pourrais les refaire maintenant, sans les changer, à Halifax ou à Victoria et, de fait, je les ai déjà répétées.

À l'Association des hebdomadaires de langue française du Canada

17 août 1964

M. LE President, invités d'honneur, mesdames et messieurs : Votre invitation de prendre part à ce congrès m'a causé beaucoup de plaisir et je l'ai acceptée avec empressement. Mais je dois vous dire que la joie que j'ai eue à vous rencontrer et la chaleur de votre hospitalité ont contribué à augmenter ce plaisir. Je vous remercie des gestes d'amitié et des gentillesses que vous m'avez manifestés depuis mon arrivée parmi vous ...

En lisant le programme de cette réunion, j'ai été intéressé par la liste impressionnante des journalistes qui se sont succédés à la présidence de l'Association des hebdomadaires de langue française du Canada. Il serait trop long de repasser toute la liste mais les premiers noms suffisent à retenir l'attention : Louis Francœur – sûrement l'un des plus grands journalistes de l'histoire canadienne ... Edouard Fortin, un ancien député de la Beauce qui a non seulement fait une belle carrière, mais qui a su laisser après lui des fils qui continuent, avec succès, la tradition familiale. L'un de ceux-là est aujourd'hui ministre du travail dans le gouvernement de la province de Québec, un autre est le président de ce banquet, parce que vous lui avez fait confiance depuis deux ans comme président de votre association ...

Mr Chairman, you have the right to be proud of your association and of each of its members. The role of the weekly press is of the greatest importance, in encouraging local initiative, in circulating news and information, and also in moulding opinion at the primary levels of human activity; that is at the family level, at the municipal and local levels. It is the man himself, the human being, that you are especially interested in, rather than in the mass of men. You are familiar, of course, with international politics and national problems, but you serve mainly the local or regional economy. That important, that vital role, only you can fulfil effectively.

This work is accomplished throughout Canada by more than a thousand weekly newspapers, but it must be noted that you, gentlemen of the French-language press, make a further and distinctive contribution; you play an essential part in safeguarding and developing French culture in North America.

Le Canada est riche et privilégié par plus d'un côté, mais surtout parce qu'il est le dépositaire et l'héritier de deux grandes cultures.

Votre association dépasse les cadres géographiques de la province de Québec puisque ses membres se recrutent aussi dans les provinces de l'Atlantique, en Ontario, et dans les Prairies. Vous êtes donc l'image même du Canada français qui s'affirme partout au pays. Il est important, je crois, d'accentuer sans cesse ce fait et cette reconnaissance pour faire

du Canada un pays vraiment bilingue avec deux cultures de base, auxquelles d'autres sont venues ajouter pour notre plus grand avantage.

L'unité canadienne traverse présentement une autre période difficile.
Ces difficultés proviennent de causes communes. Depuis quelques années, les Canadiens ont plus que jamais conscience de l'envahissement
culturel américain et ils sentent que le contrôle sur leur économie leur
échappe graduellement. Par contre, ils réalisent que leurs niveaux de
vie, qu'ils ne veulent pas voir diminuer, dépendent dans une très large
mesure de l'exportation de nos produits aux Etats-Unis et de l'importa-
tion de capitaux américains. Ils sentent donc que l'envahissement qu'ils
regrettent est la source même de la prospérité qu'ils désirent. C'est pourquoi ils réalisent que leur indépendance politique ne peut pas être très
efficace pour prévenir un envahissement devenu inséparable de la prospérité.

Cette situation fait naître inévitablement la frustration. Un très grand
nombre de Canadiens anglais éprouvent des regrets et se retournent vers
le passé. D'autres sont tentés d'abandonner la lutte et de devenir américains. La plupart, toutefois, ont décidé de réagir positivement à l'envahissement américain, d'accentuer leur identité, et de se rapprocher
davantage des Canadiens français.

En somme, la solution au problème de l'envahissement n'est pas dans
la fuite mais dans la lutte. Quand on ne peut prévenir cet envahissement,
il faut tenter de l'assimiler et de le contrôler ...

A strong and united Canada is essential if we are not to be absorbed
in some continental society, and thereby lose our own separate traditions
and cultures – French and British ... Some Canadians, however, are
beginning to ask themselves: why should we worry about "saving"
Canada from the American "invasion" if we don't believe in a Canada
to be saved, in a Canada which is greater than its provinces? I believe
that there is such a Canada of which we should all be proud to be
citizens – whether we speak English or French.

To keep and strengthen its identity and its character, therefore, is the
great task which faces Canada. It means reshaping our political and
economic society in terms of the problems and needs, not of yesterday
but of today. It means that both the founding races must meet together
more and become better acquainted. I am convinced that such closer
relations will be mutually profitable. I also think that the common
sources and the similar nature of so many of the problems of English-
and French-speaking Canada will give us a chance to get closer and to
understand each other better as we try to solve them. Basically, we have
the same problems, on this continent and in the world, and to find the
right solution we need each other. In this respect, at least, we are
inseparable.

We are also inseparable in the sense that hundreds of thousands of
English-speaking Canadians reside in Quebec, and nearly a million of

French-speaking Canadians live outside Quebec. This latter fact has been officially recognized by the government of Quebec, when it created a Department of Cultural Affairs. Quebec, in this special sense, is more than a province, it is a motherland; but a motherland in a confederation – in a national partnership.

Le rapprochement entre les deux groupes exige entre autres choses que le Canada anglais prenne davantage conscience des aspirations du Canada français et que celui-ci ne s'impatiente pas trop s'il trouve que cette prise de conscience est lente à se manifester. Des progrès véritables sont marqués d'une génération à l'autre. Par exemple, la doctrine de Bourassa sur le nationalisme canadien, qui était attaquée comme une hérésie il y a une génération, est maintenant acceptée par la presque totalité du Canada anglais. En somme, si nous n'évoluons pas tout à fait en même temps, nous évoluons au moins dans le même sens. C'est là l'essentiel à mon avis.

Il est nécessaire de reconnaître que dans un sens historique et culturel notre pays est principalement formé de deux peuples, et que ces deux peuples doivent avoir des droits égaux et une chance égale dans l'expansion de l'économie et aussi dans la direction de cette économie. Mais nous devons aussi reconnaître qu'il existe une nation canadienne qui, précisément, réunit ces deux peuples qui ont fondé et fait grandir notre pays. Le jour où nous ne pourrons plus parler d'unité canadienne dans notre pays, le Canada aura cessé d'exister et alors nos deux cultures seront en grave danger ...

Notre fédéralisme doit être conçu de façon assez souple pour permettre l'existence d'un gouvernement canadien qui soit fort dans les limites de sa juridiction afin de jouer pleinement son rôle au sein des grandes nations du monde, tout en assurant le progrès et le bien-être de la population canadienne. Egalement nous voulons donner aux provinces toutes les attributions et tous les pouvoirs que leur confère la constitution, ainsi que les moyens d'exercer ces pouvoirs.

Je tiens à répéter que nous devons arriver à un fédéralisme coopératif, c'est-à-dire une formule fédérative exempte de tout esprit de centralisation inacceptable.

A la clôture de la récente conférence fédérale-provinciale, le Premier ministre du Québec a tenu à souligner que le régime confédératif est entré dans une ère nouvelle. Je suis convaincu que des rencontres plus fréquentes permettront aux dirigeants des gouvernements des provinces et du pays de trouver des solutions aux problèmes actuels, et je ne doute pas qu'un organisme permanent pourra également jouer un rôle important dans les relations fédérales-provinciales. Tout cela permettra une meilleure compréhension de nos problèmes respectifs et aussi des problèmes communs. C'est dans la compréhension que s'établissent les bonnes relations, l'amitié, et la collaboration ...

On admettra, par ailleurs, que le Canada a aussi besoin des moyens d'être lui-même et d'agir pour le Canada, tant sur le plan intérieur que sur le plan international, surtout dans les efforts d'assurer la paix et la sécurité dans le monde. Autant pour assurer le relancement de notre économie que pour la continuation de notre rôle dans le monde, nous avons besoin d'un Canada uni. Une unité dans la diversité, une unité d'action à titre d'associés, d'associés égaux. C'est au sein d'un Canada en bonne santé que les aspirations du Québec peuvent se réaliser ...

It is in this spirit of sincere co-operation that Canada must face her future, and I have no doubt that the newspapers of Canada, and especially the weekly press, will help bring about the collaboration which is indispensable ...

There is no more important problem facing this country – apart from peace in the world and work for the people – than the maintenance and development of the Canadian confederation, on the foundation of equal partnership; the only foundation that makes possible a Canadian nation. I believe that there can be such a Canadian nation within which the two basic cultures can develop in full and equal partnership.

I know that this can only be done if each group respects and understands the position of the other and each appreciates fully the contribution of the other to the building of the Canadian confederation. But I know that it *can* be done. I believe also, as I have already said, that while Quebec is a province in this national confederation, it is more than a province, because it is the heartland of a people. In a very real sense it is a nation within a nation.

I refuse to believe that in an insecure and dangerous world where universal brotherhood is now the alternative to universal extinction, where the crying need is for men to come together rather than break apart, I refuse to believe that in this world all Canadians cannot live together in friendship and understanding, rejecting the dangerous counsel of extremes wherever it comes from, so that together we may achieve a great Canadian destiny.

36

IT was an emotional moment for me when I returned to the Assembly of the United Nations as prime minister of Canada after an absence of more than six years. The UN had changed, of course, but many of my friends from other delegations were there and warmly welcomed me back. Nothing gave me greater pleasure than the welcome I received from the journalists, the members of the Secretariat, the guards, the elevatormen, the waitresses in the restaurant.

My speech in the general debate reflected the improved international atmosphere. It was no longer necessary to take part in the polemical warfare with a Vishinsky in terms that were customary in those earlier years when the "cold war" was really hot.

This one was, I suppose, a typical Canadian UN speech. It advocated a permanent UN Peace Force; it confined itself to practical proposals for improving UN operations with a minimum of philosophical ideas about peace and humanity; and it was short. I remembered the days when I had been president and had been forced to listen to long and windy discourses.

Before the Eighteenth Session of the United Nations

19 September 1963

MR President: Some years have passed since I last had the honour to represent my country at the United Nations. My first words on my return must be to reaffirm Canada's strong and continuing support for our world organization and our desire to do what we can to help realize the ideals of its Charter.

From this rostrum, I am happy to recognize many old friends and respected colleagues. But I am also conscious that the Assembly of 1963 reflects the great changes that have taken place in our world organization since I was last here and which, in turn, reflect changes that have taken place in the world. Not the least of these changes is the admission of many newly independent states whose distinguished representatives now add their wisdom and influence to the Assembly's deliberations ... Of all the changes of the past few years, none has been more dramatic than the emergence of new and free nations in Africa. This emergence has had a profound impact on the political evoluton of the United Nations and on international affairs generally. It has added heavy responsibilities to our organization in many fields of activity. It has given new and urgent emphasis to two major questions of our time – colonialism and racial discrimination – both of which can exist in many forms and have no common political pattern.

New states have brought United Nations membership closer to the goal of universality. They have also brought inescapable problems of growing pains. This process of growth and adjustment is bound to be difficult. It requires patience and tolerance and understanding on the part of all members, new, as well as old. Many of the newer members are small states with large problems of political, economic, and social development. But the old, big powers have also been facing new and gigantic problems. Many of these result from their own great strides in science and technology. These advances have given entirely new dimensions to the threat of war and even to human survival. They have also made possible a new era of progress and plenty, surpassing any previous human accomplishment, but which is now restricted to a small minority of the world's people. The challenge to the world community, then, is a dual one.

The problem of armaments, especially nuclear armaments, must be solved before scientific advances move it beyond man's reach. The disparity in economic and social development between nations must be corrected before it creates an unbridgeable gulf between "have" and "have-not" nations. It is the duty and interest of all members of the United Nations to see that this swift march of science and technology does not lead either to the universal destruction of war or to intolerable differences between nations in human welfare. Only through constructive and co-operative international endeavour can these two fatal results be avoided.

The Congo crisis has once again shown that these two things, security and welfare, are inter-related ... It has also raised again in an acute form the main problems of peace-keeping by the United Nations; problems of political control, executive direction, financial means, and administrative co-ordination. From the Congo, new experience, not yet fully assessed, has been added to that gained from earlier peace-keeping operations.

Canada does not share the doubts which have been raised about the nature and purposes of this United Nations action. We felt that intervention in the Congo was a response which this organization had to make, a duty which it could not shirk. We believe that this kind of important, if limited, peace-keeping activity has now moved beyond the stage of first experiment. It has become a practical necessity in the conduct of international affairs, and should be provided for as such.

A main task of our organization, therefore, should be to strengthen and improve its capacity in this field, learning from the failures and successes of the past and seeking more effective ways to perform this function in the future. There will, of course, always be some situations in which the UN should not be asked to intervene because failure is bound to be the result. There are tasks which are undesirable or impossible for the UN. But there will be other situations where its intervention will be important, and even essential, for keeping the peace, for preventing small conflicts developing into big ones. For these, there should be the advance international planning and preparation without which no national government would think of acting.

I am aware that a few members disagree categorically with this peace-keeping concept of the United Nations. They argue that most of the peace-keeping operations of the past have been illegal. They would have us believe that the most challenging phrases of the Charter preamble are hollow, that the first purpose enunciated in Article 1 has no practical application. Other members are cynical, doubtful, or indifferent. Both categories reflect attitudes which have compelled the organization to improvise in carrying out tasks which have been imposed on it by the decision of the Assembly or the Security Council. Those who are responsible for the necessity of such crash action are often the first to criticize when the results are disorderly, delayed, or inadequate.

The Secretary-General in a recent speech has emphasized the advantage it would be "if countries would in their national military planning make provision for suitable units which would be made available at short notice for UN service and thereby decrease the degree of improvisation necessary in an emergency." We should now support this appeal by putting into effect these arrangements, which are increasingly becoming necessary. These would include a compact planning team of military experts which would provide the advice and assistance which the Secretary-General should have for organizing emergency peace-keeping operations.

National governments can also improve their own arrangements for assisting such operations. My own country now maintains forces, trained and equipped for the purpose, which can be placed at the disposal of the United Nations on short notice anywhere in the world. In case we are required to do more, we have recently given the Secretariat detailed information on what we can most readily provide to meet requests for assistance.

In this co-operative peace-keeping activity, we have been associated with many states and in many places – in Kashmir, in Palestine, in Gaza and Sinai, in Lebanon, in the Congo, in West New Guinea, and Yemen. Each situation has posed its own problems and suggested its own solutions. But always, our own experience has taught us one thing – the importance of advance planning and organization, both within our national establishment and within the international organization. We would be happy to share our experience with others who have participated with us in UN peace-keeping operations in the past, as well as with those who might wish to do so in the future.

To this end, we propose that there should be an examination by interested governments of the problems and techniques of peace-keeping operations. This could lead to a pooling of available resources and the development in a co-ordinated way of trained and equipped collective forces for UN service to meet possible future demands for action under the blue flag of the United Nations. The Scandinavian member states, in their formation of a composite Nordic contingent for UN police and peace duties, have shown the way. We should now make further progress along those lines.

There are other fundamental UN questions to be dealt with – of constitutional reform, organization, and administration; of financing and procedural methods. At the root of all of them lies the question of basic attitude toward the organization: "What kind of a United Nations do we want?"

We believe that most members want the United Nations to be an effective international instrument for practical and positive action in carrying out UN decisions ...

To be fully effective, United Nations machinery and organization should adequately reflect the present membership, without giving undue weight to any single factor, whether it be military or industrial strength, population or financial contribution, politics or race or geography.

To this end the Security Council and ECOSOC should be enlarged in order to permit a better balance in their composition. We should not confine our interest, however, to representation. We should be even more concerned about powers and functions. I am thinking particularly of the Security Council. Its record in recent years has been one of diminishing returns. We are all aware of the main reason for this – the lack of the essential unanimity among the great powers. That unanimity is still lacking but this year, for the first time in the postwar period, we can perhaps begin to hope that improved political relations between the great powers may make possible the restoration to the Security Council of the high executive function it was designed to fulfil.

We might also consider how to modify the Council's function to make it more effective as the instrument of political action for the United Nations. Indeed, the time may be at hand for a Security Council which can keep continuing watch on the affairs of the organization as a whole in much the same way as the executive committees operate in the Specialized Agencies. If the enlarged Security Council were given a properly balanced composition with sufficient safeguards on voting rights, it could conceivably become the main arena for political decision on questions which require urgent action. It could assume responsibility for many of the items which now lie heavily on the agenda of the General Assembly. Such a Council could be in session virtually throughout the year and make it possible to cut drastically into the excessive time and energy now consumed by Assembly proceedings.

There is another change that might be considered. The United Nations will inevitably remain the central world forum for international discussion and recommendation on a wide range of subjects. We already have regional groupings of states – in Europe, Africa, and Latin America. Other groupings conceivably may be formed. The time may have to come to correlate the activities of these regional groupings more closely with those of the United Nations. It is possible to envisage a stage in the evolution of the UN when regional assemblies may be used for regional problems in search of local solutions or for the preparation of broader treatment at the United Nations.

The Charter acknowledges the part to be played by the regional arrangements or agencies in the conduct of international relations. In the economic and social field there is a growing tendency to delegate responsibility and authority to the UN regional commissions. Why not adopt a similar approach to some, though obviously not all, of the political questions which may face us in the United Nations? ...

The first concern of the United Nations is the keeping of the peace. If we were to fail in that, the whole brave human experiment will have failed. But, second only to the keeping of peace, the great purpose of international statesmanship today must be to help to improve the living standards of all the world's peoples. The role of the United Nations in this field is necessarily limited. But if we wish, it can be one of great and lasting significance. Experience is more and more underlining the central significance and compelling urgency of economic and social questions. Their importance is rightly symbolized, as the Secretary-General has reminded us, in the naming of this as the Decade of Development. It is now focused on the forthcoming United Nations Conference on Trade and Development. Canada has been honoured to serve on the preparatory committee for that conference.

The problems of economic development and of trade expansion are fundamentally the same. This is easy to forget, when the development policies of individual countries so frequently call for reduced imports of particular commodities. But the purpose of development is to raise the level of real incomes. And, important though it is to reduce the barriers which limit trade, yet the main impetus to expanding trade must come from the improvement of incomes. In other words, economic development – raising real incomes – is itself the underlying basis for trade expansion. Higher incomes within a country do not, however, automatically improve a country's ability to trade. The improved incomes must be related in the long run to increased international earnings through exports. Aid programmes, essential as they are, are only a means of bridging a gap until export incomes increase.

In the complex structure of the world economy today, trade and aid are tightly linked. No amount of aid will create permanent, stable growth unless it is soon accompanied by developing means of increasing exports. Accordingly, all the members of the United Nations – developed and developing economies alike – have a common interest in seeking two-way co-operation which will benefit giver and receiver alike. The success of this and other similar efforts, essential for peace and prosperity in the world, will largely depend on freeing economic and technical co-operation from political controversy ...

While most members recognize the proven value of the United Nations and want it to continue in effective existence, with a substantial role in our world, there are signs of decline and deterioration which could threaten its future use, its very existence. Fortunately, there are also signs of improvement in relations between the "superpowers" which give the UN a new opportunity. There is a little more benevolence, a little less bitterness.

The United Nations is a unique political mirror reflecting, often magnifying, occasionally distorting, the dreams and the distresses of men. So what will the Eighteenth Assembly show?

The picture could be a more cheerful one. The feeling today of crisis and collision is not as oppressive as it has been in the recent past. There is an encouraging contrast between the international climate at this General Assembly and that which hung like a dark shadow over the last.

None of the great issues has been resolved. There is recurring tension in and around Berlin, in Laos and Vietnam, in parts of Africa, along the Sino-Indian frontier, in the Caribbean and elsewhere. But there seems now to be more of a will to seek peaceful settlements. This improvement may soon fade before the test of policy and action, but it exists now. And we should take full advantage of it.

Its most striking evidence is the recent partial nuclear test ban treaty between the three nuclear powers, since adhered to by more than ninety states. Even by itself, that treaty is immensely valuable in putting to an end the poisoning of the atmosphere which sustains all life on our planet. But it must be viewed beyond its own terms. It showed that great powers were able to agree on something important in spite of the fears and tensions of cold war. The global sigh of relief that followed the treaty was due not only to the ending of atmospheric pollution but to a feeling of hope for further progress toward peace. In particular, the time seemed closer when the long frustration of disarmament negotiations might be replaced by some positive measures of agreement.

It would be intolerable if our hopes for a rational response to the challenge and the fear of universal destruction were once more to be dashed. I cannot believe that this will happen. I cannot believe that there are not sensible solutions to the problems of the relations of seven hundred millions of Chinese with their neighbours; or to those of a divided Germany, a divided Korea, a divided Vietnam. I do not accept the permanence of the Berlin Wall as a symbol of a divided world. I reject the theory that Arabs and Jews must forever be hostile. I do not believe it is the destiny of Cuba to be permanently alienated from former friends and neighbours on this Western Hemisphere; or for whites and non-whites to be permanently embittered in Africa because of racial policies which are bad and bound to fail.

I do not claim that there are quick and easy solutions to these problems. There are none. But there is a better atmosphere in which to begin the earnest and persistent search for them. In this search, the United Nations can play an effective role, but only if it puts its own house in order.

It is not the sole instrument for international co-operation. It has no supranational authority. It is no substitute for national foreign policy or bilateral diplomacy. The Charter rightly recognizes that there are other peaceful means of solution, regional and limited collective arrangements, outside the United Nations but consistent with its principles which member states can employ.

Nevertheless, the United Nations alone serves us all. It provides the only world assembly to protect and advance human rights, freedoms, and welfare, to reduce and remove the causes of conflict. Whether it can discharge its great role and fulfil its great responsibilities, depends on us.

When the United Nations fails, its member governments fail. When it succeeds, the people, the plain and good people of all the world, succeed.

The League of Nations was eighteen years old in 1938. That was the year of appeasement, of unawareness, of failure of heart and nerve. The eighteenth year of the United Nations begins with a better balance sheet in a better climate. This is the Assembly of opportunity. It could be the Assembly of achievement and action.

37

IF the introductory observations to this speech are longer than the speech itself, it is because I wish to include in them the text of the toast to Canada proposed by General de Gaulle, to which my remarks were a response. I do so to give my own reply more meaning,

and also because the sentiments expressed in the President's speech contrast so vividly and depressingly with those three and a half years later when he came to Canada and which are referred to later in this book.

The exchanges printed here were made at a magnificent dinner given in my honour by the President at the Elysée Palace when I paid an official visit to France in January 1964 as prime minister of Canada. General and Madame de Gaulle were very friendly and considerate hosts to us on this occasion, and my private talks with him were most interesting and illuminating. I have often thought of this visit and those talks in view of subsequent developments.

The text of General de Gaulle's remarks on this occasion was as follows:

Monsieur le Premier Ministre,

La visite que vous nous faites est une visite d'amitié. Vous témoignez ainsi des liens de sympathie qui, longuement, ont été tissés entre le Canada et la France et qu'ici nous ressentons vivement. Certes, ce qui se passe dans les domaines de l'âme, du sentiment, de la langue, de la culture, et ce qui peut se passer au point de vue économique et à maints autres égards entre nous, Français en France, et ceux des habitants de votre vaste territoire qui sont notre peuple installé au Canada, ne laissent pas de nous émouvoir et de nous intéresser très spécialement et très profondément. Cependant, il ne saurait y avoir dans cette solidarité particulière et naturelle rien qui doive contrarier les heureuses relations de la République française avec votre Etat fédéral.

En lui, nous voyons un allié fidèle et vaillant, dont le sang a coulé à flot sur notre sol pendant les deux guerres mondiales, qui aujourd'hui fait partie de notre camp, et auquel sa situation, à la fois atlantique, arctique, et pacifique, confère, dans la défense éventuelle du monde libre, une importance essentielle. En lui, nous reconnaissons une considérable réalité économique appelée, grâce à ses ressources et à ses capacités, à une expansion assez grande pour assurer son indépendance, ce qui est la condition même du désir que nous avons ici d'accroître nos rapports mutuels. En lui, enfin, nous saluons un ensemble de valeurs humaines qui, dans la grande affaire du monde d'aujourd'hui, autrement dit dans le développement des pays qui s'élèvent en civilisation, joue déjà un rôle fécond autant que désintéressé.

A Toast to the President of France

15 January 1969

M. LE Président, j'ai été profondément touché par les paroles que vous avez prononcées et par l'éloquence émouvante avec laquelle vous avez rendu hommage à mon pays et à mes compatriotes.

Vous me permettrez de vous exprimer toute la gratitude que nous ressentons, mon épouse et moi-même, pour la réception chaleureuse que vous et Madame de Gaulle nous avez réservée. Nous ne l'oublierons jamais.

Je reviens en France – comme toujours – avec une certaine émotion; avec une conscience profonde de la longue histoire que nos pays ont partagée; et avec le souvenir vivace des tragédies et des victoires de notre propre époque, auxquelles nous avons également participé.

Le Canada, par son histoire, la langue, et les traditions d'une grande partie de notre population, est une partie de la France. Mais la France est également une partie du Canada, à cause des cent mille soldats canadiens qui reposent en paix sur ce sol sacré.

Je voudrais à ce moment répéter certaines paroles prononcées à Montréal par notre bien-aimé Gouverneur général – que vous connaissez bien d'ailleurs, ancien Ambassadeur du Canada auprès de la France – et qui m'a prié, Monsieur le Président, de vous transmettre ses amitiés les meilleures et les plus sincères. Le Général Vanier disait à cette occasion :

Une partie de la France nous appartient. Je réclame toute le terre française où reposent les nôtres. Les Canadiens morts ou vivants y seront toujours chez eux. Nos morts reposent loin du sol natal, il est vrai, mais les fleurs de France ornent leurs tombes et les cœurs français les entourent d'une affection profonde et reconnaissante.

En s'exprimant ainsi le Gouverneur général parlait au nom de tous les Canadiens.

Des hommes et des femmes, pionniers de la Vieille France, ont implanté une nouvelle société en Amérique du Nord, et leurs descendants, avec ceux de la nation britannique et de chaque race européenne, en ont fait un grand pays qui s'étend sur tout un continent et qui est maintenant au début d'une expansion nationale encore plus grande.

Au cours des trois siècles de son évolution, à travers toutes les vicissitudes de son histoire, le peuple du Canada a conservé les liens avec les deux mères-patries. Nous n'oublions pas que nous sommes héritiers de la plus haute civilisation occidentale, tout en développant notre propre vie nationale dans le vaste panorama de l'Amérique du Nord. Dans notre société canadienne, les descendants de premiers colons français représentent presqu'un tiers de notre population et ils apportent, et continueront d'apporter, une contribution dynamique et créatrice à notre expansion et à notre progrès.

Voilà, M. le Président, dans quel esprit je rends visite à la France, l'excitante jeune France d'aujourd'hui, qui comme le Canada brûle les étapes dans un nouvel âge de découvertes, d'expansion, et de changements.

Cet après-midi nous avons eu des entretiens sur quelques-uns des problèmes diplomatiques de ce nouveau monde, sur la façon pacifique et constructive avec laquelle il faut chercher des solutions, sur la manière dont les hommes et nations libres peuvent collaborer au cours des années à venir dans ces recherches. Dans ce domaine, M. le Président, nous au Canada, nous croyons que la France peut jouer un rôle de premier plan, un rôle digne de la gloire de son passé et des réalisations de l'heure présente tout comme des promesses de son avenir.

Vous n'avez là que l'une des raisons qui nous font désirer que nos liens politiques, économiques, et culturels avec la France soient plus forts et plus étendus. Nous croyons que ceci peut être réalisé pour notre avantage mutuel et en harmonie avec ce groupement plus vaste de nations auquel nos deux pays participent, ce groupement qu'il faut maintenir dans un monde, à la population grandissante, qui peut paraître déjà trop petit, où chaque nation ne peut sauvegarder ses valeurs et sa survivance nationales qu'en collaborant avec d'autres pour assurer la paix et la sécurité.

Je suis très heureux des mesures qui ont déjà été prises pour rendre encore meilleure la collaboration entre nos deux pays. J'ai bien confiance que d'autres encore seront prises dans les années qui vont suivre.

En terminant, M. le Président, qu'il me soit permis de dire que tous les Canadiens, d'expression anglaise comme d'expression française, ont pour vous des sentiments de grand respect et de profonde admiration. Nous vous tenons – et il en sera toujours ainsi – comme l'un de nos plus grands chefs au cours de la guerre; comme celui dont le courage et l'esprit de détermination dans les jours sombres n'ont été égalés que par sa foi dans la victoire finale et sa dignité et sa modération lorsqu'elle a été obtenue. Votre nom est devenu synonyme d'honneur, de loyauté, et de dévouement. Nous nous réjouissons de la nouvelle prospérité et de la nouvelle influence de la France sous votre direction. Au moment où le matérialisme a dominé tant de nos valeurs, vous avez fait valoir les plus hautes qualités de l'humanité et ceci non seulement pour votre propre peuple. Le génie et la gloire de la France débordent ses propres frontières et enrichissent la vie et l'alliance des hommes libres – en Europe et par-delà l'Atlantique.

Animé de ces sentiments et comme chef du gouvernement de mon pays, je porte un toast à l'honneur de la France, à son illustre Président, et à son grand peuple.

38

THE Parliamentary Press Gallery dinner is a light-hearted occasion held each year, when the members of the Gallery entertain their guests, and themselves, by skits which lampoon, in song and verse and even worse, the foibles and follies of government and politics. Their special victims are the party leaders, who sit at a head table; and the most special of all is the prime minister of the day. These selected victims are supposed to be highly amused, or at least look so, by the shafts directed at them. But they do have a chance to reply with a few shafts of their own. The dinner is wound up by the speech of the evening from the governor general and then the real "winding up" begins, which lasts far into the night and is greatly enjoyed by all who survive.

This was my first opportunity as prime minister to address the diners, who were far from being an expectant and hushed audience. The words spoken on these occasions are always and scrupulously unreported (not necessarily because they are unheard). But I am sure I will be forgiven for violating this sacred pledge, seeing that I am betraying only myself. And it is six years later ...

At a Parliamentary Press Gallery Dinner

22 February 1964

THIS is the occasion to make our annual obeisance to the power – if not the glory – of the press, to issue our paeans of praise and gasp our profound admiration for everything you do and say and write – no matter how dubious it may be. It is our tribute, as politicians, to what you can do to us or for us – proof that we will never wear the red badge of courage in this kind of political warfare.

In this spirit, the rationale which requires our attendance at these dinners is simple but compelling. In the perhaps less than immortal, but nevertheless profoundly penetrating, words of one of your own critics – it is comforting to think that you have some – "You can't very well criticize the fellow who got you sloshed the night before."

Now that I am prime minister, it is more than ever necessary for me to respect this hallowed tradition. So I would like to insist, with all the emphasis at my command and leaving no cliché unturned or platitude unexplored, that yours is the weapon of freedom in the scabbard of dedication; in your hands is the sword to strike down tyrants; yours is the one indispensable piece of ordnance that cannot be stolen from the armoury of democracy.

I have only one favour to ask of you tonight. If granted, I will promise you better working accommodation and greater alcoholic facilities. It is that next year you permit us, the politicians, to put on the customary and hallowed postprandial variety performance so that *we* may have the privilege of etching your virtues, of singing about your admirable qualities, and lampooning your detractors.

We must know at once if we are to be asked to do this because we will need all the intervening time to prepare. The lyrics will be by Bert Herridge, the music by Walter Gordon – with "outside help" – and the producer will be George Nowlan, with the deputy producer, or rather the officer in charge of the Quebec side of the production, Leon Balcer.

Badinage aside, I want to express my appreciation and awe at being your guest tonight, for the first time as prime minister. I owe all of my present eminence to you, of course, and, occasionally, I am grateful.

If you ask me how I feel about my new dignity, I can only reply: it's a job; pays well; has problems, such as Banks and Bomarcs; also has perquisites, such as free aspirin and free advice.

The Press Gallery, of course, adds to my problems and to my pleasures. You keep me alert so that I will avoid saying anything except in words of such crystal clarity that I could not possibly be misreported or misconstrued.

In this respect, I try never to forget the experience of the Red Dean of Canterbury who had proclaimed Chicago to be the most evil city in the world. Later when he visited the city, he was met by an army of irate reporters. The first question: "Do you plan visiting any of our houses of prostitution?" The Dean's reply: "Are there any? Where are they?" The report – a big black report – next day read: "The first question asked by the Red Dean of Canterbury on arriving in Chicago was: 'Where is there a house of prostitution?' "

As for headlines, which, after all, are the only journalistic things that matter, they are, of course, outside your control – or, so far as I can gather, anybody else's.

There was one recently, for instance, above the report of a hunting accident which boldly stated: "Father of Fourteen Shot; Mistaken for Rabbit."

But we politicians must not complain about being misquoted. That isn't cricket – or even good politics. Nor must we ever appear annoyed or even seem to hold a grudge over journalistic maltreatment, however shocking. A permanent grudge, you know, can lead to bitterness and wounding words.

Perhaps some of you may remember a story that Viscount Alexander was fond of telling. Two British school boys developed a bitter hatred for one another in prep school. The reason was simple. One fagged for the other. Out of that relationship, they developed a mutual loathing and a determination never to speak to one another once they got out of prep school. Well, as all British schoolboys do, these two proceeded on through university, one going to Eton and Oxford, the other to Harrow and Cambridge, and both rose later to the top. By the time they next met, forty years on, one was an admiral of the Queen's Navy, the other the Archbishop of Canterbury. They were both awaiting a train, the Admiral in his gold braid uniform, and the Archbishop, who had become very corpulent, in his flowing clerical robes. The Archbishop recognized the Admiral first. Approaching him, he said, "Tell me, porter, when does the next train leave for Brighton?" The Admiral, recognizing his old enemy, replied immediately and without hesitation: "I'm sorry, madam, I don't know, but, even if I did, I wouldn't advise you to travel in your condition."

If we in Parliament ever were tempted to complain about you of the Gallery, we should remember the impossible life you lead, the impossible demands made on you by your owners and editors. How you put up with it on the paltry salary you receive is almost beyond comprehension. Compared with what you have to submit to, my treatment by John Diefenbaker or Judy LaMarsh is merciful and gentle. What a profession you belong to!

I recall a friend who was a very tough managing editor of a west-coast newspaper. He had a reporter in the far north covering a rescue operation in the dead of winter. The reporter was filing three or four stories a day, but this still didn't satisfy the manager. He went after his city editor to get that blanketyblank guy up there off his seat and file four or five times as much. The city editor, showing unusual compassion, said: "Bill, he only has two hands." To which the managing editor replied: "Well, then, fire the crippled bastard."

That, of course, would never be the kind of relationship that could possibly develop between myself and the Gallery.

I have composed a little sonnet which comes close to that relationship and touches also on that happy breed of special assistants to prime ministers and other ministers, whose role in government does not always receive from you – or the opposition – that deep and understanding appreciation it deserves. I apologize for this sonnet to John Milton, who was himself a clerk of Parliament and spent much of his time, I am reliably informed, preparing government answers in the Long Parliament to long, irrelevant, stupid, and unnecessary questions. This sonnet is entitled: "The Press Gallery Lost, or Paradise Regained":

> When you consider how your days are spent –
> Nights too – revelling and sharpening knives,
> What do you tell them, those that are your wives?
> Lodged with them useless, all your talents bent
> To darkest deeds, in efforts to present
> The false account of news and money spent,
> Brooding lest travelling free may be a sin, and thinking
> We better serve who pay – and do no drinking.
> See you, dark O'Hagan* how he strives
> With practice occult to shape men's lives;
> And when the hero's image by you is bent
> He mutters "There's no vision," turns on Kent,†
> Not realizing gallery wails are more the tacit
> Outgrowth, not of news provided, but of Bassetts.

Et maintenant, mes amis, je vais continuer en français ...

No, perhaps on second thought, I had better not. I have already spoken too long in my other official language. If I go on, I will be accused of imitating Rich Little and, far worse, of holding up: His Excellency, the Governor General.

39

IN the electoral campaign of 1963 I stated, as leader of the Liberal party, that I would introduce a motion for a distinctive Canadian

* My press officer, Richard O'Hagan
† My special assistant, Tom Kent

national flag within two years of assuming office as prime minister. I took office in April 1963 and, after discussions with my colleagues and the Liberal caucus, introduced the necessary resolution into the House of Commons on 15 June 1964.

The first announcement to the country of my intention to take action on a matter where action had been postponed for so long was made in this speech to the annual convention of the Royal Canadian Legion in Winnipeg on 17 May 1964.

I chose this occasion deliberately, though I might easily have arranged to speak to an audience which would have given my views a friendlier reception. I thought, however, that, outside Parliament, the Legion had the right to be the first to hear my statement. I had no illusions about their reaction for I knew their official views. But I got a fair, if somewhat hostile, hearing. It was naturally a difficult speech to make in the circumstances.

The flag resolution included a specific maple leaf design. It would have been easy to have asked a parliamentary committee to recommend a design. But that had been tried before and had meant indefinite postponement. So I decided that, if the resolution were to go to a Commons committee, it should go in a form which included a design put forward by the government.

This was done, but the design was changed by the committee in its report to the Commons, without, however, losing the principle of distinctiveness. This change resulted in stronger backing for a Canadian flag from the opposition side than might otherwise have been the case. I therefore advised the members of our party to support this new red and white design which was simple, attractive, and Canadian, as it would secure maximum approval in the House.

The introduction of the flag resolution was followed by six months of vigorous, emotional and, at times, bitter debate. It ended on 14 December 1964. As prime minister I had the last words. They appear later (as selection 42) and the interruptions reported in Hansard give some idea of the strength of the feelings that were involved. It was a historic night in the House of Commons when the resolution was adopted by 163 to 78. The scene after the vote was taken was very emotional and one not soon to be forgotten. Canada, at last, had her "distinctive national flag."

The other flag statement included in these papers (44) was the one I made one cold February morning when, after all the formalities had been completed, the red Maple Leaf Flag was raised for the first time and flew proudly from the staff high up on the tower of Canada's Parliament Building.

To the Royal Canadian Legion

17 May 1964

MR Chairman, honoured guests, and members of the Royal Canadian Legion: I am honoured to be here with you tonight as a veteran, as a member of the Legion, and as prime minister. I am proud to have witnessed your opening ceremonies and am deeply moved by them. I congratulate most warmly all who participated in your impressive Colour ceremony and in conceiving this visual act of remembrance. I wish all Canadians could witness it ...

When it became known that I was going to have the honour of opening this twentieth Legion convention, I got a good deal of advice as to what I should discuss – or *not* discuss. There was one compelling subject, of course, which I had to refer to: national unity and certain problems which affect that unity, for instance, federal-provincial relations within our confederation.

On this subject, I will say only this: the provinces have new problems and greater responsibilities and must have, among other things, the financial resources to deal with them. The provincial governments will play, I believe, an increasingly important part in our national progress. But this need not be, and must not be, at the expense of the federal government. In our system, the federal government must remain strong in authority, resources, and leadership. I do not consider that I was chosen to preside over its decline or its dissolution – and I do not intend to do so.

I do intend, however, to do everything I can to maintain the closest co-operation with the provinces inside a confederation which must remain strong and united ...

There is one subject which I was advised not to mention at all – the flag. That advice, of course, was well meant. It was also impossible to accept. Members of the Legion are aware of my government's commitments, made by our party some years ago, to ask Parliament to decide on a distinctive Canadian flag within a certain period of time. For my part, I am very much aware of the Legion executive's current attitude towards government policy on this subject.

This mutual awareness of our attitudes, I believe, precludes any possibility that I should appear before you tonight and attempt to dodge the flag issue. After all, you are men who know what it means to go into battle! So I intend to talk briefly, but frankly, about this issue: to put my own feelings, my beliefs, my judgment squarely and honestly before you. You would expect me to do this and I believe it is my duty. I expect dissent. I also respect it.

This question of a national flag, however, is only part of the larger

question of national unity which I have already mentioned. There is
unease and division in Canada today which is a threat to that unity;
and this, ironically, at a time when our country is admired, respected,
and envied throughout the world. The only anti-Canadians I know of
are inside our own borders.

When I went overseas in 1915 I had as comrades in my section men
whose names were Cameron, Kimura, English, Bleidenstein, DeChapin,
O'Shaughnessy. We didn't fall in, or fall out, as Irish Canadians,
French Canadians, Dutch Canadians, Japanese Canadians. We wore
the same uniform, with the same maple leaf badge, and we were proud
to be known as Canadians, to serve as Canadians, and to die, if that had
to be, as Canadians. I wish our country had more of that spirit today, of
unity, "togetherness," and resolve; the spirit that was shown by Canadians in time of war when the survival of our country was at stake. Well,
the survival of our country as a united and strong federal state is at stake
today ...

What we need is a patriotism that will put Canada ahead of its parts;
that will think more of our future destiny than our past mistakes; that
rejects emphatically the idea that, politically, we are, or should become,
a federation of two associated states – some kind of prewar Austria-
Hungary. We should have none of such separatism or of petty, narrow
nationalism of any kind.

I am a Canadian; very proud to be one. But this does not make me
less proud of my British heritage or my Irish origins. It makes me all
the more anxious to bring that inheritance to the service of my country.
So it would be if I were of another race and spoke another language.

I am a Canadian who speaks English. There are millions of others
who speak French and have constitutional rights and privileges as
French-speaking Canadians which must be respected and recognized.
There are also others – and they are an increasingly important segment
of our population – who, while they may speak one of the two official
languages, also have an ancestral language which they use, traditions
and a culture of which they are proud, and which are neither French
nor Anglo-Saxon. But we are all, or should be, Canadians – and un-
hyphenated, with pride in our nation and its citizenship, pride in the
symbols of that citizenship.

The flag is one such symbol. For Canada, it has changed as our
country has grown from colony to self-governing dominion to sovereign
independence; to a nation respected among nations. Canada made this
change by peaceful evolution, gradually and in a way that did not
weaken the bonds with the mother country. That phase of our political
evolution is now completed.

Our ties to the mother country do not now include any trace of
political subordination. They are ties of affection, of tradition and
respect. As a Canadian, I don't want them destroyed or weakened. But

they have changed, and the symbols of Canada have also changed with them. This is an inevitable process. In World War I, the flag that flew for Canadian soldiers overseas was the Union Jack. In World War II, in January 1944, the Red Ensign came officially on the scene, though the flag designated for the first Canadian forces overseas and presented as such to General McNaughton on his departure for Europe was a different one, with the three joined red maple leaves predominant.

I believe that today a flag designed around the maple leaf will symbolize – will be a true reflection of – the new Canada. Today there are five million or more Canadians whose tradition is not inherited from the British Isles, but who are descendants of the original French founders of our country. There are another five million, or more, who have come to Canada from other far-away lands, with a heritage neither British nor French. I believe that a Canadian flag – as distinctive as the maple leaf in the Legion badge – will bring them all closer to those of us of British stock and make us all better, more united, Canadians.

Would such a change mean any disrespect for the Union Jack or its rejection from our history? No. I would not agree to that. I have served under the Union Jack in war and I have lived under it in peace. I have seen it flying above the smoke and fire and crashing bombs in London's blitz. I have seen it flying proudly in some desperate times in an earlier war. I know it stands for freedom under law, justice, and the dignity of man; for the glorious history of a brave breed of men. The Union Jack should still be flown in Canada – not as our national flag, but as a symbol of our membership in the Commonwealth of Nations and of our loyalty to the crown.

In taking this position, I know there are others, as patriotic as I am, who disagree, honestly and deeply. Such an issue is bound to raise strong emotions. Symbols, whether badges, flags, or anthems, have a deep emotional meaning. That is why they help to make a nation great, help to inspire and nourish loyalty, patriotism, and devotion among those who make up the nation. An emotional reaction is roused when there is any suggestion that old symbols should be discarded or adopted to new conditions and new needs.

You will recall the great Legion debate just a few years ago, in 1960, when you were choosing a new Legion badge; you will remember the arguments put forward in defence of your executive's decision on that new badge. As described by your then president, Mr Justice Woods, it was correct according to heraldry, was distinctive, and embodied the right symbolism to represent those things the Legion stood for. It was strictly your own, and could not be confused with the badge of any other organization. Its central dominant feature was the maple leaf.

Writing about this central symbol, Mr Justice Woods said at that time: "Consideration was given to some other form of emblem to represent Canada. As a matter of fact, a number of those who have criticized the badge asserted that the Maple Leaf was not a good Canadian symbol. Your council, however," – and he was referring to your executive council – "were of the opinion that it was a widely accepted Canadian symbol. This certainly is true in Europe. Our troops wore it on their caps and uniforms in the First World War. It appears on the flag of the Canadian Army. It appears on our national Coat of Arms. It appears on the shields of our provinces." Mr Woods then added:

When it was pointed out to us that it was improper to multilate the Union Jack by placing the Maple Leaf over it we did not see how we could properly carry this on in the new badge, so we removed the Union Jack and this left the gold Maple Leaf. We decided to change its colour to red. We put a white background so that it would stand out and this in conjunction with the blue on the Legion scroll below gives you the red, white and blue which we, of course, wanted to retain.

You will recall also that the suggestion made at the time, that the question of your new badge should be determined by referendum throughout your membership, was rejected by your executive as impractical.

As in the case of your new badge, so it is with any question of changing symbols. It asks a lot of human nature to expect ready acceptance of something that is going to alter that which is venerated and has been for long honoured by so many. Any suggestion for change is bound to provoke strong criticism as well as support. This is all part of the democratic process.

We who are elected to serve Canada in Parliament owe those who elect us more than the advocacy of non-controversial ideas. We owe Canada our best judgment, and we fail Canada if we fail to exercise that judgment, or if we pass our responsibility for judgment back to the electors who sent us to Parliament.

I believe most sincerely that it is time now for Canadians to unfurl a flag that is truly distinctive and truly national in character; as Canadian as the maple leaf which should be its dominant design; a flag easily identifiable as Canada's; a flag which cannot be mistaken for the emblem of any other country; a flag of the future which honours also the past; Canada's own and only Canada's ...

No one would deny that we have a responsibility to the past. But we have also a greater responsibility to the present and to the future. Moreover, our responsibility to the past will be best fulfilled by being true to its real substance and meaning. May I quote the words of Premier Stanfield of Nova Scotia in this connection, on 6 April last:

Surely, however, it is not necessarily patriotic for me to insist that something I value highly must be adopted as a national symbol if it is objectionable as a national symbol to a large number of Canadians. Surely the Canadian thing for us to do is to find symbols which are mutually acceptable. Let us emphasize what we have in common. Surely we can have a national anthem and a flag that unites Canada.

In the same spirit the Canadian Chamber of Commerce not long ago adopted the following resolution: "That the Parliament of Canada formally adopt and authorize a distinctive national flag," because, as the resolution said: "A distinctive national flag would be a strong, unifying influence, consistent with the status of full nationhood."

But I want to add this, ladies and gentlemen, that while I am concerned about this whole question of national symbols, national anthem, national flag, and all they mean to our country, I am even more concerned with making Canada the kind of country – with freedom, economic security, social justice, and opportunity for all – over which we will be proud to have our flag fly.

People are more important than emblems ...

40

IT seems to me that a selection of Pearson papers would not be complete without a contribution from that member of the family who, though very rarely speaking herself in public (one is enough in the family, as she says), made possible most of the other contributions in this book. After all, if I had not married Maryon Moody, I never would have occupied the positions which made authorship of this kind possible.

This was a Ladies' Day at Campobello, New Brunswick, when both Mrs Johnson and my wife did the honours at the opening of the Roosevelt International Park. I am told that, in this role, they were both noticeable improvements over their husbands on similar occasions.

Mrs Pearson Speaks

20 August 1964

MR Chairman, Mrs Johnson, Premier Robichaud, Governor Reid, Commissioners, Distinguished Guests, Ladies and Gentlemen:

First may I say how happy I am to be here today with Mrs Johnson and to share with her in this unique ceremony. On behalf of my husband and the Canadian government, I welcome her most warmly to Canadian soil, though the actual ground we are standing on is now, in a sense, half Canadian and half American.

As others have already said, it is this that makes our gathering here indeed unique. We mark the official opening of an international park in Canada – honouring the memory of a great statesman of the United States.

Although Franklin Roosevelt was not a Canadian, the summers he spent on this Canadian island made it part of him and contributed to shaping his character and his interests. For it was here that, as a boy and as a young man, President Roosevelt learned to fish and hunt. It was here he strengthened those qualities of courage and resourcefulness, of foresight and leadership, which later were to characterize his service not only to his own great nation, but to free men everywhere.

I hope I may be excused if I mention some of my own personal recollections of this great man. My first, most vivid memories of President Roosevelt go back to those dark days of 1939–41. My husband was in London among the bombs and the fires, I was alone in Ottawa with my children. I remember listening to the President's fireside chats to the American people pleading the Allied cause against Nazi Germany; and I remember how I prayed that his voice would be heard with understanding and, ultimately, with accord.

Later when we were living in Washington, from 1942 to 1946, I had the privilege several times of meeting him and talking to him. And I remember how deeply I admired and respected his courage in the face of his physical disability.

Then one dark day in April 1945, I came home from the hospital where I was working as a nurse's aide and there at the embassy, waiting to see my husband, was "Scotty" Reston of the *New York Times*. He told me Mr Roosevelt had died. I will never forget the shock, the deep personal sorrow, and the wave of fear I felt for the future of the free world without him. And I knew that that awful feeling of loss would be felt as deeply by millions of Canadians and Americans, and shared by free men around the world, on that lonely day.

These are some of the reasons I feel so proud and so privileged to be here today, to have a part in dedicating this international park to the memory of that great president, Franklin Delano Roosevelt, and why I want to record Canada's sincere gratitude to Dr Hammer and his brothers for the generous gift of this historic cottage and these grounds which are now the common possession of our two countries.

I hope the park will give pleasure to many people and, in so doing, will enrich for all time the memory of one of history's great men.

41

THE hundredth anniversary of the Charlottetown Conference, which had led to confederation, was celebrated by a federal-provincial conference of the heads of the Canadian governments meeting in the same city and, indeed, in the same room of the same building where our Fathers of Confederation began to "build better than they knew." It was a moving occasion and, in a sense, the beginning, and a very impressive one, of our Centennial celebrations.

At the Federal-Provincial Conference, Charlottetown

1 September 1964

IT is a great honour to speak in this chamber on this centennial anniversary of Canada's first confederation conference; to meet with the premiers of all the provinces around the same table where those men of vision conceived a great new nation a hundred years ago. I think today of the words of the sixtieth chapter of Isaiah: "A little one shall become a thousand and a small one a strong nation. The Lord will hasten it in his time." The Lord has hastened it in our time.

I share in the gratitude we all feel to our host, Premier Shaw, for the delightful and uniquely "Island" welcome we have received. History tells us that our forefathers from Canada were not met by any such welcome when they first arrived here for the conference a hundred years ago. It also shows that when they left Charlottetown, exhausted by hard work and open-hearted hospitality, they were happy in the warmth of a new fraternity and the hope of a new nation. That hope has been realized, and the fraternity is also with us today.

It is of course most fitting that a federal-provincial meeting should have been convened here to commemorate the centennial of the Charlottetown Conference. This was the point of time and place at which the grand but distant vision of Canadian confederation emerged as a desirable and attainable goal. The Charlottetown Conference was also the first of the intergovernmental meetings of which today's is a direct descendant, meetings which have in effect become a permanent part of our national governmental structure, and through which we can cooperate to keep our federal system effective and acceptable.

Today, a hundred years on, there are constitutional, racial, and regional tensions in Canada. At times they seem to endanger our very survival as a nation, for strains of the present always create doubts about the future, in a nation no less than in an individual. This doubt is seized by the cynics and the faint-hearted, to belittle the Canadian experiment and diminish its achievements. To counter such defeatism we should spend more time rejoicing in our achievements, less in moaning about our difficulties.

Social unrest, economic pressures, federal-provincial differences, difficulties of the kind that are felt today have tested every Canadian generation; and no generation has failed to meet the test. Nor will *we* fail – we who enjoy riches and resources beyond the wildest dreams of those men who met here in 1864; but only if we face our problems in the spirit and with the resolve of our forefathers.

The Fathers of Confederation combined a remarkably clear and sure sense of purpose and direction with a single-minded dedication and determination to reach a goal. Within three years they converted their dream into the reality of a federal state, now grown beyond their imaginings.

If it is to continue to grow – as it will – we must acknowledge the strains imposed by our times on the national structure bequeathed to us; we must acknowledge them without being daunted by them. We must define them. And remove them.

For that purpose, we must have a sense of political realism, a passion for justice, and a gift for compromise. We must also recognize that the basic partnership of our two founding peoples and the enriching diversity of our national pattern remain our greatest source of strength and progress.

We must not over-dwell on yesterday, or even on today. We plan for the future, and it is the future on which we have to agree. For we cannot turn back the clock. We cannot by our wish or our command restore to our problems the simple shapes, the neat black-and-white alternatives, of less complicated times.

To solve them, we must recapture the faith of our predecessors and restore their purpose in our national life. We must reaffirm those principles on which they agreed, and which are still valid. But in following them, we must be willing to modify procedures unsuited to our own times.

First among our national goals, the prerequisite to all others, economic, social, or cultural, is national unity. This does not mean and cannot mean uniformity. It does mean Canadian identity, with the symbols and even more the spirit and the pride to foster such identity. It does not mean subordination in any way of provincial rights or the alienation of provincial authority. It does mean a government at the centre with powers strong enough to serve Canada as a whole.

Let us here declare, and let our accord be broadcast for all men to know, that this nation – conceived in the hearts and minds of those who met in this place a century ago, nurtured through twenty-one Parliaments and now embracing half a continent and ten provinces – has no intention of falling apart and every intention of moving forward to greater things.

Let us agree that whatever may be the difficulties facing our federation, whatever our differences, we are resolved to keep our union strong, our federation healthy, and our nation one before the world; that we accept our responsibility to the past; but, even more important, that we will discharge our obligations to the future.

Gathered here in Confederation Chamber on this the first day of September 1964, let us vow to do our part in lifting our country beyond the jeopardy of forces or factions which would divide it; to strengthen and safeguard its federal system; and to accept as our highest purpose trusteeship over the concept of a Canada fortunate in the duality of its origin and the diversity of its development; but a Canada greater than the sum of its parts.

Let us acknowledge freely that these goals will not be easy to reach; that in their pursuit we must show tolerance and patience as well as strength and determination. But let all Canadians know that these *are* our goals. Their acceptance can itself be a strong unifying force.

Finally, let us ask God's help and His blessing in our task. In this spirit, Canadians will never betray the faith of those we honour today, or the heritage and the hope of those into whose keeping we pass our trust tomorrow.

42

From the Commons Flag Debate

14 December 1964

MR PEARSON Mr Speaker, I should like to begin by calling attention to the fact that this debate which is now coming to an end has seen 270 speeches in the house –

AN HON. MEMBER How many on your side?

MR PEARSON – 190, plus, of which have come from the official opposition.

MR DIEFENBAKER And we successfully changed the thinking of the government on the first flag.

MR PEARSON I have been criticized in the house for not having spoken enough in the flag debate.

MR MONTEITH You finally were flushed out.

MR PEARSON I wonder if my hon. friend could contain himself for about twenty minutes ... Mr Speaker, when I rose to conclude the debate as prime minister, the hon. member for Bow River (Mr Woolliams), who has had a good deal to say about closure, rose in his place, as was his right, to prevent me from closing the debate. I have twenty minutes, Mr Speaker, and if the house wishes to give unanimous consent I would be very glad indeed to take only half of that time and give the last ten minutes to the Leader of the opposition if he would like to have them.

SOME HON. MEMBERS Oh, oh.

SOME HON. MEMBERS Hear, hear.

MR DIEFENBAKER Mr Speaker, when the Greeks produce gifts we recognize what they mean. The Prime Minister is trying to explain away a situation in which he is throttling Parliament and is tearing down the flag which has flown over this country for 100 years. He is trying to be facetious at a time like this.

MR PEARSON Mr Speaker, I was trying to be courteous and co-operative and give half of my time to the Leader of the opposition. I was offering to give him the last ten minutes in this flag debate which began last June. Perhaps I should have learned from experience that offers of co-operation of that kind to that quarter usually do not get a very friendly reception. This debate has gone on for a long time, Mr Speaker, and in order to preserve to Parliament the right of decision it was necessary for the government to invoke a rule which I hope will only be very rarely invoked in this Parliament, the rule of closure.

SOME HON. MEMBERS Oh, oh.

SOME HON. MEMBERS Hear, hear.

MR PEARSON Otherwise we would have made a farce of parliamentary debate on this matter and the minority, the opposition, would have had the right to prevent a decision on a matter of the greatest possible national importance.

SOME HON. MEMBERS Hear, hear.

SOME HON. MEMBERS Oh, oh.

MR DIEFENBAKER We accepted our responsibility.

MR BELL May I ask a question?

MR PEARSON Mr Speaker –

MR BELL How could we prevent this decision, Mr Prime Minister?

MR PEARSON By the action you are taking now, by intervening to prevent discussion.

The motion of the government [for closure] was sustained, Mr Speaker, by representatives of every party in the house, including the deputy leader of the Conservative party.

Mr Speaker, when the right hon. gentleman talks closure, and when he realizes his deskmate, the deputy leader of his own party, voted for closure, how is he going to reconcile that? A decision was taken, and we continued the debate.

We have had a vote this evening on an amendment to the motion to concur in the report of the committee, which would have sent the report back to the committee with instructions to have the Red Ensign as the flag.

MR MONTEITH All you want to do is to crucify it.

MR PEARSON I have too much respect for my hon. friend to pay very much attention to that interjection.

MR MONTEITH I have a lot of respect for you, too, but not when you talk that way.

MR PEARSON On the vote this afternoon on the Red Ensign, a straight-forward vote for the retention of the Red Ensign, the result, I believe, was 162 to 80, or two to one against that motion.

Now, Mr Speaker, we are approaching the end of a long, hard, and sincere fight by hon. members opposite for what they considered to be the right national flag for Canada. I have never denied them that right, nor have I ever denied the sincerity with which they made the fight.

AN HON. MEMBER You denied the people that right.

MR PEARSON I denied the people no right. The people are represented in this Parliament, and 162 of the representatives of the people in this Parliament, representing every party, voted against my right hon. friend and his supporters. All right, Mr Speaker, that fight in this Parliament is over.

AN HON. MEMBER That's what you think.

MR PEARSON The fight is over in this House of Commons. Now, Mr Speaker, we approach the main motion and the main motion is a report of a committee, representing all parties in this house, a report containing a recommendation which was concurred in by the members of all parties in this house, recommending to this house a red maple leaf flag as the emblem of Canada. This is our flag for the future, but it does not dishonour the past. I hope that Canada can go forward as a united, strong, and progressive country, with this flag as its emblem.

MR DIEFENBAKER The right hon. gentleman has done everything to divide the country.

MR PEARSON Will the right hon. gentleman contain himself for two or three minutes longer, and then we will vote.

MR DIEFENBAKER When the right hon. gentleman starts giving me advice, I say to him, you have done more to divide Canada than any other prime minister.

MR PEARSON I think we should be sympathetic to the right hon. gentleman because he is feeling the frustrations of failure.

MR DIEFENBAKER Mr Speaker –

SOME HON. MEMBERS Order, sit down.

MR DIEFENBAKER I challenge the Minister of National Health and Welfare (Miss LaMarsh) because she was the one who said, with exquisite femininity, "Shut up and sit down." I say to the Prime Minister, is he experiencing the happiness of having throttled discussion in Parliament? Is that what he is experiencing at this time when a flag is being born?

MR PEARSON Before I was interrupted by the right hon. gentleman, that master of parliamentary procedure, I was trying to say that this is a good flag, and it is Canada's flag, an emblem of which we and our children can be proud and under which Canada can go forward; the red maple leaf flag. Surely, Mr Speaker, when the dust of controversy clears away, when the bitterness of debate is over, we can all in this house rally around the red maple leaf Canadian flag. I know the atmosphere does not appear very propitious across the chamber for appeals, but I make an appeal even at this late date in the debate. I appeal for us all to forget divisions and differences of this debate and to rally behind this red maple leaf Canadian flag.

MR DIEFENBAKER May I ask the Prime Minister a question?

MR PEARSON Yes.

MR DIEFENBAKER He is telling us of the wonders of the red maple leaf flag. When did he change his mind, after saying the three maple leaf flag represented our heritage, and the one maple leaf had none?

MR PEARSON Well, Mr Speaker, that is a very easy question to answer. We submitted this matter, at the request of the right hon. gentleman, to a committee representing all parties in this house. This committee did not see fit, by a majority vote, to accept the design I preferred. I accept the design recommended by the committee, and I ask my right hon. friend to do the same thing. Surely there is nothing disgraceful, Mr Speaker, nothing could be further from disgrace, than to accept as the emblem of our country a flag which has one red maple leaf on a white background representing what we have stood for in this country in war and peace. Why cannot my right hon. friend forget the passions, the prejudices, and the bitterness of the fights of the past few months and rally around this Canadian flag and make it the emblem of unity in this country? Why can he not do this? I ask him to do what we would have done, if the amendment had been carried.

MR DIEFENBAKER A flag by closure, imposed by closure.

AN HON. MEMBER The great divider of Canada.

MR PEARSON All right, Mr Speaker, there is no use making an appeal; that is obvious. I regret very much that a man who has attained such prominence in the public life of Canada for so many years would take this attitude at the end of this debate on a matter of this national importance.

I will make one final suggestion, Mr Speaker, and that is that if this

motion carries – and it is going to carry, that is clear, from the vote this afternoon; there is every likelihood of this motion carrying – surely hon. gentlemen opposite do not wish to be put on record as voting against a design which is going to be our national flag.

MR MONTEITH Oh, nuts.

MR PEARSON I ask them, Mr Speaker, that when you put this motion no hon. member in this house vote against the design which is going to be our flag. Mr Speaker, I do not ask them to vote for it. I ask that there be no recorded vote so that we will not be in a position in this house of having hon. members vote against what will be our national flag.

MR MONTEITH Don't be crazy; I am going to be recorded.

MR PEARSON I make this appeal to them. They can turn it down with insult and contumely if they so desire. On this side of the house there are Canadians as loyal to the past as any hon. gentlemen opposite, and they will vote for this flag.

SOME HON. MEMBERS Hear, hear.

MR PEARSON There are Canadians on this side of the house quite as loyal to our past and quite as hopeful of our future.

MR NUGENT On a question of privilege, Mr Speaker, I consider the remarks of the right hon. gentleman an insult to members on this side of the house.

MR PEARSON All right, Mr Speaker. We on this side have made the appeal. They have turned it down with jeering and insult. We on this side, and a good many on the other side of the house will vote with pride and confidence in the motion you are now about to put before the house ...

43

THIS was another party occasion on which I was expected to give a political speech. It was at a time when the government, and I particularly as head of it, was under bitter, continuous, and often, as I saw it, most unfair attack in Parliament over alleged corruption and scandal within our ranks. There were occasions during these weeks when I became disgusted that the whole business of politics could descend to such levels and indeed when I abhorred my own participation, and the necessity for it, in this kind of conflict.

It was also a time of strong conflict and controversy between the two basic language groups that – constitutionally and racially – make up the Canadian nation. I often wondered then whether there could ever have been another period in Canada's Parliament which was so difficult, so debasing, so violent. But I recalled history and realized that this sort of thing has always afflicted parliamentary institutions in Canada and, indeed, in other democratic countries. It is, however, a luxury that could more easily be afforded and accepted in those earlier days than at present when parliamentary responsibilities are so much greater and the stakes, in terms of a nation's future, so much higher.

It was in the mood of those months that I gave the Toronto Liberals some of my views on political leadership which are included in these few extracts from a longer speech.

To the Toronto and District Liberal Association

14 February 1965

It has been a year when political leadership has not been easy and when one leader, I speak only for one, has often longed for a life with more leisure, some privacy, and no autographs. That day, no doubt, will come.

But meanwhile, I feel fine and will continue to give every ounce of energy I possess, every quality of heart or mind I have, to the discharge of the responsibilities entrusted to me. I am eager and anxious to face the work ahead and I am happy in the doing of it. The satisfaction one gets from serving Canada in this way far outweighs the frustrations, set-backs, and the nastiness that is at times inescapable from politics.

We who are chosen for high office have an obligation to give direction and leadership. Today the leadership that is required is not for victory in war but for victory in the search for the solution of political, social, and economic problems in a country whose people, as a whole, enjoy one of the highest material standards of living in the world, but who are uneasy, at times perplexed, and worried about the pressures that divide within or pull from without. Today political leadership must be steady and persistent, never forgetting ultimate national objectives in the face of immediate and disconcerting diversions.

It does not have to be and, so far as I am concerned, it will not be the kind of leadership which shouts and spellbinds, which plays on false emotions and narrow prejudices, which prefers the easy and immediate cheer to the hard and ultimate achievement. This kind of leadership has never saved a country, but it has destroyed more than one. In government and party, leadership must bring about unity through co-operation – a close and creative working-together. As the Editor of the Halifax *Herald* put it the other day:

What it all boils down to is that the times are out of joint, in a peculiarly Canadian way, and that no political leader can look like Sir Galahad as he goes about his business. None will, if it is to survive. Attempting to reconcile what appears to be the irreconcilable will continue to be the task of Prime Ministers. The job will be even more difficult than that faced by their predecessors.

While the difficulties are there, it is easy, but wrong, to exaggerate them into defeatism and see in them the danger of immediate collapse; to ignore the progress made in their solution and the reality of achievement. From defeatist exaggerations there often come a host of simplified solutions for salvation. Every problem becomes a national crisis in which every adult Canadian worth his salt must be putting in sleepless nights awaiting the magic arrival of some Lochinvar, whose vigour and enterprise, combined with bold certitude and sheer strength, will solve all our problems immediately and with ease. These are crisp and comforting conclusions but oversimplified and fanciful.

Mature people – and Canadians are a mature people, despite the lamentations of some of our chroniclers – can be trusted to keep the Jeremiah and the medicine-man equally in perspective. Canadians know and accept, without being overwhelmed by them, the obstinacy and complexity of our problems and our challenges. Today they ask of their leaders not incantations or panaceas, but honest and intelligent hard work.

Leadership also means insistence by the leader on high standards of political conduct and action in government. When these standards are betrayed, then those who betray them must go. But leadership also means refusing to yield to unfair partisan and popular pressures, by sacrificing to such pressures those who do not deserve it. No government can strengthen its position by injustice. I think I have already made my position clear on that score. I said some weeks ago in Winnipeg:

Every specific charge in Parliament, of default in duty or betrayal of trust, which is seriously made, should be investigated at once through a full and fair enquiry conducted in a way which will command public confidence.

If there are findings which require action by the federal government, that action must and will be taken, without fear or favour. Nothing should be hidden, and no wrong doing, if any is found, should go uncorrected. However, while the guilty must always be punished by responsible action, the innocent must not be ruined by ruthless and irresponsible words.

That remains my position.

There is, in all politics, a vital relationship, a subtle balance, between the play of political passion and the faculty of human compassion, as there is between the exercise of power and the necessity for agreement. Any politician today must be aware of the importance of what is called "the image." But this does not mean that, if you save the surface, you save all. Indeed, the man of integrity in public life will never sacrifice the substance for the surface.

On this subject of politics and political leadership, may I quote Dag Hammarskjold, who said in a speech on 14 June 1953:

Politics is no mere play of will and skill where results are independent of the character of those engaging in the game. Results are determined by the consistency of the actors in their efforts and by the validity of their ideals. Contrary to what seems to be popular belief, there is no intellectual activity which more ruthlessly tests the solidity of a man than politics. Apparently easy successes with the public are possible for a juggler, but lasting results are achieved only by the patient builder.

That is a good philosophy to keep in mind ...

44

On the Inauguration of Canada's National Flag

15 February 1965

On 5 September 1945 an Order-in-Council was passed declaring the Red Ensign to be Canada's national flag pending a decision of the Parliament of Canada.

Such a decision was made in December 1964 after long and vigorous parliamentary debate and careful committee consideration and recommendation. As a result of this decision by the Canadian Parliament and on the advice of the government of Canada, Her Majesty, our beloved Queen, was pleased to issue a proclamation that the flag we are about to raise today should be the flag of Canada.

So, at noon today, in this eighth month of our ninety-eighth year as a confederation, our new flag will fly for the first time in the skies above Canada and in places overseas where Canadians serve.

If our nation, by God's grace, endures a thousand years, this day, the fifteenth day of February 1965, will always be remembered as a milestone in Canada's national progress. It is impossible for me not to be deeply moved on such an occasion or to be insensible to the honour and privilege of taking part in it.

There are many in this country who regret the replacement of the Red Ensign by the Red Maple Leaf. Their feelings and their emotions should be honoured and respected. But I am sure, now that the decision has been made by the representatives of the Canadian people in Parliament assembled, that all Canadians, as good patriots, will accept that decision and fly with pride our national flag.

This ceremony today is not a break with history but a new stage in Canada's forward march from a group of separate, scattered, and dependent colonies to a great and sovereign confederation stretching from sea to sea and from our southern border to the North Pole.

No step by which we have advanced to our present position among nations has been an easy one and none has been taken without some nostalgia for the past. This is inevitable in the succession of new beginnings that mark a nation's progress, as they do the course of human events; for each brings to an end a stage for which deep attachment often lingers.

The patriotic motives that have led Parliament to adopt a new Canadian flag do not include disrespect for our past or for the emblems of that past. We salute the future, but we honour the past on which the future rests.

As the symbol of a new chapter in our national story, our Maple Leaf Flag will also become a symbol of that unity in our country without which we cannot grow in strength and purpose; the unity that encourages the equal partnership of two peoples on which this confederation was founded; the unity also that recognizes the contributions and the cultures of many other races. And so the new flag, joining but rising above the milestones of our history, today takes for the first time its proud place as the emblem of Canada: "The Maple Leaf our Emblem dear."

May the land over which this new flag flies remain united in freedom and justice; a land of decent God-fearing people; fair and generous in all its dealings; sensitive, tolerant, and compassionate towards all men; industrious, energetic, resolute; wise and just in giving security and opportunity equally to the people of all its cultures; and strong in its adherence to those moral principles which are the only sure guide to greatness.

Under this flag may our youth find new inspiration for loyalty to Canada; for a patriotism based not on any mean or narrow nationalism, but on the deep and equal pride that all Canadians will feel for every part of this good land.

God bless our flag! And God bless Canada!

45

An interview of the type I had with Pierre Berton on this occasion is never an easy thing to do and often not very satisfactory. So many questions are thrown at you suddenly that there is always the chance of a quick reply being not only inadequate but misleading. This is especially so as there is never time to go into the subject in any depth before you are invited to move into another question. More than once I have fallen a victim to this danger. When it happens, you can only blame yourself, of course, because, even if the question is designed to lure you into a pitfall, you should be able to avoid it, especially if you have had some experience in sessions of this kind.

The excerpts from the interview which follow provide a good illustration of this process of question and answer with a very shrewd, well-informed, and tough questioner as the inquisitor. When you are in an election campaign, and what you say can be seen as well as heard, the operation is even trickier. Your expression and your manner, as you try to deal with questions are, of course, as important in creating an impression as the words you use.

In the transcript, however, only the words matter. I'm not sure whether in my case this is an advantage or otherwise. I know I always felt much more comfortable with an interviewer or taking part in a discussion than I did when I was alone in front of the camera, under instructions to give the feeling that I was talking to a family in a living-room. But the "idiot box" was never a substitute for a family, so far as I was concerned; and I am not, and never could be, a good enough actor to make it appear so.

On Television with Pierre Berton

12 September 1965

MR BERTON Good evening. Welcome to the programme, Mr Pearson.

MR PEARSON Thank you.

MR BERTON Now, because there is an election on, I am going to ask you some tough questions. First, let's talk about the elections. The Toronto *Telegram*, the day after the election was called, reported that one of the reasons for this that you gave was that a poll by your people showed you would get 160 seats. Was there such a poll taken?

MR PEARSON Well, if there was I have never heard of any result of that kind. We have been taking soundings, surveys across the country for some weeks, indeed some months ... They're encouraging. I believe they indicate that we should get a clear majority in the House of Commons, as the feeling of the country is at present.

MR BERTON In other words, if the polls had been discouraging, you might not have been so quick in your announcement.

MR PEARSON A major reason for an election at this time is for one party to have a majority in the House of Commons, with the stability and continuity of government that this should represent.

MR BERTON You said, Sir, that the election was really up to the opposition, but you were never defeated by the opposition in Parliament. You've got a great deal of legislation through. Why do you feel that the opposition –

MR PEARSON I don't think I ever said an election was up to the opposition. There are two ways it can –

MR BERTON Well, I have a transcript of our talk, and that was the phrase you said, it was up to the opposition.

MR PEARSON When we were in office, a year ago, if the opposition had voted us out as they threatened to do at that time, and as they've tried to do, we would, of course, have had an election. So we were in a period of uncertainty ...

After two years and four months of minority government, with the uncertainty that this creates; with the opposition parties saying all summer that we are a government that does not deserve to stay on; a corrupt and a bad government; throw the rascals out ...

MR BERTON They said they would only throw you out if you didn't clean out the mess, whatever the mess may be.

MR PEARSON We feel that the time has come for an election. They have challenged us in terms which, we think, should be taken to the people.

MR BERTON Let me talk to you about strong government, because this is one of the issues in the election.

MR PEARSON Yes.

MR BERTON Let me ask you this question: If you had had a majority government in Ottawa, would the scope of the Dorion inquiry have been as broad as it was as a result of the NDP forcing you to widen those terms of reference?

MR PEARSON Yes. The scope of the Dorion inquiry would have been sufficient to have done the job that the Dorion inquiry did. True, the original terms of reference of the inquiry were altered as a result of parliamentary discussion. That is done sometimes in majority governments as well as minority governments. They were altered, but the original terms of reference were quite sufficient for Justice Dorion to have investigated this matter as he did.

MR BERTON But, surely the NDP would not have been able to force those broader terms and allow more witnesses to have been interviewed and put on the stand if you had had a majority government, because it was a threat that they would bring you down that forced this. That's pretty obvious, if you read Hansard at the time.

MR PEARSON What you have said is that a minority government has to operate all the time under the threat of being brought down.

MR BERTON Is that not a good thing sometimes?

MR PEARSON It's a good thing sometimes, of course, but it's not a good way to conduct government in a parliamentary system; to have a minority under the gun of an opposition majority at all times. If we had been been a timid government, we wouldn't have brought in these controversial measures which we did, even in a minority government. We did, but it took us a long time to get them through. It took us six months to pass the resolution establishing a Canadian national flag. We didn't need six months for that.

MR BERTON Let us turn to one controversial area of your government and that is the events surrounding the Dorion inquiry. Back on 2 September, last year, your Justice Minister sat down beside you in an airplane. He told you a bribery investigation was under way in high levels of government. He named a parliamentary assistant, and you forgot about this.

MR PEARSON You put it inaccurately. He sat down beside me in an airplane on the way back from Charlottetown for a few minutes. He said there was an investigation going on of an allegation of a bribe having been offered to an executive assistant of a minister in the government, and there are many executive assistants in the government.

MR BERTON He named the executive assistant.

MR PEARSON He may have named the executive assistant. If he did, the name didn't mean anything to me at that time. At that time I didn't know by name all the executive assistants in the government. I said to him: "Are you looking into this matter? Are you investigating it?" He said: "Yes, we are." I said: "That's fine, go ahead."

MR BERTON But two weeks later, that executive assistant, who Mr Favreau said he named, was fired by his boss, Mr Tremblay.

MR PEARSON Well, he was told to go off on leave until the investigation was completed.

MR BERTON Well, he vanished. Did you not know about this? Didn't you connect this name with what Mr Favreau said to you?

MR PEARSON I certainly did not. When a minister tells an executive assistant to go off on leave while he is being investigated, it's not inevitable that such things get to the prime minister who has many other matters to deal with. It was essential that this matter should get to me when the investigation was completed and the report was ready to be made, and that was done. As soon as that report was made, I took the action that was required.

MR BERTON But, it seems to me, Sir, that Mr Favreau was remiss in not mentioning to you that another man under investigation was in your own department, that is Mr Rouleau, who was your own assistant.

MR PEARSON As soon as that name was brought to my attention, when the report was submitted by the Minister of Justice, action was taken in regard to that particular member of Parliament within two or three hours. I don't know how much faster you could act than that.

MR BERTON You couldn't act very much faster, but couldn't Mr Favreau have let you know that this was going to happen, faster than that?

MR PEARSON Well, Mr Favreau brought the report to me and to the Cabinet as soon as he could – when it was completed. I'm not going to analyse his own particular conduct in regard to whether he should have told me earlier in the investigation that this name was under consideration.

MR BERTON The electorate is going to analyse it, and your opposition is certainly going to analyse it.

MR PEARSON Of course.

MR BERTON ... What we are faced with here, surely, and let me put this bluntly, is that a gang of international thugs, connected with a sleazy matter, connected with dope, undoubtedly connected with the Mafia, in some way were able to reach their finger into the highest levels of government. Their hands got in here, didn't they?

MR PEARSON The way you put it, "they reached their finger in the highest levels of government," I don't accept that description. They were in touch with an executive assistant in the government. They were in touch with members of Parliament who didn't know they were a "sleazy gang of criminals," as you put it, and those members of Parliament were asked to intervene with the minister to see what was going on. As soon as the investigation was completed, as soon as it was referred to Cabinet, and that was very shortly after its completion, action was taken on these matters at once by the government ...

MR BERTON But, during this election campaign, your judgment in keeping Mr Favreau in the government is going to be questioned. People are going to say that Mr Favreau was more than remiss ... The question is going to be asked of you: how could you keep a man in the Cabinet at all, who had made those obvious errors?

MR PEARSON I think that that is a matter of judgment. I'm very glad that Mr Favreau is still serving Canada in the Cabinet. He is a man of ability and honour.

MR BERTON Let me ask you, Sir, if the story is true that you wanted to keep Mr Favreau in the justice department.

MR PEARSON I don't know where you get these stories.

MR BERTON Well, this has been published.

MR PEARSON Well, it's not true. As soon as the report was published, Mr Favreau and I had a conversation at lunch, and we agreed that he should leave the justice department, and go into another portfolio. Any stories you may have heard to the contrary are false.

MR BERTON Right. Well, we have your word for that on the record. It is said, Mr Pearson, Bruce Hutchison once wrote that you had no killer instinct; he said you are not ruthless enough as prime minister. Now, let's get some comment from you on this, because this is what we are dealing with. A lot of people said you should have cut Favreau's throat and thrown him out.

MR PEARSON All right. This is a matter of opinion. I don't know what you mean by "the killer instinct."

MR BERTON Well, Mr King had it. Mr King didn't suffer anybody who made an error; he chucked them out, and he was a pretty stiff prime minister.

MR PEARSON Perhaps you should read more carefully Mr King's diaries. When Mr King decided that the time had come for a Cabinet minister to go, he went. But Mr King kept a lot of ministers in his Cabinet, I think quite rightly, who had made mistakes and turned out to be even better ministers after they had made the mistakes.

MR BERTON Let me ask you one final question on the Dorion situation, and it's this: if Mr Eric Nielsen had not stood up in the House of Commons and blown this thing wide open, would the public ever have known the details that they learned through the Dorion Inquiry?

MR PEARSON Once the report was made to us, in the terms in which it was made, that report would have been acted on whether Mr Nielsen had initiated an investigation or not.

MR BERTON This was the RCMP report?

MR PEARSON Exactly! – and remember also –

MR BERTON And, Mr Dorion criticized the RCMP for not going far enough.

MR PEARSON: Remember also that the particular man, the executive assistant who, in the report, has been most criticized, is now before the courts.

MR BERTON Oh yes, we understand that we can't comment on his culpability; but still, another of your Cabinet ministers was before the courts, and he was fired pretty summarily last January, wasn't he?

MR PEARSON Yes, but I thought you said I didn't have the killer instinct!

MR BERTON Touché, Mr Pearson. Let me ask you this: last spring, or early in the year, you wrote out a code of ethics for your Cabinet ministers ... Should it really be necessary to spell out a code of ethics at all for high officials? Shouldn't this be taken for granted? Were some of them not resentful that there was a code of ethics sent around?

MR PEARSON You should never have to talk to civil servants in terms of ethics, and you don't. You don't have to talk to political leaders in terms of ethics, or rather you shouldn't have to. I think it was a good thing, however, to remind the ministers at this particular time, and especially ministerial staffs, who were new and inexperienced many of them, of the ideals we are serving in politics, and the things we have to live up to in politics.

MR BERTON Were any of the ministers resentful that they had been reminded of something that many of them, I think, would have taken for granted?

MR PEARSON Not to my knowledge.

MR BERTON Now, I must ask you one more question in this area. This is a very difficult situation, but is it a matter of concern to you that several of these recent political scandals – in fact, I think all of them – have involved French-Canadian Liberals?

MR PEARSON It's a matter of concern to me that the criticism from partisan sources should have been centred against political persons from Quebec. I think we should keep these things in perspective, not only in respect of the so-called political scandals that are alleged, when they often are exaggerated unfairly, but also in terms of our country as a whole. There are unfortunate things that go on from time to time in public life, in business life, and even in journalistic life. We are having difficulties now in Queen's Park in respect of certain financial exposures. I am not going to talk about scandal in the Ontario government because of that, or say that Queen's Park is worse than Quebec. There have been difficulties in other parts of Canada. So, I don't think we should look at this matter at all in terms of Quebec versus the rest of Canada, or French Canada versus the rest of Canada. There is no better way than that of stirring up enmity and division inside our country ...

MR BERTON Let me ask you about the Bilingual and Bicultural Commission. In its preliminary report it is said that this is a most critical period in our history since Confederation. It's talking about the French-English dialogue, if you want to use a kind word. Do you agree this is the most critical period?

MR PEARSON No, I don't believe this is the most critical period in Canada since Confederation. We have gone through some very critical periods before; we have gone through them and come out of them. This is a serious time in our history in regard to the adjustment of federal-provincial problems, and in regard to relations between the English-speaking and the French-speaking elements in our country. We are going to face these problems. We are going to solve these problems and, as a result, we will come out stronger than before.

MR BERTON Do you think Messrs Dunton and Laurendeau* are crying wolf there, when they call this a crisis?

MR PEARSON I don't criticize them a bit for expressing their own views on the seriousness of the situation. I think it is a very good thing to expose problems, if you are going to solve them.

MR BERTON Did you ever complete the questionnaire, incidentally, that they sent around to the MP s?

MR PEARSON No, I didn't.

MR BERTON You didn't answer that?

MR PEARSON No, I didn't. I thought some of the questions were quite unnecessary. I was annoyed by the questionnaire, and the form in which I got it, so I did nothing about it.

MR BERTON I see.

MR PEARSON I have some rights as an independent citizen too, you know.

MR BERTON Let me ask you a few questions on foreign relations. Though I don't think these will be election issues, still, they're important. It seems to me that you had much more rapport with Mr Kennedy than Mr Johnson.

MR PEARSON I don't accept that. I have seen more of Mr Johnson than of Mr Kennedy, because of the tragedy of Mr Kennedy's early death. He wasn't in the White House for very long after I took office. The two men are so different themselves that the kind of relationship any

*The co-chairmen of the B and B Commission

person would have with them is bound to be different. If you're wise, it would be different. For me, it has been very friendly in both cases, I assure you.

MR BERTON Was Mr Johnson equally friendly after you made the speech urging a pause in the Vietnam war, in his own country? He was supposed to be very angry.

MR PEARSON He couldn't have been more friendly with me afterwards. We had a good friendly argument about this, which is a good test of friendship, believe me.

MR BERTON He smiled while he was arguing, did he?

MR PEARSON Yes, and he smiled afterwards and he took my arm and led me down to the plane and wished me well. He sent me a friendly letter a few days later and we went over some of the points again.

MR BERTON Mr Pearson, in what way does our policy in South Vietnam differ from the US policy, if it differs at all?

MR PEARSON We haven't the same responsibilities that the United States have in Vietnam, and our policy is bound to differ. That's why we have to be very careful in our criticism of United States policy. We have to recognize the fact that they have the responsibility. Our objectives are the same. They want to get out of Vietnam and do their best to ensure that a government is set up in Vietnam which meets the wishes of the people. So do we. They are not going to stay in Vietnam one hour longer than they have to.

MR BERTON Let me get back to the election in the moment we have left. If you are beaten this time –

MR PEARSON Now, why do you want to say that?

MR BERTON Will you retire from politics? Or will you stay on?

MR PEARSON If I am beaten this time, the party might wish me to retire from politics.

MR BERTON I think that's possible. It's probably also possible of your opposition. Is it true that you tried to get Jean Lesage into the federal Cabinet?

MR PEARSON No.

MR BERTON You never tried? The story is that you tried and he said if you'd guarantee him he would be your successor he'd take it.

MR PEARSON Why do you believe all these stories, Pierre?

MR BERTON I didn't say I believe them. I'm trying to find out from the horse's mouth whether they are true or not.

MR PEARSON Well, that's not true, I assure you.

MR BERTON You called an election this year on television. This is the first time that that medium has been used rather than the press. Why?

MR PEARSON Well, it was a way of reaching more people in a shorter time than a press conference. But, of course, the television statement I made was given to the press exactly at the same time.

MR BERTON So, you gave the press and television equal time. In that sense, Mr Pearson, you're a good politician. And, the half hour is over. We haven't covered all the issues, nor could we, but they will be covered in the weeks to follow.

46

I TOOK advantage of the conferring on me of the Atlantic Award in Springfield, Illinois, to give my views on NATO at a time when earlier hopes that it might develop into an Atlantic community had diminished, when indeed it was entering a new and difficult period which, in my view, required a reassessment of the purposes and direc-·tion of the organization. My thesis was that NATO had to be re-examined in the light of the conditions of 1966, not 1948, and necessary changes made accordingly, so that the European members would have more responsibility for NATO and the USA less, without, however, any weakening of the lines across the Atlantic or of collective security. I was proposing not abandonment but adjustment.

At the Atlantic Award Dinner

11 June 1966

IN conferring on me an Atlantic Union Pioneer Award this afternoon, you have done me high honour for which I am very grateful. You have confirmed my admission into ranks of the Atlantic Pioneer Corps and have chosen for the confirmation this historic setting of New Salem and Springfield, steeped in memories of one of the towering figures of history.

At the same time you have added to my feeling of grateful appreciation by coupling my name with those of Christian Herter and Adlai Stevenson, as recipients of the Atlantic Award. I know, as you do, how much we owe to these two men. Not only the United States and Canada, not only the Atlantic community, but the whole world is in their debt ...

As I look back on the years through which we have passed since the second great war of this century, I am struck by the fact that our destinies have depended so very much on the vision and leadership of a few men, on their understanding of what, at a particular moment, was the right way out of danger, and the right way to move ahead. These rare individuals had always before them an ideal of human brotherhood, of a world at peace and with freedom. They also had a firm and confident sense of direction in trying to achieve their ideal. Chris Herter and Adlai Stevenson are such men. Clarence Streit is another ...

NATO – the Atlantic alliance – is an encouraging, if imperfect, reflection of this ideal. It has served us well for the past sixteen years. NATO could hardly have achieved its political and its military expression, however, if the yeast of the Atlantic unity idea had not been at work before the treaty of 1949 was signed ...

In 1948 it was our hope that Western Europe and North America working through co-operating national governments could provide a nucleus of military strength, economic prosperity, and political stability, around which a global balance could be re-established and the extension by force of aggressive communist imperialism be stopped. We did not know at that time whether this would be at all possible. We did not know, whether, if it were possible, it would take five, ten, twenty, or fifty years to accomplish. We certainly cannot even say today that it has been accomplished. But we *have* reached a kind of equilibrium in which we can live together, the communist states in Europe and ourselves, with hope for progress to something better than mere co-existence.

Indeed, some of our troubles today are the results of our successes in these recent years. In 1948 we were anxious and frightened – with cause – at the threatened extension westward of totalitarian communism into those European countries which, while still free, were badly shaken in their political confidence and almost completely disrupted in their economic life. After the war our problems were of immediate, not ultimate survival. But today we are concerned with longer-range problems of peace, of prosperity, of development. This is a measure of our progress.

Once the course of history has been changed, even a little, we are prone to look back and regard that change as inevitable. But in 1945, as we looked ahead, there seemed nothing inevitable or certain about the reconstruction of a democratic, prosperous, independent Western Europe. There seemed nothing inevitable about a change in the old American habit of peacetime isolation, which had been dominant for 150 years. It was far from inevitable that countries which had never in peacetime pooled any part of their sovereignty would do so now, and together organize a collective defence system that, in the conditions of the modern world, might prove effective enough to deter another war. We were up against physical destruction, economic stagnation, and political defeatism. Vast human and material resources had been blown away and destroyed in war. Out of this waste and weariness could we really construct something new that might help to meet and solve our problems?

Well – it was done. Gradually, hesitantly, painfully, but steadily, things were done. An alliance that was designed to be more than military was welded together in peacetime. Its members began to believe in the possibility of a secure peace – of a good life. Indeed, as the years went by, many even began to forget or ignore the continuing dangers of a yet more horrible war. So they became impatient with the structures and the processes that had made their own comfortable conclusions possible. Some people and some governments began to fall back into those historic nationalist grooves which had been the source of so much of the bloodshed and conflict and chaos they had recently endured. With recovery came impatience and doubt and some distrust.

We should have seen what was happening in the Atlantic alliance and countered it. Indeed, in December 1964 Canada did propose in NATO a reassessment of the nature of the alliance in the light of these changing conditions. Little was done.

Unhappily, it is man's weakness to cling to the ideas, the institutions, and the habits of the past instead of adapting them to the needs of today and tomorrow. So it was with NATO. The weight of inertia and a vested interest in a new status quo, felt especially among the most powerful governments of the alliance, made it difficult to find anyone in a responsible position on either side of the Atlantic who was prepared to come forward and specify in any detail what should be changed. A lot of people were talking about the need for change but nobody, no government, in a position of power was really doing much about it. Then abrupt and unilateral action by France thrust change upon us. Crisis – as always – forced our hands.

We should have acted earlier and not under the compulsion of events. We should have tried to move forward together to a closer international association in order to remove the risk of sliding backwards. In these matters, there is no standing still. Surely the course that should have been taken – should *still* be taken – is clear.

Today, facts, compulsions, and opportunities lead inexorably toward closer international association and away from the self-sufficient sovereignty of the nation state. The jet planes that fly, the rockets that range in outer space, the universal revolution of rising expectations, combined with the speed of technological change which make their realization possible, all these make it essential that we move ahead in the field of political and social organization in a way which is at least remotely comparable to our technological and scientific progress.

We can begin with the "like-minded" Atlantic nations, who have already acquired a sense of community and a habit of co-operation, but we must include ultimately all mankind. The world is too small for less, yet we continue to boggle even at the first careful steps. If there is anything that has been made crystal clear by the grim experience of half a century, it is that neither peace, security, nor prosperity can be achieved or maintained by national action alone – or by national policy alone.

So this is no time to weaken in our support for the NATO alliance, because it is having difficulties. We must solve these difficulties. But we must not stop there. We must move forward with new resolve toward an international community with common political institutions, which covers more than a single continent, and spans the Atlantic.

It must also be more than a military alliance. Try as we might, however, we have never been able to make NATO much more than that. An alliance for defence only, however, is an anachronism in the world of 1966, especially when nuclear power is not shared, by possession or by control, among its members. As Professor Hans Morgenthau has put it: "It is no longer possible to rely completely on the promise of a nuclear ally to forfeit its very existence on behalf of another nation." A guarantee of nuclear support against aggression simply does not now have the credibility that would make it a fully effective deterrent and therefore a guarantee of security.

I repeat, we must develop common, unifying political institutions which would provide for collective foreign and economic policies, as well as genuinely collective defence. Nothing less will be adequate to meet today's challenge of jets and rockets and hydrogen bombs.

As a leader of a government, I am very conscious that politics is the art of the possible. Anyone with political responsibility must think in terms of what can be done at any given time, of what public opinion will accept. He must not allow the best to become the enemy of the good. Nevertheless, if we don't keep the best always before us as an eventual and essential objective, not only will we never reach it but we may even fail to reach more immediate good objectives. Nor should we always wait for a crisis to force us to act.

In 1940, Great Britain – only a few years before, cool and confident behind its channel – proposed full union with France. It was the moment when continental Europe was about to fall a victim to the Nazi aggressor. The offer was too late. Offers made in the imminence of defeat and collapse for radical and immediate action to implement ideas which the day before yesterday were considered as visionary and unrealistic always *are* too late. Do we have to have panic before we can make progress?

At this moment there is no panic, but a feeling of discouragement which is more likely to work not for the transformation of NATO into something better, but for its reduction into something less. This is a very real danger. French policy has underlined it.

General de Gaulle has rejected Atlantic defence integration. He has ordered France's withdrawal from the North Atlantic Defence Organization. In doing so, his procedures have been brusque and his ideas understandably disturbing to France's friends and allies. It would be foolish, however, to push the panic button over this. By doing so, we might merely push France, not only from the NATO military organization, but out of the Atlantic alliance itself. And France does not want to leave the alliance.

It would be short-sighted, also, not to realize that the attitude of Western Europe to American commitments in Europe is changing, just as the attitude of Eastern Europe toward Moscow is changing.

We should not try to throw all the blame on France and General de Gaulle for recent NATO developments. Some of General de Gaulle's decisions, I know, have been disconcerting and seem to indicate a return to a kind of nationalism from which France has suffered as much in the last fifty years as any country in the world. Before we condemn, however, we should try to understand what is behind France's recent actions. France is not, has not been, and will not be, satisfied with an Atlantic organization or an Atlantic alliance of independent states dominated by the United States of America. France, and not only France, feels that continental Europe is now strong enough (in large part because of the generous assistance of the US) to be given its rightful share in the control of the policies of the alliance.

While France is not alone in this feeling, only de Gaulle has translated it into policy and action. If he has gone too far in that action, as I think he has, if he is on the wrong course, we should not drive him further in that direction, but try to bring him back to the right course by seriously re-examining the purposes and the organization of NATO in the light of 1966, not 1948. We should have done it years ago. If the reason for General de Gaulle's action is his belief that the other allies will not consider any change to NATO to meet new conditions, let's take positive action now for the necessary reforms. Surely it doesn't make sense any longer to take the position that NATO is sacrosanct and mustn't be altered. Our reaction should be just the opposite.

In short, merely to rail at General de Gaulle, because he is demanding for France a position in the Atlantic alliance equal to that of Great Britain and somewhat closer to that of the United States, is to show a dangerous misunderstanding of the situation.

May I refer on this point to some observations in Max Frankel's penetrating article, "Our Friends, the French," in the April number of *Freedom and Union*. Mr Frankel is somewhat critical of his own country's share in the responsibility for NATO, as he puts it, "becoming an anachronism whose defensive or military purposes were long ago overtaken by technological change and whose diplomatic purposes we have never managed to define or construct." He believes that not de Gaulle's stubbornness, but a long chain of events and conflicting governmental policies, including those of the United States, have caused the present disarray.

I do not see the Atlantic nations going forward together to a secure and hopeful future without France. Therefore, we must find a way out of our present NATO difficulties so that France can fully participate in the march to greater, not less, Atlantic unity.

We must not give up the ultimate vision of closer Atlantic unity just because some clouds are obscuring the immediate future of NATO. Indeed, a new move forward to realize the greater vision may help remove some of the nearer clouds.

We must now look at the picture ahead of us with the courage and imagination we showed seventeen years ago when the NATO pact was signed. Taking this same cradle area of the Atlantic nations, we must ask ourselves what sort of Atlantica would we like our children to inherit from us in five years, ten years, twenty years. What vision of the future can we hold up as a rallying point, as an objective of policy, without pretending that it *must* turn out the way we wish, but convinced in our own minds that, given good will, dedicated hard work, and a certain amount of good luck, it *could* be that way?

This forward march must be Atlantic, and not merely European or North American. But it must provide for more control by Europe of its direction and its character – a Europe, moreover, which would include Great Britain.

I realize that a united Europe, would, in its political, economic and military decisions, be more independent of Washington than is the case now. But what is wrong about this?

There are those who worry about the "separateness" of such a European development and who would therefore prefer to concentrate now on the federal union of all the Atlantic peoples, even at the expense of earlier European union. If we are realistic, however, we may have to accept at this time the more practical immediate objective of a united Europe, not as an obstacle to, but as a stage on the way to, Atlantic union.

If we cannot at present achieve Atlantic federalism, it may be necessary to acknowledge the realities of the situation and, as North Americans, work with Europeans in the hope that in the longer sweep of history both European and North America will come to realize that their respective affairs can best be harmonized in a wider union. Meanwhile, if an intervening stage of European unity is necessary, it must be taken not in continental isolation but in close Atlantic co-operation and understanding.

As I try to grope my own way towards a concept that would make sense for North America, and for both Western and even Eastern Europe, I am convinced that we cannot insist on retaining NATO in its present form as the only foundation for building a genuinely international structure more appropriate for the future. I am equally sure that continentalism either of the European or North American variety is not the answer.

Finally, I believe that only the United States can give the effective lead required for Atlantic unity. Without her active participation and support, nothing can be done; at least on the broad front which is essential. Without her leadership we will be driven back to national or continental solutions for the organization of security and for progress.

So we in other countries should be heartened by the fact that one hundred and eleven senators and congressmen from thirty-four states, and from both parties, along with ex-presidents, former presidential candidates, and governors, have co-sponsored or supported the resolution on Atlantic unity. The list includes two names that mean much to all free citizens throughout the world, President Truman and President Eisenhower. With this kind of backing, with this kind of understanding and vision, who dares not take this initiative seriously?

Years ago, long before the North Atlantic Treaty or the United Nations Charter were signed, even before the United States or Canada had ever been heard of, when the Sioux and the Blood Indians hunted over the western prairies, their young men on coming of age would retire alone to some hill or mountain. There, in solitude, fasting, watching, they would seek before entering on their adult years to look at themselves for the best that was in them; to purify their thought and their feeling; and to seek the guideposts they would try to live by as men. This solitary vigil they called "Crying for a Vision." Now, more than ever before, we need as individuals, as nations, to "cry for a vision"; and then, with devotion and persistence, to strive for its realization ...

What we seek is new and unprecedented. But so is our world. Abraham Lincoln once said: "As our case is new, so we must think and act anew." Today, we must think anew and act anew.

47

THEN came Centennial Year – one of celebration and rejoicing, of looking back with pride and forward with hope. Canadians needed such a year, because our country had been going through a period of dissent, division, and too much self-depreciation. We needed a lift and Centennial Year gave it to us, at least for a time. Preparations for it had been imaginative and comprehensive. Never did a country have a better year-long birthday party, culminating in the great 1 July celebration on Parliament Hill which the Queen so graciously honoured with her presence.

As prime minister, I had to participate in much of the ceremonial. It was a stern but happy test of the social durability of my wife and me and of the wearability of my striped trousers. All stood up well. There were official visitors from more than forty countries and all, except three, were given an official welcome at Parliament Hill on their arrival in Ottawa; the President of France left before reaching Ottawa; the Prime Minister of the UK was called back to deal with an emergency and could return only in January 1968; the President of the USA was able to spend only one day in Canada and, as that also included a short visit to Expo 67, there was no time for any ceremonial welcome during the three or four hours he spent in Ottawa.

Thanks to the magnificent work and organization of many people, the visits – with all the complicated and difficult protocol, hospitality, and security arrangements involved – went off without a hitch, or at least any hitch that I could detect, except one for which I was solely responsible. I started my speech of welcome on one occasion before the guard had presented arms and just as the band was getting ready to play the national anthem of Ruritania.

The particular inclusion in this book is my short address one cold December night when I welcomed in Canada's centennial new year and then lit the Centennial Flame in front of the Parliament Buildings. For a few horrible seconds, it looked as if I might fumble this major ceremonial assignment, as the flame appeared reluctant to catch on. I never was very good at causing instantaneous fire. But the critical and dark moment passed, the flames lit up, and Centennial was well and truly and formally initiated. It was a wonderful year. It would be even more wonderful if its spirit could continue to animate and inspire our national life.

On Lighting the Centennial Flame

31 December 1966

ONE hundred years ago our country was born. For this we honour men of vision and purpose and high endeavour. Lesser men would have failed or, more likely, would not have tried at all.

The task at times seemed impossible. So did that which followed: the consolidation and expansion of the new country until, strong and free, it spanned the continent from sea to sea and reached toward the Arctic.

Tonight, one hundred years later on Parliament Hill in Canada's capital, with the lighting of this flame, with pride in our present and faith in our future, we open officially our centennial celebration.

As this symbolic flame burns, so let pride in our country burn in the hearts of all Canadians, where the real meaning of Canada must ever be found. If I may put it in the words of the Canadian poet Charles Bruce:

> This heaped geography ...
> What is the blend of fear, strength, song and dream
> Slowburning in its heart?
> ... There is no answer but the wordless answers
> That live in flesh, in nerves, heart, blood and bone;
> The moving images that crowd our dreams ...

Tonight we let the world know that this is Canada's year in history. It is a time to measure, with grateful hearts, the achievements of our past. It is a time to face with confidence the test and the opportunity of the future. It is a time to assess our national condition. It is a time to appreciate the honourable place we hold in the world community gained by sacrifice in war and service in peace.

Economically, we have become a rich society and a great industrial power. We have built new dimensions of progress and welfare into the Canadian way of life. The boundaries of freedom and opportunity have been expanded for every Canadian.

Out of our experience in nation-building, we are forging a new principle of democracy, the principle of political and economic unity in racial and cultural diversity.

History and geography, man and the map, have made Canada a particular kind of community where we can show this unity in diversity that all mankind must find if we are to survive the perils of a nuclear age.

Much has been done in Canada. Much remains to be done for Canada. We have laid a strong foundation on which to build in our second century. If we have the will and the goodwill there is no limit to our progress.

It is my hope and my belief that as we continue to work out Canada's destiny, our national spirit and our national purpose will shine – as this Centennial Flame now shines before us here – humbly but strongly before all the world as an example of what men and women working together can do to build the good society.

Tonight we begin a new chapter in our country's story. Let the record of that chapter be one of co-operation and not conflict; of dedication and not division; of service, not self; of what we can give, not what we can get. Let us work together as Canadians to make our country worthy of its honoured past and certain of its proud future.

God bless Canada.

48

THIS was one of those occasions when veterans get together, fight again old battles, relive the glories and the miseries of active service, and remember old comrades who didn't "make it." As it was the fiftieth anniversary of Vimy Ridge, a Canadian victory with a significance deeper than military, my dinner companions were with few exceptions over the three score years and ten; but they were young again on that memory-filled night.

Vimy – Fifty Years After

9 April 1967

Mr Chairman, ladies and gentlemen: This is a very moving occasion and I feel very privileged to be allowed to be with you. I have been asked to say a few words to you as prime minister of our country, but I like to think of myself tonight in the terms of my original military designation: 1059 Private L. B. Pearson. Later I did become an acting corporal. Then there was a setback, and I got a commission!

Tonight we remember with pride and with sadness the men who gave their lives on Vimy Ridge. We also honour those who survived and especially those who are with us tonight. Our memory goes back half a century. Each of us will have his own thoughts of those days, those weeks, those months, and those long years; thoughts of courage, and of loss, and of sacrifice, of mud and boredom, and the delights of leave; above all, of the close, wartime bonds of comradeship and friendship, born of shared experiences and shared dangers. War has been called hell. It is the ultimate folly, the very worst of man's inhumanity to man. But war does bring out qualities of unselfish working together, of common resolve, of unity of purpose, of subordination of self to a cause; qualities that could do so much to settle our national problems and remove our national difficulties if we could but show them in action in the less demanding and the more dividing times of peace.

The sufferings and the sacrifices of the soldier on active service should give us a sense of proportion about our contemporary discontent and complaints. But they don't. Memory fades and, in any event, only a minority now have these things to remember. So the imperfection of a picture on the television screen or a plane being ten minutes late will cause more grousing than an order in war which is obeyed without complaint, but which might mean death. All is relative. Battles far away are for history, without, it seems, especially for the young, much relevance to the circumstances of today. But the spirit of those days is relevant to the search for solutions to the problems we have today.

I was not at Vimy. Indeed, if I had been I might not be talking to you tonight. During those April days, I was at a place of almost incredible contrast to the awful chewed-up slopes of that ridge. I was at an Oxford college whose gardens were becoming beautiful with the new green of an English spring. It was a place of quiet and lovely serenity, an improbable place to learn about infantry tactics and a startling contrast to what was going on a few miles across the channel. I was there because after two years or so of obscure service as a private soldier in the Mediterranean theatre and the Balkans, the General Staff agreed that I should become an officer, though up to that time I had given no indication that I could be of any great assistance to them in winning the war.

In any event, in April 1917 I was then a cadet. Because it was a British training battalion, I was a "gentleman" cadet. Many years later I had the privilege, as I know some of you had, of taking part in the pilgrimage to Vimy on the nineteenth anniversary of the battle, when King Edward VIII led the parade to the most beautiful of all the war memorials, one whose design represents all that is most enduring in human life and human values: gallantry, sacrifice, compassion, justice, truth and knowledge, death, sorrow, peace, and the cross; a monument which stands on 250 acres of land which by deed of the French government and by the will of the French people is forever Canada.

I should not try to repeat the story at Vimy. It has already been told tonight, and who am I to repeat it to those who themselves were the story; of that night of 8 April 1917 when all was ready for the assault, gun flashes lit up the sky, and the noise of shelling helped to cover the movement of troops moving up? What is today a peaceful hill, surmounted by those two commemorative pylons communing with the open sky, was on that day, as you know so well, a turmoil of moving men, of spouting earth, of drifting smoke, and driving sleet. There may have appeared to be confusion. In reality there was order, discipline, and determination out of which came success.

I'm no military expert or even a military historian, but Vimy, I believe, was the first example of new skill and imagination in the organization and planning of an attack. It led to a brilliant tactical triumph, though unhappily within a higher strategy that for three years was stolid, unimaginative, and tragic in its bloody futility.

Vimy was more than a battle. It has become for Canada a symbol. It is a symbol, as were many other and even bloodier battles, of the courage and the self-sacrifice of Canadian men. It is also a symbol of the coming of age of Canada as a nation, a nation which was brought to birth in the emotion of that time with a unity sealed by blood. May we always keep that feeling of togetherness and unity in this country.

On that day in April 1917 nobody asked in the Canadian Corps whether the soldier next to him came from British Columbia or Nova Scotia; or whether he spoke French or English. It was enough to wear the maple leaf badge and be working, and fighting, and dying together.

It all happened that day when the Canadian Corps of four divisions, together for the first time as one Canadian formation, went over the top and took the ridge. That impregnable bastion, as it has been called, had withstood those fierce earlier assaults of very gallant French and British soldiers. It was a very proud moment in our history. But it was only one heroic episode in the worst, and perhaps the most stupid, bloodletting in human history, where generals in the highest places of command on both sides were fighting earlier wars in an obsolete and obstinate way and where men died in masses to prove them wrong.

Perhaps some of you will recall the order of the day issued in ringing terms after the first magnificent success of the Canadians at Vimy. The order was to keep the beaten enemy on the run and exploit the victory. The way was open. The emptiness, indeed, the mockery of those high-sounding, if sincere, words was soon made clear when the Battle of Arras, of which Vimy was a part, bogged down into the old trench warfare while General Neville's French offensive shared the same fate.

The lesson of the tactical success of Vimy Ridge and the strategic failure of the whole spring warfare of 1917 was not learned, and soon Passchendaele followed – perhaps the worst horror of all during those terrible years. It is well to remember the human wastage that can come from war, especially as we honour the men who lost their lives in war; especially the wastage that comes from fighting a wrong war in the old way.

I think it is wise to remember this now, in the face of changes in the world since 1944. A new war, if it were ever allowed to occur on a large scale between great powers, is now further removed from the ideas and tactics of World War II than World War I was from Caesar's campaigns in Gaul. There will be no front lines, no barrages, no great expeditionary forces crossing the ocean, no time to train masses of civilians. It will be nuclear missiles and a devastated planet – and all in a matter of hours. We should think and plan accordingly.

None of this dims in any way the imperishable heroism of the men whom we are honouring tonight. That will never die and has become a proud place in our national heritage. Nor does it deny the truth that no nation is great unless its citizens are willing to die for the things they deeply believe in. But Vimy also means that we must now use our powers, not to win a war but to prevent it. We must use power for peace.

Here Canada does not and cannot act effectively alone. Nor can any other country. That's another lesson of Vimy and we shouldn't forget it. Soldiers of Britain, France, and Canada all took part in that 1917 spring offensive. Soldiers of France in their tens of thousands, men of Britain and Canada, have all died in attacks on Vimy Ridge. Indeed, on the larger scene of the war, it was only by the collective action of many soldiers from many nations, fighting men dying together, in accord with plans which at last were agreed together, that victory and peace were ultimately won.

The soil of France or of Belgium, in 1918 or in 1944, could not have been liberated by national action alone. Nor can an attack on France or Belgium or Canada or any other country today be deterred by national planning and power alone. Only by collective action for collective defence with collective strength under collective control can there be maximum deterrence against aggression. Surely this means subordinating national sovereignty and even national feelings and prejudices – and national pride at times – to the necessity of maintaining the peace by international action which must go far beyond the old military alliance systems of other years now proven to be so inadequate.

Indeed, that inadequacy might have lost the first great war if the

crises and dangers of 1918 had not forced the co-ordination of planning
and operations and command in France. Why is it that so often in
human history only crisis and danger can force the course of wisdom?
One would think that the countries that have had the most bitter experience of the inability of national effort and national arms to secure
national safety, or prevent enemy occupation, would be the very first to
appreciate the importance of collective action through a strong and
cohesive coalition for policy and for defence, such as NATO could and
should be.

But tonight we think not so much of these things as we do of our
comrades who fought and died at Vimy, and also of that greater host
of French and British who lie buried in those fields and who silently
and together and forever mount a guard of honour – Canadian, British,
and French – over the memorials to our dead.

The glory of those who fell at Vimy has been eloquently celebrated
in a poem written by Raymond Card of Toronto on the pilgrimage of
1936. It's called "Vesper at Vimy." I'm sure many of you have read
it and it includes these words:

> Their chantry chapel is the night;
> The dews of eve the mourners' tears;
> The stars the altar candles bright,
> Endowed through everlasting years.
> Oh! Time shall wait on time in vain,
> And Envy die of self-accord
> Before a stouter deed shall claim
> A prouder laurel for the sword.

That is how Canadians will always think of the men of Vimy.

49

I GOT a great deal of pleasure talking to this banquet of political
scientists and economists. The latter had by this time created a
separate academic organization for themselves, and this was the last
banquet at which they all sat down together as a single group. Separatism was rearing its ugly head!

I could hardly resist the opportunity to strike a blow, well above
the belt, of course, on behalf of those practical and practising political
scientists who are known as politicians, a breed which is continually
being subjected to the slings and sneers of non-politicians, including
at times some academics who reserve their political science for the

classroom, the learned journals, or, more and more these days, with mixed results, for the TV or radio. Of course, now that I am a professor again, and haven't been asked to advise the government or even to work on a royal commission or task force, I can more fully appreciate the critical academic side of the picture.

To the Canadian Political Science Association

8 June 1967

Mr Chairman, I am both happy and nostalgic at being here tonight to celebrate with you. I may say I rather underestimated the power and prolongation of your celebrations because I asked my car to come back at ten o'clock! It never used to be that way in my day at a university; not only were we prohibitionists, we were poor.

I wish I could have been here, Mr Chairman, for some of your programme. I have been looking at it. It's an evidence of the wide range of your intellectual curiosity. I would have loved to have attended the seminar on political behaviour, especially to have listened to the paper on apathy and political stability! I might have even learned something from the survey research seminar at 1:30 this afternoon on the political outlook of Canadian voters. Unfortunately it was about the November 1965 election and I can't do anything about that.

It is right, of course, that you should be curious, because curiosity as every scientist – political or otherwise – knows is one of the enduring and persistent characteristics of man. It's also the main force behind his own and his society's progress. Indeed, the curiosity of the scientist, political or social or natural, has been behind most of the changes that are now sweeping over the world with a speed and a scope which is bewildering. Of course, politics, naturally, could not escape the impact of man's curiosity. It is indulgence in this urge to explore the meaning of social and political and economic behaviour, to explore it in an objective and intellectual way, that makes one a political scientist or, if you prefer, a political theorist. Anyone who conducts his exploration in an unscientific way is merely a politician.

It is, of course, quite impossible to combine the two approaches, though contemporary experience shows that they may be practised successfully in succession, with eager and inquisitive men and women switching from one to the other in transitions that are more valuable to the political scientist than they are to the politician.

Naturally, I admit to some prejudice in this matter. But I have always felt that a plunge into the untidy moat of practical politics improves the nature and contentment of life, as well as the practicality and the reality of activity on return to the ivory tower. I hope there are those here to-night who will agree with me. I apologize, at least to myself and perhaps to Miss Jewett, for this unfortunate reference to "the untidy moat" as if it were something muddy and stagnant. I beg you not to despise the profession of politics. It's the second oldest in history, much more reputable even if less rewarding than the oldest, whether you define politics as the science and art of government, or, more originally, as one of my professors did at Toronto many years ago, as "the skilful use of blunt instruments."

The political scientist, without I think the same incentive as the politician, recently seems to be turning his mind and directing his restless academic curiosity and his intellectual assurance to the new ultra-modern world of communication. Indeed, a prominent Toronto TV and radio newspaper columnist pointed a few days ago, with some anxiety, to those "university people" – he was thinking of political scientists I'm sure, and I quote him – "who are now engaged in establishing communications as a new academic discipline." Incidentally, why do we have to use this word discipline all the time? The professors are getting as bad as the Pentagon in inventing jargon. Anyway, this columnist attributed this interest in communicating to "the dazzling ascendancy of one of their own, Marshall McLuhan," whose adoption, as he put it, "by the media as the latest public guru merely heightens the frustration of all his ivy-covered colleagues." Then came Mr Braithwaite's most caustic observation:

The more the academics study communications, the more they come to realize that the essence of the subject is the thing itself, the act of communication. And though they pay lip service to the precept that the most valid form of communication is the simplest – one man speaking to one man, or a small seminar – their ambition really is to have access to the newspapers, to radio, and most of all, to television.

Well, I might not go quite so far as that, but I must confess that my confidence in my own ability to do anything intelligent in the practice, if not the exposition, of politics is rapidly becoming eroded by the radio and TV commentaries of political scientists, or even worse, of those political non-scientists who haunt the galleries of Parliament and the corridors of government offices. Both the scientist and the non-scientist in this field of national and international politics often speak and write with an easy assumption of infallibility which I have never been able to muster since I left the University of Toronto. I find this depressing, but not destroying.

I was reading a book the other day – Eric Hoffer, *The Temper of Our Time* – a very good book, I thought, in which he said that political commentaries always flourish in a time of political disarray. The fact is, of course, the political disarray is due largely to an excess of political commentaries!

Confronted with the continual frustration and worry brought about through practical considerations getting in the way of intellectual and political perfection, I get discouraged when I listen to the confident voice of academic omniscience on everything from the recognition of Red China to the base price for industrial milk.

I am comforted, however, by the thought that, God willing, I may soon be academic again, starting where I left off, somewhat to my own surprise, in 1928. Soon I will again become a learned authority instead of merely a Cabinet leak. Mr Chairman, I may even qualify to become a member of one of your associations where my experience over the years may help speed up the move toward bilingualism and biculturalism and stop the drift toward separatism in learned societies.

I must stop this lighthearted banter or I'll run the risk of being charged with mocking the solemnity of this impressive academic occasion. True, it is designated in the programme as merely a "banquet," with myself as guest speaker. Yet it must have been considered by you to be a very important occasion because there is an asterisk after the word banquet and a footnote, which reads: "accompanying order form must be returned immediately to the Secretary-Treasurer to reserve a place." I am deeply flattered by this tribute to Caesar by God.

There can be little dispute today over the need for a more scientific, a more rational, a more systematic approach to the practice of politics and to the work of government. But there is still a great deal of room for dispute as to how this need should best be met, or indeed if it can ever really be met in popular democracy. Much of the advance in human well-being through economic progress that has been made during recent decades, for example, has resulted from organization and specialization. The experience of your own association during the last couple of years illustrates this point.

From one body embracing all the major social sciences, your membership will soon be divided, perhaps it has already been, into three separate groups: the Canadian Sociology and Anthropology Association established last year; the Canadian Economic Association to be established I believe this week; and your own Political Science Association with its membership devoted only to political science *per se*.

I don't want to criticize this breaking apart. After all, as a political party we Liberals are dedicated to the liberalizing of divorce laws. I assume that these moves are intended to make each of your "disciplines" more effective and to encourage a greater distinction in your separate efforts to discern and explain the laws of human behaviour and human progress. I hope these purposes will be realized, because the work of the social and political scientist has never been so important as it is now.

In this era of ceaseless and often turbulent change, people in your professions face unprecedented challenges, as we do in politics, in helping to chart new social directions and in assessing their values. But if it is important to pursue your studies of human problems, needs, and values within your separate professions, I believe, as Vincent Bladen has already indicated, that the interrelationship of your specialized studies should not be lost sight of. This trend toward organization and specialization has, I know, increased efficiency and maximized results, but it has also created new and difficult problems; how, for instance, to ensure that the individual retains at least some ascendancy over the organization, over the institution.

There may be some of you, of course, who are tempted to take refuge in your own personal academic delving, preferring individual intellectual adventuring to organized action and rejecting as a shade indecent participation in established forms of political action and the exercise of political power.

I have one idea which will make this immunity, I hope, a little more difficult – at least so far as part-time participation in political matters is concerned. In the House of Commons at the present time, a committee is studying reforms in our rules and procedures. We are also trying out a number of changes in actual practice. Among other results, I would like to see some proposals made effective so that our various parliamentary committees could make much greater practical use of the knowledge and special skills of our political and other social scientists.

I think it would be beneficial both to Parliament and to the academic community if it were easier than it is now for committees to employ experts, even on a short-term basis, from the social sciences to give greater depth to committee studies of one kind and another – that is, if we can find any experts who are not already being employed in royal commissions or task forces. I think it would also be useful for a committee studying certain bills or resolutions to be able to bring a few specialists to Ottawa to work as advisers to the members of Parliament on that committee for the duration of such a study. Widened opportunities for the social scientist to gain personal acquaintance and experience with the day-to-day operations of our parliamentary system would, I think, be almost as beneficial to the halls of higher learning as the academics' presence and advice would certainly be beneficial to our parliamentary activities.

I'm going to mention only one other area of Canadian political activity where I think there is a greater need for co-operation between politicians and political scientists. That is in the field of external aid. The need to develop more effective and useful relations between the developed and the developing areas of the world has become as much of a challenge to our domestic policy as it is to our external policy. If free civilization is to survive and grow, and there are times these days when we wonder whether that's going to happen, we must very soon find vastly improved methods for extending the benefits of modern industrial and technical progress to the whole world community of man. The rapidly advancing technology and the complex interrelationships of today's global society demand that the fundamental problems of man be dealt with on an international and an interprofessional basis.

The challenge for international development is to find new instruments for concentrating more interest and more resources on the application on a global basis of the latest technology to the solution of man's economic and social problems. One idea for a new Canadian initiative to meet this challenge which is being considered by the government is the establishment of a research centre for international development. It might even be on the site of Expo 67. After nearly twenty years of trial and error in this field of international co-operation, we have learned a great deal about what can and what cannot be done. But at the present time, there is no single institution in the world that acts as an internationally recognized focal point for concentrating research and study in this field which holds such a vital challenge to all of humanity.

The excitement of using new techniques for the purposes of peace and universal human progress, instead of for war and universal destruction, is simply not getting across, either to the statesmen or to the people of the developed countries. So the Canadian government is looking into the possibility of building on the inspiring theme of "Man and His World" created by Expo this centre for international development that might focus, in a continuing way, this heightened Canadian awareness of the development problems and challenges confronting mankind at the present time.

We cannot, even if we wished, become a great power in a political or military sense. But we have already proven in our peace-keeping efforts that we can make a good contribution to world order. Perhaps it will now prove possible for us to add a new dimension to our modest role in the world community by providing for this centre for research.

This idea, this plan, if you like, is one of long-range importance. But this doesn't mean it can be postponed too long. Unfortunately, however, most of today's political problems have to be dealt with by a government on a day-to-day, almost an hour-to-hour, basis. That's what I meant when I once said that government is the adminstration of the unintended – or the unexpected. It's all too true that in the vastly more complicated and more numerous and more pressing problems that now face those of us in government, the important often has to give way to the merely urgent. It's one of the great weaknesses of democratic governmental structures at the present time.

Changes are rushing in on us from every direction and they will not be put off while we retire to an ivory tower or a trout stream to brood over their significance or what we should do to adjust to them. We haven't time. We're expected to have found an answer yesterday. That's only one reason why I ask your indulgence for that harried non-specialist and pragmatist, the politician; the sweaty man who works in the centre ring of the dusty circus of everyday life, who must daily juggle the dream against the reality, and walk the tightrope between what is and what ought to be. Indeed, it is one of the dangerous ironies of the present condition of politics that at a time when the need for reflection and thought has never been greater, the practising politician has less and less time to think before he must act.

The political scientist, on the other hand, whose chief purpose is to be a thinker-in-depth about the problems and trends in our politics, is often removed from the compulsions, pressures, and limitations that influence and at times determine political action. That, of course, is why he is so much wiser. I know you will agree with me, that even the wisest political thought can have better practical results if it acquires first-hand experience with political action or with the processes leading up to such action.

It's exciting and exhilarating – I've experienced it – to dream of great schemes for political and social advancement. Indeed dreams, translated into practical action, are the stuff of progress. But dreams that merely result in theories and the kind of research that specialists in any field are sometimes tempted to divert themselves with, often produce very little but euphoria.

As one who has known both the shelter of academic halls and the anonymous security of the civil service, I have at times had my own doubts about the wisdom of venturing forth, with wary shield and uncertain sword, among the lions in the open forum of party politics. But that's where the action is today. Without action we can't make progress no matter how brilliant our thoughts may be. Whatever his party affiliation, and whatever his personal talents, every member of the House of Commons has at least proven himself a successful warrior on the hustings, exposing himself, his ambitions, and his pride openly to the verdict of his peers. If the standards of our political battles are not so high as some of our spectator columnists and ringside warriors would like, then I suggest they should try to move openly into the lists themselves.

After all, the arena of Canadian politics remains today one of the last strongholds of truly free and competitive enterprise. It is a big and open ring where anyone, and particularly anyone who is certain he could do better than the present combatants, is free to throw his hat in and have it kicked around. In my own experience in this arena I have not escaped without some bruised political muscles and even a drop or two of spilled political blood. But out of my own experience, and notwithstanding sins of omission and commission, I have come to be proud of the good things that those of us who are in the midst of the action manage at times incredibly to achieve. That's a sufficient solace for the less rewarding aspects of the life we have to lead.

As a matter of fact, I wear my bronze badge of politician with a pride that grows with the passing years. My satisfaction, if not my pride, was increased some weeks ago in this regard when I read a lecture by a very distinguished political scientist, poet, university administrator, gunner, ex-civil servant, and friend, Douglas LePan, which included what I thought to be some perceptive and certainly generous words about my present profession. He said in this lecture given at Queen's University:

> To the extent that those called on to rule are trying to do that, however fallibly, however imperfectly, I can see no reason to deny to those in positions of responsibility the tribute that is their due because of the necessity and difficulty of their task. They have nowadays little support from tradition or from authority in the family or the church. They must deal with forces that are largely out of control and which they must yet try to curb. They work with the possibility of annihilation, of world-wide annihilation, always at their back ... The causes of revolt, particularly of revolt among the young are deeper than they have ever been before. There are no widely-recognized religious or philosophic systems to redeem the world from meaninglessness. And yet, in the midst of these difficulties, they must go on.

Well, Mr Chairman, whether I go on or not, this speech must not go on any further.

Thank you.

50

HER Majesty's visit to Expo began gloomily because as we disembarked from the *Britannia* the rain came down in torrents. But the skies cleared and it was a great day, without any incidents except happy ones. The high spot on the programme, though a last minute addition to it, was the ride over the grounds on the mini-rail. The security people had earlier vetoed this as too risky, but during the morning I instructed those responsible to restore it and make the necessary arrangements which meant that I had to take full and personal responsibility. I was certainly glad to do this, the only drawback being that the luncheon was rather rushed and had to be shortened. The Queen and Prince Philip considered this, I am sure, to be no drawback.

My remarks were certainly less formal than those customary on such occasions. If this disturbed anybody I can assure you that it wasn't the Queen.

Expo—and a Welcome to the Queen

3 July 1967

I WOULD like to welcome Your Majesty and Prince Philip to our Expo, in the presence of some of those who had the major responsibility in making it possible. Premièrement, le Premier ministre du Québec, dont le gouvernement assume une partie des dépenses – peut-être pas autant que le gouvernement fédéral, naturellement, mais une bonne partie; also the Mayor of Montreal whose irresistible imagination and dynamic energy made the whole thing possible in the first place; and then the commissioner general, Mr Pierre Dupuy, and his chief associates who are here today and who have faced and overcome every obstacle in the conversion of a dream into a reality.

I wish that all those who directed this project, who planned and worked for it beyond the call of duty so that Expo might be finished on time and be the success it has been, I wish they could all be here today to receive our thanks.

Notre Centenaire, dont la manifestation la plus spectaculaire est l'Expo 67, offre à tous les Canadiens l'occasion d'être vraiment fiers. La présence de Votre Majesté, Notre Reine, et de Votre Altesse Royale au milieu de nous pour partager cette fierté et ce bonheur est pour nous un bonheur et une grande joie.

I read the other day that Expo was an achievement in human excellence, perhaps unmatched in history. The writer then went on to leap verbally from superlative to hyperbole – but naturally without exaggeration. After all, we Canadians are famous for our modesty and restraint. We are a factual people given to sombre and at times satirical self-analysis. No wonder we get a little unbalanced by exposure to the psychedelic experience of Expo and other exciting Centennial achievements.

One of the most welcome features of our Centennial Year is the keen and friendly interest being shown in Canada by observers from abroad. Expo and Centennial are making it apparent to the world at last that we are not merely an Arctic extension of the United States of America. It has been most refreshing to have outsiders analysing us for a change, instead of subjecting ourselves to that introspective self-examination of our national psyche to which we have become accustomed.

A London journalist even went so far the other day as to admit that Canada now existed, not merely as a fact, but also as an idea and an ideal. Certainly there could be no more dramatic and impressive expression of the idea and the ideal of the Canadianism we celebrate this year than Expo 67.

Canada may have dressed in borrowed clothes in the past, as that same London journalist put it, but I hope I won't be considered irreverent if I remind him that no longer is our national costume a union jacket worn with star striped trousers! Her Majesty is groaning at my "wit." I don't blame her.

Expo has two main purposes which I think it has achieved. It was designed to make us all conscious of our global neighbourhood, of "Terre des Hommes," of the inescapable interdependence of all people in a shrinking, crowded, little planet, and of the fact that every man on this planet is linked to every other man.

L'Expo également – en notre année du Centenaire – nous a rapprochés, à l'intérieur même de nos frontières, nous a fait prendre conscience de la destinée de notre pays et de tout ce qui s'y accomplit, ce qu'aucun autre projet n'aurait pu faire.

By one of those accidental miracles of history that sometimes quite suddenly crystallize a country's true character, we have achieved in Montreal through Expo and in Canada through our Centennial, the portrayal of a developing Canadian personality, both for the present and I hope for the future; a personality in which we can take pride, but without, I hope, conceit or smugness.

The new Canada is as modern as the day after tomorrow. But it appreciates, I hope and believe, what the heritage of our past means to our future, in the depth of our roots and the stability that comes

from institutions that have proven their enduring value. One of these
is the monarchy which symbolizes the political and parliamentary
freedom we have inherited, broadening down through the ages and
giving to our political life the cohesiveness which comes from continuity. It is a continuity that goes back unbroken from the budget of
1967, approved by Parliament in Ottawa, to the clerk of the exchequer
in the thirteenth century making in French a report on the state of his
treasury to a French-speaking king, who then tried to persuade a
French-speaking council to grant him more money by raising taxes,
from the people of course, particularly the wealthy ones.

La monarchie, en tant qu'institution, présente un attrait particulier
quand notre Reine et son époux et sa famille symbolisent si bien et de
façon si réelle tout ce qui nous est cher dans la vie familiale et dans
les services désintéressés et dévoués aux autres.

I am very greatly honoured and very happy indeed to welcome Her
Majesty and His Royal Highness to this very happy occasion. It is an
honour and a pleasure which I know is shared by every one of you.

51

THIS speech was to have been delivered at the government luncheon
given in honour of General de Gaulle when he visited Ottawa during
the celebration of the centennial of our confederation. That visit
never took place. The luncheon was cancelled, as was also the state
dinner planned by the Governor General that night at Rideau Hall.
The reason for these last moment cancellations constitutes an unhappy episode in our history, and the only sad political happening in
our Centennial Year.

It was not possible, however, for a Canadian government to over-
look what General de Gaulle had said in Montreal, prior to coming
to Canada's capital, where he was to convey the greetings of France
to Canada on the hundredth anniversary of that confederation which
French-speaking Canadians had done so much to make possible. The
ringing declaration by the President of France, "Vive le Québec
libre," was bound to be interpreted as endorsing the political slogan
of a faction in Quebec dedicated to the destruction of the Canadian
confederation, and especially so since there was no mention of "Vive
le Canada," only "Vive le Canada français."

The words in General de Gaulle's speech that shocked and dis-
tressed me most, however, as I listened to them almost in disbelief

on television, were those which referred to his motor journey that afternoon from Quebec City to Montreal: "Je vous salue de tout mon cœur. Je vais vous confier un secret que vous ne répéterez pas. Ce soir, ici, et toute le long de ma route, je me trouvais dans une atmosphère du même genre que celle de la libération." The "liberation" to which General de Gaulle referred in describing his entry into Montreal was the freeing of Paris from the Nazis, for which so many Canadians, with other allied soldiers, gave their lives.

A statement in reply to General de Gaulle's remarks obviously had to be issued by the Canadian government, and immediately. It was as follows:

"I am sure that Canadians in all parts of our country were pleased when the President of France received such a warm welcome in Quebec.

However, certain statements by the President tend to encourage the small minority of our population whose aim is to destroy Canada; and, as such, they are unacceptable to the Canadian people and its government.

The people of Canada are free. Every province of Canada is free. Canadians do not need to be liberated. Indeed, many thousands of Canadians gave their lives in two world wars in the liberation of France and other European countries.

Canada will remain united and will reject any effort to destroy her unity.

Canada has always had a special relationship with France, the motherland of so many of her citizens. We attach the greatest importance to our friendship with the French people. It has been, and remains, the strong purpose of the government of Canada to foster that friendship. I hope that my discussions later this week with General de Gaulle will demonstrate that this purpose is one which he shares."

Shortly after it was issued, General de Gaulle returned to France. No one could have been other than unhappy over the circumstances which brought about his departure.

My Undelivered Toast to General de Gaulle

27 July 1967

Nous sommes honorés de recevoir aujourd'hui parmi nous un grand homme d'Etat. Nous sommes particulièrement heureux de reconnaître en lui la France, l'une de nos mères-patries. Au nom du Canada, au nom de tous les Canadiens, je souhaite la plus chaleureuse bienvenue au Président de la République française.

Lors de ma visite à Paris en 1964, M. le Président, je vous disais mon désir de voir se multiplier les relations entre nos deux pays. Ce n'était pas là une phrase polie que me dictaient les circonstances. A vrai dire, ce désir avait sa source dans la nature des choses, dans la nature même du Canada.

Car le fait français est partie essentielle de notre identité. Ce fait le gouvernement canadien a voulu lui donner sa pleine expression. C'est pourquoi nous avons travaillé avec le gouvernement français à élargir notre coopération et à l'étendre à de nouveaux domaines.

There are three countries with which Canada has particularly close relations and with which we have special ties of friendship. Britain, with whom we have historic links going far back into our history. We cherish these links. There are also our close, neighbourly relations with the United States of America, whose strength was essential to bring victory to freedom in the tragic years of two world wars and whose strength and generosity are a buttress of freedom today. Then – and this is in the forefront of our minds today – there is France, our other mother country, with whom we also have ties which go back to the very first years of Canadian settlement. It is not only in the interest of French-speaking Canadians but of *all* Canadians, of all origins and races – and there are many – that a very special relationship with France should develop in the closest and most harmonious way.

Since our 1964 conversations in Paris, Mr President, my government has sought to strengthen these relations by adding to the bonds of sentiment and history between our two countries a solid structure of shared interest and practical co-operation. Much has been achieved, through political consultations, parliamentary visits, cultural and scientific exchanges, economic missions, and the like. Much remains to be done. I look forward in particular to a continued exploration of the possibilities for further co-operation in the scientific and technological fields, where both our countries have important achievements to their credit.

French-speaking Canada, especially and naturally, reaches out to France with a deep and strong affection. But English-speaking Canadians also welcome the fuller recognition in Canada of French culture and traditions; of the French language as a positive and valuable asset in the development of our country into a strong and united confederation from sea to sea; with a Canadian destiny and Canadian identity of its own on the North American continent; where the "French fact" is *not* isolated in a sea of 200 millions of North Americans who speak English, but finds a national home where, indeed, it has been for 350 years.

France has always stood for law and liberty as the solid foundation of enduring and enlightened human progress.

De la mode à l'architecture, de la technique à la philosophie, les créations de la France s'inspirent d'un sens profond de l'équilibre, qui est au centre de l'esprit français. Les valeurs humaines qui sont la France, nous voulons tous les partager. Elles sont indispensables à toute société qui se veut libre et ordonnée dans un monde libre and ordonné.

The basis of Canada's strength and her unity is the Anglo-French dualism of our origin. But it is a dualism which must be a partnership, something of which all Canadians are becoming more and more conscious. To this dualism we have added diversity, for Canada has been fortified and enriched by the cultures and talents of many peoples and many races.

Nous n'avons pas peur de nos diversités. Elles sont notre richesse commune.

Indeed, our ideal – which we are achieving – of unity in diversity is not only essential in Canadian life, it is the pattern for good international relations.

Mais avec cette diversité même, nous continuons à bâtir une vaste fédération canadienne unie, d'un océan à l'autre, des grands lacs jusqu'au pôle nord; un pays fort de ce patriotisme canadien dont nous vibrons en cette année centenaire, fort par la prospérité dont peuvent jouir tous les Canadiens, fort enfin par la contribution que nous pouvons faire ensemble à la paix du monde.

Our two countries have had a long common history since those days when Canada was New France. We have been partners and friends in peace and war. Twice in this century we have fought side by side, and many thousands of Canadians who rest forever in the sacred soil of France have made it part of Canada. In those tragic years of war we learned (or did we?) that co-operation and collective action was the only key to victory and, hence, to the survival of the national values that we cherished and wished to retain. We have learned also in the years between war – or I hope we have – that neither peace nor prosperity can be secured by national action alone.

Today the facts of modern life, its compulsions and opportunities, lead toward closer, not weaker, international association. Fragmentation – national or international – is not the answer to our problems. Nor is cultural absorption and political centralization. It is cultural diversity and political unity. If we can't achieve this in Canada, what hope is there for the world?

Notre pays est fondé sur la coopération entre Canadiens anglais et Canadiens français. Le dialogue entre nos deux grandes familles culturelles doit se poursuivre, il doit prendre toute son ampleur. Pour sa part, mon gouvernement compte poursuivre son effort pour exprimer pleinement à l'étranger, au Canada, et dans son sein, la présence française dans ce pays. Ceci ne peut que conduire, j'en suis certain, à des liens de plus en plus étroits entre la France et le Canada.

In April, 1950, speaking in Ottawa, you said that Canada is "a state which has found the means to unite two societies, very different in origin, language and religion; which exercises independence under the British crown and forms part of the commonwealth; which is forging a national character even though spread out over three thousand miles alongside a very powerful federation; a solid and stable state." We remember those words with deep appreciation.

Excellences, messieurs, je lève mon verre en l'honneur du Président de la République française et aux liens séculaires qui unissent nos deux pays.

52

My wife and I had decided long before Centennial Year that I would retire from political life on my seventieth birthday, or as near it as was possible. The responsibilities of Centennial Year made an announcement of this intention impossible before December of that year. Meanwhile, I had to keep my plans secret, for obvious reasons, and even to give the impression that there was no question of withdrawal from the leadership.

There have been some weird and purely fanciful reasons for my decision to resign, given by some who write about these matters. The facts are simple. As stated above, I had long since decided that at seventy it would be time for me to retire.

So on 14 December I told my surprised colleagues in the Cabinet of my decision and read the letter sent to Senator Nichol that morning, I stopped all discussion and argument on the matter by saying the decision was irrevocable, left the Cabinet room, walked across Wellington Street to the National Press building, and held a press conference, the report of which follows in part.

I would have given much to have been able to announce at the same time that the convention to choose my successor would be held in three weeks, but I was told categorically by one or two party officers, whom I had consulted the day before, that it would take at least three months. So the convention was not held until April 1968.

The intervening period, for a leader of a minority government who had announced his retirement and with seven of his colleagues soon to throw their hats officially into the leadership ring, was a rather difficult one.

I Announce My Retirement

14 December 1967

I'VE asked you to meet me, gentlemen, for a few minutes this morning, not primarily to talk about that day next week when we'll be discussing housing with the provinces, but to read you a letter which I have just sent to Senator Nichol, president of the National Liberal Federation.

13 December 1967

Dear Senator Nichol:

I wish to inform you of my decision, taken after lengthy and serious consideration, to resign from the Leadership of our Party. I feel that this is the appropriate time for me to take this step.

I do not need to tell you that I have reached this decision with great regret but I am convinced that it is the right one. I will soon have been in public service for forty years, nineteen of those years as Member of Parliament for Algoma East, and, for the last ten, I have had the great honour and privilege to be the Leader of the Liberal Party; and for nearly five years the Prime Minister of our country.

No Leader of a political Party could have received more loyalty, support and friendship than I have. For that, and for the opportunity to serve my country through the Party, I will always be deeply grateful.

I would like to ask you, as President of the Liberal Federation of Canada, to take at once the necessary steps to organize a national convention at an appropriate place and time. Until that convention has chosen my successor I will, of course, continue to serve as Leader of the Party.

Yours sincerely

That is the letter I sent to Senator Nichol this morning. The purpose of this press conference is simply to read it to you. In that sense this is not a general press conference and this is the only matter that is before us this morning; the only matter I would like to talk about.

Q Mr Prime Minister, do you have any idea of the date on which this convention will be held?

A I understand from the talk I've had with Senator Nichol that it will take three or four months. When he arrives, and I've asked him to come, he'll be able to give you a little more detailed information on that subject. I should think some time around the end of April would be the date.

Q What are your plans for your retirement over the years?

A My plan at the moment is to carry on as prime minister until a successor to the leadership of the party has been chosen. That's my immediate preoccupation. There are some very important things in which I hope to take part during these three or four months, particularly the constitutional conference in February and developments arising out of it. When the time comes for me to leave the leadership of the party after a convention has chosen my successor, I'll be retiring with my wife to our little "rose-covered cottage" in Rockcliffe!

Q Sir, will you indicate in any way your preference as to a successor or do you propose to have it completely without any signals from you at all?

A I will indicate in no way any preference for any successor. I will have nothing whatever to do with that aspect of party activities ...

Q Do you expect that the House of Commons will be closed down until after the convention or will it open again in January?

A The House of Commons will open at the regular date. The decision that I announced this morning will have no bearing on that. We have been discussing in Cabinet the date for the resumption of the session in January. It will also be discussed by Mr MacEachen with the other House leaders and the decision will be reached, I should think, today. The House will resume in January and I'll carry on during the resumed session ...

Q Mr Prime Minister, there will be no new session perhaps before the convention?

A We want to finish certain pieces of legislation. Then we will prorogue in the normal way. There may be a few days between the end of this session and the new session. We will have an Easter recess in the normal way and the leadership convention will be held, perhaps, during that Easter recess. I'm not sure. That will have to be determined ...

Q Sir, I wonder if you could tell us whether your decision, the timing of your decision, represents any change in your original plan as you formed it a year or so ago, and what factors led you to make this decision at this time.

A I had always anticipated that I would be retiring from political life, and the leadership of the party, during this year. I had at one time thought that perhaps the best time would be in the spring, or in early summer after the session. Then Centennial Year occurred with all the duties that were involved, and the privileges and the pleasures that were also involved. It didn't seem possible to leave during the summer or early autumn, until the Centennial activities were over. I then made up my mind to retire toward the end of Centennial Year. I thought that it would be wise for me to announce my decision before the parliamentary recess. As we will be recessing, I expect, next week I thought I would do it this week. There will then be a month of parliamentary inactivity ...

Q Sir, up to this point, what has been the greatest satisfaction and the greatest disappointment of your career as prime minister?

A Perhaps we should have another pre-Christmas press conference where I could reminisce and give you all the material that will be appearing shortly in my autobiography! I don't want to scoop myself. I'll be doing a lot of writing. Mr Diefenbaker and I, no doubt, will be meeting each other in our daily walks in Rockcliffe. We will be exchanging views as to how we're getting on in our respective memoirs. I've had a great many satisfactions during these ten years of leadership; a great many rewards. I wouldn't say that my actual introduction to leadership was the high spot of my career. I'm thinking of the day I got up in the House of Commons and moved my first motion. After that I had no place to go but up!

Q Sir, will you be staying on as the representative of your riding? ...

A I expect to, for the time being. Here again I have been given a very good example by my predecessor as prime minister. He, I understand, will be for some time the member for Prince Albert. I'll be the member for Algoma East. We might find ourselves on the same Parliamentary committee! ...

By the way, I should have mentioned I will not be a candidate in the next general election, for membership in Parliament. I'll cease then to be the member for Algoma East ...

Q Mr Pearson, I'm a little confused at one point that you said you would be sitting on the same committees ... then you say you won't be running again.

A I'm talking about the present Parliament. I don't expect to be a candidate in the election for the next Parliament. That is one of the things I'll regret most in my public career – not continuing, if I was chosen as their member, to be able to serve the best constituency in Canada. Mr Anglin, will you send that up to Algoma East?

Q Will there be any transitional period after the leadership convention – would you stay on as prime minister?

A No – it will be only a matter of days, once the new leader has been chosen before I leave. He should take over as quickly as possible. Well, good-bye, c'est la vie.

53

As I have included the remarks I made to the first Parliamentary Press Gallery dinner as prime minister, I thought that it might be of some interest if I included my "absolutely last appearance" as well.

Adieu to the Parliamentary Press Gallery

30 March 1968

I THANK you for your kindly reception.

"De Morturis nil nisi bonum," which, to you who are only bilingual, means those who are dying get a bonus.

I am aware, of course, that both the "newly arrived" and the "dear departed" get generous and flattering things said about them. In between, you are strictly on your own – for better, or at a press gallery dinner, for *verse*.

This is my tenth appearance on your programme as a guest speaker and positively my last. Next year I expect to be on the other, the paying side, as the gallery correspondent of the *Manitoulin Expositor*. Also, I hope by then to have successfully led a revolt against the old press gang who have run these shows for so long to their own ill-concealed delight if not to that of everybody else; especially their victims who have to display those sickly smiles.

If there was ever an activity that positively groaned for new, imaginative, and decisive leadership, this annual show is it. If it hadn't been for the scintillating contributions from this side of the table over the years, each dinner would really have been a ghastly flop. Flop is the right word.

Ten of these salvaging contributions have come from me. I was looking over them today, thinking that I might use one again, like an old sermon. But I soon realized that, so ebullient were they all in their perceptive wit, that every single one would have been remembered by the members as if it had been given yesterday, especially, of course, as the members are the "same old crowd" each year.

As for me – to add to my civil service pension, which has *not* been increased – I am going to put these ten pieces together as an "Anthology of the Best Canadian Humour" and sell them to the Mortuary Monthly or to Art Buchwald.

Tonight, in my swan dive at this function – which has always been so close to my heart and, because I have always been a guest, has never touched my pocket – my mind is caught in the tempestuous excitement of the Liberal leadership contest, the most exciting horse-race since this morning's "Grand National" and with almost as many entrants and obstacles. I have been agonizing over who should be selected – not so much for the good of the country, or even the good of the party, but for his own good.

My personal choice?

I keep asking myself: who has the combination of qualities – in English and in French – which would make him a fitting successor to Alexander Mackenzie and a fitting leader for Ralph Cowan? What are the qualities that the perfect candidate should have?

I know the answer from my own long and happy exposure to politics:

The well-rounded experience of Paul [Hon. Paul Martin]
The corporate efficiency of Bob [Hon. Bob Winters]
The decisive courage of the other Paul [Hon. Paul Hellyer]
The calm competence of Mitch [Hon. Mitchell Sharp]
The harmonious humanity of Allan [Hon. Allan MacEachen]
The boyish brilliance of John [Hon. John Turner]
The Lincolnian limpidity of Joe [Hon. Joe Greene]
The palpitating persuasiveness of Pierre [Hon. Pierre Trudeau]
The Irish appeal of Eric Kierans

(I have to give *his* full name because he doesn't belong to the Cabinet Old Comrades Club and therefore may not be so well known to you).

These are the qualities that are essential. A good new leader *must* have them. Yet, I insist, I am not available. I've even burnt my draft card. So I just don't know what is going to happen. But when one arm attached to some tired, ecstatic body is lifted high in victory at 2:12 am on Sunday, 7 April, in the words of the old Scottish ballad: "*I* will not swoon, nor utter cry." In fact, I will fly to Ireland on the next plane to see how that separated island – without the excuse of two languages – is getting on.

Tonight, as I look back, I cannot refrain from assessing for your benefit my own triumphs and disasters as leader: after all *you've* done it often enough for *me* – especially the disasters.

In the former category – successes – I put at the top the vote on third reading of an unpopular tax bill on 19 February, which we lost by only two, when it could easily have been twenty-two. That night – as the tropic waves lapped against a golden Jamaica beach – Mr Mackenzie King came to me in a dream and murmured: "Well done, good and faithful servant, but hurry home or disappear for good."

Then I think of the time I went to Camp David to order LBJ to stop bombing North Vietnam or else; and got away alive and happy to tell the tale, which no one believed.

Then there are the 476 recommendations of the Glassco Report we have put into effect while rejecting out of hand the Auditor General's extravagant demand that his salary and staff be trebled.

These are things that I will savour in retirement – as I watch the sun set behind Harrington Lake and wonder who is fishing there now.

But the record was not all of triumph. It had its occasional failures and even regrets.

I do not forgive myself for the occasional refusal – born of obstinacy out of experience – to take the advice of the pundits of the Press Gallery on each issue that arose. I paid for that neglect almost as heavily as I would have if I had done what they advised.

My sixty days of decision were too decisive. I failed to get three maple leaves on the flag and I lost the blue border. I failed to get Vancouver into the NHL or Gabon into the Canadian confederation. I failed to realize that unification of the armed forces should have been preceded by unification of the Cabinet. I was wrong in relying entirely on the Sermon on the Mount as the guideline for Cabinet solidarity.

But I treated these failures, as I did my successes, with a stoic and rather touching calm.

So I leave you, with head held high, chins up, step steady, conscious of a job half-done; confident also that the verdict of history will be: Après lui – le déluge.

54

THE first night of the leadership convention was devoted to saying farewell to the old leader before beginning the serious and exciting work of choosing a new one. "Pearson Night" was one which the Pearsons – we were all there, wife, children, and grandchildren – will remember for a long, long time. My wife and I were deeply moved by the reception we received and deeply grateful for all that it represented in friendship and support by so many over so long a time.

It was not easy for me to put my feelings into words as I thought of my ten years of leadership which were now ending: years of troubles and discouragement, but years also of achievement and of happy excitement.

After I finished my speech – and the cheers died down – I was presented by Senator Nichol with the most original and intriguing "going away" present that any leader of a political party, I feel sure, has ever received. The conventional pattern for such an occasion would have prescribed an oil painting of myself looking like a statesman for the ages; or, on a humbler note, a warm dressing gown and very comfortable slippers; or even an encyclopedia or two. But the young, swinging, disestablished, progressive party that I was leaving to my successor decided that I should receive a very new, sleepy, West Highland puppy who behaved like a little gentleman as he was deposited in my somewhat nervous arms and who has since given a great deal of pleasure to many members of the Pearson clan. He is called Toby.

At the Liberal Leadership Convention

4 April 1968

ON 16 January 1958, when I was chosen Leader of our party, I pledged myself to do my best to justify your choice. I also said: "I am quite sure – being human – I will make mistakes, but I can promise you that they will be honest mistakes for which I will not have to apologize to my conscience."

Tonight, as I hand back to the party the trust and the honour I received from it that day, I acknowledge, and regret, those promised mistakes, while I am happy and grateful for any good things I have done or good results I have helped to achieve. I am also comforted by the remark of a wise man, "Failures are made only by those who fail to dare, not by those who dare to fail."

I would wish to begin tonight by thanking you, very sincerely and very warmly, for your support and your loyalty since that day ten long and exciting years ago when I was chosen to lead our great party. Without the friendship and encouragement you have given, I could not have carried on during one of the most difficult periods of political development in our history. I will always be deeply and humbly grateful for the privilege that was given me of working with you in service to Canada and our party.

In expressing my feelings of gratitude, I will merely mention – to spare them embarrassment – those closest and dearest to me, my wife and my family. They have made my life happy and good, no matter how heavy the burdens may have been. I think also of those with whom I worked so closely, especially in those days of opposition when we had to reconstruct a defeated and shattered party.

Then there were my Cabinet and parliamentary comrades; my loyal and hard-working office staff to whom I owe so much; the party workers – right across the country – so many of whom are at this great convention. Without your selfless and untiring effort we would have accomplished little.

Nor can I omit mention of my own constituents of Algoma East, some of whom are present tonight. If they had not elected me to Parliament eight times, I would have had nothing to retire from. Indeed, I would have been retired years ago.

I am not going to boast tonight about our years of office. Après tout, Paul Cézanne a déjà dit, "Le sentiment de sa force rend modeste." But I do take pride in what we have been able to do for Canada, what we have done to keep our party truly Liberal, with a Liberalism that is attuned to the changing conditions of today, yet does not betray those principles that are of enduring value.

Liberalism remains an essential political doctrine, and will so remain as long as there are evils to be removed and improvements to be made. But today, Liberalism must adapt itself to new conditions. We live in a new world, more bewildering than brave. Our party, for success, or even survival, must adjust itself to inevitable and revolutionary change.

The Liberalism of today and tomorow must be founded not only on freedom and opportunity for the individual, but also on improvement in the quality of life. It must show itself in policies designed to recognize the individual's right to basic social security and to seek happiness in his own way in the world in which he lives, while recognizing also that this right must be limited by the necessity to maintain and protect the rights of society.

The areas in which the new Liberalism can now best operate are those

that are concerned with conditions of life far removed from those of
only a few years ago when our party doctrines were formed. So it is foolish to reject, or ignore, ideas and policies merely because they would
have shocked Queen Victoria; even more foolish than to seize on them
merely because they are new and different.

Today Liberalism must tackle problems which our grandparents
never heard of: the quality, as well as the material standard, of life;
urban development and housing; communications on land, water, and
in the air, even into outer space; the constructive use of our increasing
leisure, as machines do more work in less and less time with fewer and
fewer people; air and water pollution and the slaughter on the roads;
protection of the consumer against fraud and against "chemistry";
greater concern with education, research, and adult training; above all,
the building of the new federalism with a new Canadian unity which
accepts duality and diversity as the pattern of development, and which
could be the model for an interdependent world.

The party that now will win, and deserve, the support of the people
is the one that best understands, and adapts well to the requirements of
change; that can face reality with a minimum of fear or illusion; that
has courage to act according to the compulsions of today, not the conventions of yesterday.

Liberals must be the liberators – not the kind of liberator who rebels
against society and withdraws from reality or responsibility, but the
kind who rejects extremism, either reactionary or anarchic, and who
fights intolerance, prejudice, discrimination, and every form of injustice.

Our party must march into the future with confidence and without
doubt. We can leave to conservatism and to socialism the placid satisfaction that comes from adherence to the out-of-date dogmas and
slogans of yesteryear. While this party must be as modern as the day
after tomorrow, it must not cut itself from the past, or betray proven
and ageless values, or scorn the lessons of experience as a guide to action.
A party can die of convulsions as well as stagnation.

Liberalism, in short, must help Canada to come to terms with the new
age. If it does not, it will cease to have much relevance to the issues and
the people of 1968. How to meet today's needs will be the main test of
the party in the days ahead, and of its new leader.

As we gather to choose this new leader, we can be very proud of
those men who, having served the party with ability and distinction, now
seek a responsibility which includes the crushing burden – I can testify
to that – of directing the government of the country, at a time when
the difficulties that face us are equalled only by the certainty of a glorious
Canadian destiny if we solve them. A party is fortunate in having among
its leaders men of this calibre, all with experience, energy, high quality,
and a deep devotion to Canada.

Political leadership in a democratic state, as again I can testify from experience, and especially in a federal, continental, bilingual state like Canada, is a hazardous and demanding occupation, subject to slings and arrows, brickbats and, of course, bouquets. Its difficulties are increased by the growing number and complexity of problems, because government now intervenes, for better or worse, in practically every aspect of the citizen's life, regiments him from before the cradle till after the grave. It is not only because of all this that the political leader grows prematurely worn and old and haggard. It is because problems are compounded by the impatient feeling, often by the insistence, of his masters, the people, that there is a quick and clean-cut solution to every problem, each one of which is reduced to simple terms of black and white.

The leader has merely to find these solutions and, for this purpose, to be strong, decisive, wise, dynamic, charismatic, patient, indefatigable, kindly, and capable of inspiring unswerving loyalty, unquestioning obedience, and rapturous worship. He is expected, by the image-maker, to be a combination of Abraham Lincoln and Batman, to perform instant miracles. Then, when the poor, honest, decent chap can't live up to this image, the process of demolition begins so that another superman can be erected on the ruins.

I mention all this to give my successor courage and good cheer, as he contemplates "les grandeurs et les misères de la politique."

At this convention we are looking forward, not backward; but I make no apology for taking a glance at what has been done in the last five years by our government.

I think of the progress we have made in making life better and more secure for people; for older men and women; for the disabled and deprived; for the unemployed and the needy; for students and young people. We now have in this country a strong basic structure of social security and welfare.

We have improved our economic and financial system, encouraged trade and development, with special consideration for areas of underdevelopment. We have shown concern for the consumer.

We have unified the defence services; doubled external aid; passed far-reaching transportation, communication, and broadcasting legislation; helped the primary producer and the worker; signed the most important international agreement for tariff reduction ever drawn up; made available vastly increased financial aid to the provinces and a fairer equalization of that aid between them.

We have introduced far-reaching changes to the criminal law and are modernizing our penal system. We have kept Canada's place high in the councils of the world, at the United Nations, and in the commonwealth.

We have given new strength and spirit to those facets of national life which reach beyond national income. We have our flag, our anthem, the Order of Canada. We have given greater support than ever before to the arts and letters and sciences. We have helped to foster a new pride in Canada; a pride which came to a glorious climax in Centennial Year – that heart-warming, outpouring of love and loyalty for our country, shown in the most modest village celebration, all the way up to Expo '67, the finest fair in history.

We have, in short, changed the face of Canada and, I hope and believe, have made it better. As a government we have worked hard to bring about a meaningful and deeper unity, to build a new federalism with strong provinces and a strong central government working together in a more co-operative way than ever before and with new machinery for such co-operation.

What now faces Canada? What faces our Liberal party? And, in particular, what faces the new leader of our party?

Problems and difficulties of a nature, complexity, and importance never encountered before in peace-time. The problem of a wealth which is not fairly shared between people and regions. The problem of maintaining economic expansion without inflation; of financial stability without stagnation and mass unemployment. The problem of growth and development which will require large amounts of outside capital. Much of this will come from the United States and will, in its turn, create a problem of Canadian control or US domination.

The problem of a new and closer co-operation – especially in financial and economic matters – between federal and provincial governments. The problem of a new constitution, acceptable to Ottawa and all the provinces, continuing the momentum begun at February's conference.

The problem of social security, the structure of which must now be reviewed and pulled together, in the light of experience. The related problem caused by excessive expectations that the state can now do everything for us; that we don't need to rely on ourselves; that discipline, order, respect for authority, self-reliance, personal independence, the satisfaction that comes from hard work and honest service, that all these things are old-fashioned and should be replaced by the "Play now, pay later" mentality, both national and personal.

We are living in a fool's paradise if we think that Canada can grow great on a programme of easy work in easy stages, of each for himself and God for us all.

There is, also, the overriding problem of foreign policy and the part Canada should play in the ultimate issue of peace and war. I believe that the principles that have governed our foreign policy since World War II have been right and that their application has, on the whole, been effective. But the world has changed and the time has now come for a re-examination of the whole basis of policy. We should not shrink from this. But we should never forget one thing. Today the world – and our country as part of it – is highly irregular and unpredictable in its political and economic contours. But there is one common feature: a growing interdependence and a closer interrelationship within and between countries.

The last thing we Canadians should do is to shut ourselves up in our provinces, or, indeed, in our own country, or our own continent. If we are to be of service in the world and to ourselves and our own destiny, if we are to find our right place in the sun, we must look beyond our own national or local limits. Our foreign policy must remain based on this principle.

Finally, and governing everything else, there is the problem of national unity; of constitutional change to give this unity a new basis and meaning; of a greater understanding to give it a new depth. And we face this problem of unity at a time when there is an organized movement to destroy it.

A destiny that takes Quebec outside Canada means, simply and starkly, the end of Canada, the end of our forefathers' dream, and of our dream of a great confederation of people from coast to coast developing, for the common good, resources unsurpassed in any country, showing the world how a state of many provinces, of two basic language groups, and of many races and cultures, can combine their efforts, their talents, and their ideals to make of Canada a land of hope and happiness and equal opportunity for all.

I love my country. It is strong and beautiful and good. It is rich in its resources of man and nature. It is greatly blessed among the nations of the world. Everything that is possible in this world is possible here.

For a hundred years in good times and bad, in war and peace, Canadians have worked together to build this big and beautiful land. We have combined our efforts, linked together our overlapping loyalties, composed our differences, shared the happiness of our common achievements. Canada is our country. It belongs to us all and we belong to it. Are we to let it weaken now – and fall apart – as we enter our second century of confederation? The answer is not in our stars, but in ourselves. It is up to us.

But let us not deceive ourselves. It *could* happen here – separation and break-up. There are some, on each extreme of narrowness and bigotry, who would *make* it happen. And there is the great mass of good, grey men and women in the middle who, by their indifference, could *let* it happen.

So we who believe in our country, and our party as an instrument to serve it, must work with "a passionate intensity" to see that this doesn't happen; that the Canadian dream does not end but is realized in a Canadian destiny worthy of those who have brought us so far in our first century.

May I finish on a somewhat personal note. I am now retiring from the active sector of the political front; I have reached three score years and ten, normally the age, the Bible tells us, for permanent discharge. My difficulty is that, as I get older, I refuse to feel older, or at times even act my age. I have grandchildren whom I embarrass and exhaust. This is disconcerting. I do not believe I have come to think "old" just because I have grown older; nor, on the other hand, do I believe I am more mature or wiser at seventy than I was at forty.

I confess, however, that as prime minister, there have been times when I felt very old; when I have made a bad decision or, even worse, when a good decision has gone wrong – like accepting in February an honorary degree from the University of the West Indies. But as prime minister, I have also felt positively adolescent when I have seen a fine ideal converted into reality – a Maple Leaf Flag, for instance; or a Canada Pension Plan; or a moccasin industry for my Indian friends at Wikwemikong on Manitoulin Island.

This is just another way of saying that political leadership and the life of a prime minister has its ups and downs. What human experience has not? When it has been *down*, I felt like the person who said: "I'm a self-made man, but I think if I had it to do over again, I'd call in an expert." When it has been *up* – which has been most of the time, I felt rewarded far beyond my deserts and I have wondered how I ever earned such good fortune!

My work as your leader is now finished; my stewardship is at an end. I wish I could have done better. Perhaps I am fortunate that I have not done worse. In any event I will be measured by the record, not by a recording. And that is as it should be.

I have been greatly privileged in having been able to serve my country for so many years; in wartime and in peacetime; at home and abroad; in good days and dark ones; in the classroom, the embassy, the Commons Chamber, the Cabinet Room, and the prime minister's office.

For a long time I had the comfort and protection of relative obscurity. Then great responsibility and great opportunity came my way, without any conscious plan on my part. I remembered that I had been brought up in the belief that if I always did the best I could in any situation I had to face, remained true to the best in myself, there would be no cause for fear or loss of faith; that as Montaigne put it – my parents would have expressed it less poetically – "la plus grande chose du monde, c'est de savoir être à soi."

This is the course I have tried to follow. I hope I have achieved something along the way. If I have, it is because of the loyalty, the friendship, and the support I have received in such overflowing measure, for which I shall never cease to be grateful, and which I shall never forget. Thank you and goodbye.

Captions to the Illustrations

My favourite portrait of myself, by Gaby of Montreal
title page

Wearing the dark blue stripes of the Oxford University
Lacrosse team, 1922–23
3

There's that bow-tie, even in 1924 in a group portrait
at Victoria College
7

Visiting 10 Downing Street – improperly dressed – in the company of
Hon. J. L. Ralston and Col. Vanier before the opening of the
London Naval Conference of 1930
21

In my office at Canada House, London, 1940
35

A committee session at the founding of the United Nations,
San Francisco, 1945 (UN photograph)
62

My campaign headquarters at Massey
78

The candidate and the workers – and his wary wife – at Massey
during the by-election in Algoma East, 1948
(*Sudbury Star* photograph)
81

At the United Nations, perhaps listening to Mr Vishinsky
(UN photograph)
96

In the backyard of the parsonage,
with my father and mother and two brothers.
A homespun little Lord Fauntleroy enters a new century.
108

A fortuitous example of sartorial and postural similarities
(Capital Press photograph)
123

Khrushchev and Bulganin welcome me as a weekend guest
in the Crimea.
The hand holding the microphone belongs to René Lévesque,
then of the Canadian Broadcasting Corporation.
134

Elected leader of the Liberal party, 1958
(Public Archives of Canada)
158

Two chiefs of the Ojibway tribe at Wikwemikong, Manitoulin Island
(*Manitoulin Expositor* photograph)
182

Almost a bear-hug at the Chanticleer Inn in the Laurentians
191

Visiting the United Nations.
Left to right: Adlai Stevenson, U Thant, John F. Kennedy, LBP,
Ralph Bunche
(UN photograph)
213

Les splendeurs de la France! Leaving with the French ambassador
to Canada and his wife for the state dinner given by
General de Gaulle
220

The flag and a press conference at Dublin
240

On winning the election of 1965 – but without a majority
253

Myself in 1917, learning to fly
262

A spontaneous joy ride on the monorail at Expo
(Public Archives of Canada)
274

The Liberal caucus equips my wife and me for a cold retirement, 1968
284

My wife and Toby, 1969
294

This book
was designed by
ALLAN FLEMING
with the assistance of
ELLEN HUTCHISON
and was printed by
University of
Toronto
Press